Mortal Subjects

Mortal Subjects

Passions of the Soul in Late Twentieth-Century French Thought

Christina Howells

polity

First published in 2011 by Polity Press

Polity Press
65 Bridge Street
Cambridge CB2 1UR, UK

Polity Press
350 Main Street
Malden, MA 02148, USA

ISBN-13: 978-0-7456-5274-0 (hardback)
ISBN-13: 978-0-7456-5275-7 (paperback)

A catalogue record for this book is available from the British Library.

Typeset in 11 on 13 pt Berling
by Toppan Best-set Premedia Limited
Printed and bound in Great Britain by the MPG Books Group

For further information on Polity, visit our website:
www.politybooks.com

Contents

Acknowledgements

There are many people I would like to thank for their help with this project, which I have been working on since 2002 – and probably longer. Wadham College and the University of Oxford have granted me several periods of sabbatical leave during this time, the John Fell Fund paid for some vital editing and translating and the AHRC generously funded an extra term's leave in Spring 2010, during which I managed to complete the work. But there are also many individual friends and colleagues who have been kind enough to discuss ideas with me and correct and improve chapters, passages, and even sentences – whether because I was keen to share the excitement I felt at a new discovery or simply because I was suddenly terrified by the vastness of the task I had, perhaps foolishly, undertaken. These include Colin Davis, Jennifer Gosetti, Scott Sturgeon, Ralph Wedgewood, and my husband Bernard (who continues to regret that I did not include Ficino in my Introduction). Special thanks are due to Gerald Moore who read the whole typescript, translated the quotations, and was a great interlocutor and iconoclast. I should also like to thank my children, Marie-Elise and Dominic, for sometimes discussing Plato with me, or love, or death. The errors that remain are, of course, all my own. The study was initially inspired by the early death of John Flemming, Warden of Wadham from 1993 to 2003, who brought me face to face with mortality in a way I had not previously experienced.

Note

Material from Chapters 1 and 5 was published as 'Mortal Subjects: Passions of the Soul in Sartre, Derrida and Nancy', in *Paragraph, A Journal of Modern Critical Theory*, vol. 32, no. 2, July 2009, Theory-Tinged Criticism: Essays in Memory of Malcolm Bowie.

Abbreviations

The following offers an alphabetical key to references given within the text. Published English translations have been used where possible, though frequently altered for reasons of accuracy, or better to fit the context of the discussion. Citations from works not translated into English, or whose translations are out of print or unduly difficult to obtain, have been done by Gerald Moore. For reasons of consistency, abbreviations in the text refer to the original French titles, with full details of translations given in the bibliography. The page number is given initially for the French, followed by the English reference, which is separated by a back-slash (/).

58IC Jean-Luc Nancy, *58 indices sur le corps et Extension de l'âme*; *Corpus*, including 'Extension of the Soul' and '58 Indices on the Body' (2004/2008).

A Jacques Derrida, *Apories*; *Aporias* (1992/1993).

AE Jacques Lacan, *Autres Ecrits* (2001).

AEL Jacques Derrida, *Adieu: à Emmanuel Levinas*; *Adieu: to Emmanuel Levinas* (1997/1999).

AQE Emmanuel Levinas, *Autrement qu'être*; *Otherwise than Being, or Beyond Essence* (1978/1991).

C Jean-Luc Nancy, *Corpus*; *Corpus*, including 'Extension of the Soul' and '58 Indices on the Body' ([1992] 2002/2008).

CFU Jacques Derrida, *Chaque fois unique, la fin du monde*; *The Work of Mourning* (2003/2001).

CP	Jacques Derrida, *La Carte postale: de Socrate à Freud et au-delà; The Post Card: From Socrates to Freud and Beyond* (1980/1987).
DA	Jacques Derrida, *Demeure, Athènes: Photographies de Jean-François Bonhomme; Athens, Still Remains: The Photographs of Jean-François Bonhomme* (1996/2010).
DMT	Emmanuel Levinas, *Dieu, la mort et le temps; God, Death and Time* (1993/2000).
DM	Jacques Derrida, 'Donner la mort', in *L'Ethique du don. Jacques Derrida et la pensée du don; The Gift of Death* (1992/1995).
DS	Simone de Beauvoir, *Le Deuxième sexe* (DS II = vol. 2).
E	Jacques Lacan, *Ecrits; Ecrits. The First Complete Edition in English* (1966/2007).
EA	Gabriel Marcel, *Etre et avoir; Being and Having* (1935/1949).
ED	Jacques Derrida, *L'Ecriture et la différence; Writing and Difference* (1967/1978).
EGM	Gabriel Marcel & Paul Ricœur, *Entretiens avec Gabriel Marcel*; 'Conversations between Paul Ricœur and Gabriel Marcel', in *Tragic Wisdom and Beyond* (1968/1973).
EN	Jean-Paul Sartre, *L'Etre et le Néant; Being and Nothingness* (1943/1958).
ETE	Jean-Paul Sartre, *Esquisse d'une théorie des émotions; Sketch for a Theory of the Emotions* (1939/1994).
HA	Julia Kristeva, *Histoires d'amour; Tales of Love* (1983/1987).
HS	Emmanuel Levinas, *Hors sujet; Outside the Subject* (1987/1993).
HV	Gabriel Marcel, *Homo viator* (1944).
IRS	Jean-Luc Nancy, *L' 'il y a' du rapport sexuel* (2001).
MA	Jacques Derrida, *Mal d'Archive: une impression freudienne; Archive Fever* (1995/1996).
MHO	Paul Ricœur, *La Mémoire, l'histoire, l'oubli; Memory, History, Forgetting* (2000/2004).
MPD	Jacques Derrida, *Mémoires: pour Paul de Man; Mémoires for Paul de Man* (1988/1986).
OE	Maurice Merleau-Ponty, *L'œil et l'esprit; 'Eye and Mind' in The Primacy of Perception* (1964/1964).

OG	Jacques Derrida, *Introduction à* L'Origine de la géométrie *de Husserl ; Edmund Husserl's* Origin of Geometry: An Introduction (1962/1989).
PA	Jacques Derrida, *Politiques de l'amitié; The Politics of Friendship* (1994/1997).
PP	Maurice Merleau-Ponty, *Phénoménologie de la perception; The Phenomenology of Perception* (1945/2002).
SI	Jacques Lacan, *Le Séminaire de Jacques Lacan, livre 1; The Seminar of Jacques Lacan, book I: Freud's Papers on Technique* (1975/1991).
SII	Jacques Lacan, *Le Séminaire de Jacques Lacan, livre II: Le Moi dans la théorie de Freud et dans la technique de la psychanalyse; The Ego in Freud's Theory and in the Technique of Psychoanalysis, 1954–55 (The Seminar of Jacques Lacan, book II)* (1978/1991).
SMA	Paul Ricœur, *Soi-même comme un autre; Oneself as Another* (1990/1992).
SN	Julia Kristeva, *Soleil noir: dépression et mélancolie; Black Sun: Depression and Melancholia* (1987/1992).
SVII	Jacques Lacan, *Le Séminaire de Jacques Lacan, livre VII: L'Ethique de la psychanalyse; The Seminar of Jacques Lacan, book VII: The Ethics of Psychoanalysis* (1986/1997).
SXI	Jacques Lacan, *Le Séminaire de Jacques Lacan, livre XI : Les Quatre concepts fondamentaux de la psychanalyse; The Seminar of Jacques Lacan, book XI: The Four Fundamental Concepts of Psychoanalysis* (1973/1998).
SXVIII	Jacques Lacan, *Le Séminaire de Jacques Lacan, livre XVIII: D'un discours qui ne serait pas du semblant* (2006).
SXX	Jacques Lacan, *Le Séminaire de Jacques Lacan, livre XX: Encore; The Seminar of Jacques Lacan, book XX: On Feminine Sexuality, the Limits of Love and Knowledge* (1975/1999).
TA	Emmanuel Levinas, *Le Temps et l'autre; Time and the Other* ([1948] 1979/1987).
TE	Jean-Paul Sartre, *La Transcendance de l'ego; The Transcendance of the Ego* ([1936] 1965/2004).

TI   Emmanuel Levinas, *Totalité et infini*; *Totality and Infinity* (1961/1991).

V   Paul Ricœur, *Vivant jusqu'à la mort, suivi de Fragments*; *Living Up To Death* (2007/2009).

VP   Jacques Derrida, *La Voix et le phénomène*; *Speech and Phenomena* (1967/1973).

1

Introduction:
Love and Death

Love's mysteries in soules doe grow
But yet the body is his book.

(John Donne: *The Extasie*)

Only *we* see death.
The whole reach of death, even before one's life is
underway.

(Rainer Maria Rilke: *Duino Elegies*)

Several interweaving strands traverse this study, which attempts
to explore the relations between body and soul, love and death,
desire and passion. These have been the subjects of literature and
philosophy from their origins and it may seem a hopeless or
hubristic task to try to bring them together in a single book. But
it does not seem possible to work on subjectivity in the twenty-
first century without considering the mind–body relationship, and
an investigation of human mortality tends to lead directly or indirectly to questions of love and desire. What is more, the impulse
to undertake this work arose from an acute personal experience
of love and death that has necessarily given the book much of its
particular flavour and texture. The difficulty of reconciling philosophical reflection with experience is especially severe where
mortality is concerned, and it seems as though grieving for the
dead may never be able to escape the aporias that Derrida detects
in Freud's notion of the work of mourning.[1] It is impossible as
well as necessary to 'mourn well', that is to say to respect

individual specificity at the same time as avoiding melancholia and abjection.[2]

The focus on death inevitably brings passion into the frame, for the relationship between love and death, and passion and death, seems to be more than intimate; it is intrinsic to human subjectivity. All experience is predicated on its ultimate transience, in other words on its death.[3] It is the inevitable death of the other, be s/he friend, lover, mother, child, that gives our relationship with them its poignancy and intensity. This was the theme of all Derrida's obituary eulogies for his friends, and will be an important element of this study. Friendship, love, and passion are always already permeated by loss and death. As I look on the face of my sleeping baby or lover I am acutely aware that I cannot contain or possess the moment. As Roland Barthes points out so beautifully, this provokes the pain and pleasure of the photograph which, in capturing the moment as it passes, brings us face-to-face with death, irrespective of whether the subject of the image is still alive when we contemplate his portrait.[4] *Sic transit gloria mundi*.

But awareness of transience does not simply give human experience its ambivalent and bitter-sweet quality as we try to hold onto the moment that we cannot suspend in its flight towards oblivion; it is fundamentally constitutive of that experience. In Rilke's terms, 'we live our lives, forever taking leave'.[5] Human subjectivity does not pre-exist its relationship to the other: as we shall see, identity and alterity are mutually self-creating; indeed, one of the constants of twentieth-century French thought is precisely its sensitivity to the inescapable imbrication of self and other, subject and object, love and loss. It is our awareness of mortality that creates the lack or fissure in the self through which subjectivity is born; it ultimately prevents the closure that would ossify the subject and allow the rigid ego to take hold. In existential terms, we desire the impossible combination of liberty and identity – to know (and be) who we are while still remaining fully free. In psychoanalytic terms, we seek narcissistic closure, that is to say self-sufficiency and self-identity, but such closure would entail the death of the subject: paradoxically, perhaps, the subject remains alive and mobile only because of its relation to mortality, both its own and that of others.

It is love that makes us fear death, love of self, and love of the other: we fear losing our very selves when we risk losing what we love.[6] And it is our anguish in the face of loss and death that lies at the heart of our uncertainty about the ontological significance of the body. If I *am* my body, I die when my body dies; but this prospect of ineradicable loss (be it of self or other) is precisely what is most inimical, since it puts my very identity at stake. Consequently, I am tempted to differentiate myself from my body in a form of natural dualism. But this dualism too founders, as we shall see, on the reefs of experience and imagination: if I – or the beloved – am not to be identified with the body, what does this mean for the powerful physical affection and desire that accompanies and arguably constitutes human love? We are trapped between the Scylla of dualism and the Charybdis of materialism in all our diverse attempts to understand and conceptualize human embodiment.

It will already be clear that, looked at in this way, the question of the relationship between subjectivity and mortality is not easily circumscribed. Indeed, this became increasingly evident to me throughout the writing of this project, as the paradoxical and even aporetic nature of this relationship made closure and conclusion impossible. Moreover, since it would not be feasible to write even a brief 'history of everything', much as I might like to, the subject matter itself will of course be limited. I shall focus in particular on French thought of the second half of the twentieth century, broadly understood, starting from phenomenology and existentialism (Sartre, Beauvoir and Merleau-Ponty), ending with deconstruction (Derrida and Jean-Luc Nancy), and exploring religious philosophy (Gabriel Marcel, Ricœur, Levinas, and Vladimir Janké-lévitch) and psychoanalysis (Lacan, Kristeva, and Didier Anzieu) along the way, dipping, from time to time, into the texts of other theorists, such as Freud and Barthes. These approaches constitute the four major philosophical discourses about mortality and subjectivity of the twentieth century, and will enable us to explore how well the modern age deals with this most fundamental problematic.

Ancient and contemporary philosophers have, of course, examined these questions many times before, and I have drawn on them for inspiration and regulation as well as sparring partners. If Plato's *Symposium* and Aristotle's *De Anima* still engage modern lovers of wisdom, advances in neuroscience remind us of the very real claims of radical materialism, and analytic philosophy – by which I am surrounded in Oxford – has been a true friend in keeping me a little closer to the straight and narrow path, despite all my Continental wanderings. This introduction will attempt to situate my work fairly schematically with respect to a variety of different philosophical traditions, before passing on to a more detailed exploration of recent currents in French thought and theory. For this purpose I shall take as exemplary Aristotle and Descartes in particular, as well as some strands of the current debate between contemporary philosophy and neuroscience. Then I will look briefly at the implications of the notorious 'death of the subject' in twentieth-century French philosophy and consider how it relates to the issues of mortality, subjectivity, and passion that constitute the major preoccupations of this project.

Body and soul: some historical signposts

One of the major motifs of twentieth-century philosophy concerns the extent to which I am, or am not, identical with my body and, given the importance of this question for the conceptualization of subjectivity, it will constitute a recurrent theme throughout this book. Even the apparently materialist claim: 'I am my body', which is made by both Sartre and Merleau-Ponty (EN, 391/326; PP, 175/174), contains a syntactic dualism at odds with its intention, a dualism which Jean-Luc Nancy attempts to overcome with his formulation 'Corpus ego' (*Corpus*, 26/27) and his insistence that 'the soul is the body' (C, 67/75). But the attempt to overcome dualism goes back at least as far as Aristotle's refusal of Plato's radical separation of soul and body (though the late texts of Plato do recognize a relationship between them).[7] It is worth spending a little time with Aristotle now, not only because of the inherent interest of his texts, but more especially because his approach to the most fundamental questions of human existence – life and death, body and soul – is in many ways closer to those of the French philosophers whose work I want to explore than are the prevailing post-Cartesian preoccupations of contemporary philosophy of mind with its obsession with subjectivity, consciousness, and the problems of dualism.

For Aristotle, the soul is precisely the form of the (living) body, the vital, animating, principle without which the body would be purely material. This means that the soul is a feature of all living beings, not just of human beings, and one consequence of his interest in the principle of life is a concomitant concern with the death and decay of the body and the implications of this for the soul. ('By life we mean self-nutrition and growth and decay.' *De Anima*).[8] Indeed, it has been claimed that, in the ordinary Greek of Aristotle's day, 'the antithetical term to *psuche* was not "body" but "death"'.[9] Exegetes and interpreters of Aristotle vary widely in their understanding of his views on the body/soul relationship, but one thing is certain: his various formulations all struggle precisely with the problem of how to express the intimacy of the relationship in terms which avoid identity:

> Now given that there are bodies of such and such a kind, viz. having life, the soul cannot be a body; for the body is the subject or matter, not what is attributed to it. (*De Anima*, 412a)

> That is why we can dismiss as unnecessary the question whether the soul and body are one; it is as though we were to ask whether the wax and its shape are one ... It is clear that the soul is inseparable from its body, or at any rate that certain parts of it are (if it has parts). (*De Anima*, 412b–413a)

> Since it is the soul by which primarily we live, perceive, and think ... the body cannot be the actuality of soul; it is the soul which is the actuality of a certain kind of body. Hence the rightness of the view that the soul cannot be without a body, while it cannot *be* a body; it is not a body but something relative to a body. That is why it is *in* a body, and a body of a definite kind. It was a mistake, therefore, to do as former thinkers did, merely to fit it into a body without adding a definite specification of the kind or character of that body. (*De Anima*, 414a)

Aristotle believes that most of the faculties of the soul, such as desire, sensation, movement, are inseparable from the body, which means that his Psychology is necessarily a part of his Physics and that he is not satisfied with the apparent limitations of the expression 'passions of the soul' (or 'affections of the soul') which seems to overlook the body:

A further problem presented by the affections of the soul is this: are they all affections of the complex of body and soul, or is there any one among them peculiar to the soul by itself? To determine this is indispensable but difficult. If we consider the majority of them, there seems to be no case in which the soul can act or be acted upon without involving the body; e.g. anger, courage, appetite, and sensation generally . . . It seems that all the affections of the soul involve a body – passion, gentleness, fear, pity, courage, joy, loving and hating; in all these there is a concurrent affection of the body . . . Hence a physicist would define an affection of soul differently from a dialectician; the latter would define e.g. anger as the appetite for returning pain for pain, or something like that, while the former would define it as a boiling of the blood or warm substance surrounding the heart. The one assigns the material conditions, the other the form or account. (*De Anima*, 403a–b).

But this is not so clearly the case for the rational soul, some aspects of which (specifically the theoretical intellect, sometimes called 'nous') have an ambiguous, possibly immaterial status:[10]

Thinking seems the most probable exception; but if this too proves to be a form of imagination or to be impossible without imagination, it too requires a body as a condition of its existence. If there is any way of acting or being acted upon proper to soul, soul will be capable of separate existence; if there is none, its separate existence is impossible. (*De Anima*, 403a)

Aristotle's wrestling with the enigma of the relationship between body and soul may appear to anticipate in some ways the views of Descartes and the post-Cartesians who attempt to explain the union of body and soul in the human being, or, in more contemporary terms, the lived interdependence of body and mind, consciousness and brain; but it is important to bear in mind that his frame of reference is indisputably the attempt to understand the soul as the principle of life rather than as subjective or intentional consciousness.[11] Indeed there is no term in Ancient Greek truly corresponding to 'consciousness',[12] even though Aristotle does occasionally reflect on the question (or aporia) of self-awareness, or of how precisely we are (reflectively) aware that we see, hear or think, suggesting that all our senses 'are accompanied by a common power, in virtue whereof a person perceives that he sees or hears':[13]

> If he who sees perceives that he sees . . . and in the case of all other activities similarly there is something which perceives that we are active, so that if we perceive, we perceive that we perceive, and if we think, that we think. (*Nichomachean Ethics*, 1170a)[14]

As I have indicated, however, his preoccupation with the principle of life, and with questions such as the mortality and the necessary and intimate embodiment of the individual soul,[15] bring him far closer to recent attempts by philosophers such as Jean-Luc Nancy to bypass Cartesianism and natural dualism than to the philosophers of mind or of consciousness who currently dominate the intellectual arena, at least in analytic philosophy. And if Aristotle has been variously assimilated to the contemporary camps of Dualists, Physicalists, and Functionalists, this very variety must surely warn us that any such appropriation inevitably involves a degree of violence to the spirit as well as the letter of Aristotle's work.[16]

This is perhaps a good moment for a brief note on terminology. Not only do we need to try to understand the Ancient terminology of Soul and so on in modern terms, and *Psuche* is of course far broader than the Christian 'soul' not least because it is to be found in all living beings; but there is also a more contemporary problem: 'Mind' does not have a real equivalent in French. 'Ame' (soul) is too spiritual, but 'Esprit' (Spirit) is not much better, and has other meanings such as wit. 'Conscience' is fine as a French translation for 'consciousness' (despite the fact that in French it cannot be distinguished from conscience) but will not do for Mind either. Some contemporary French philosophers have opted to force the issue and declared that Philosophy of Mind will be termed 'philosophie de l'esprit', despite the violence this does to ordinary usage. Derrida entitled one of his collections of essays *Psyche*, and he spends many pages exploring a multiplicity of different meanings for the term. In any case, this fundamental lack of equivalence between epochs and between languages means that this book will not be able to maintain a consistent terminology throughout: my solution will be to use the terms of the philosopher in question, and to invite the reader to bear in mind the terminological pitfalls. The alternative would seem to be to abandon the whole enterprise, or else to force old wine into new bottles (or vice versa), at considerable cost.

Questions of terminology should not then deter us from attempting to situate contemporary French thought with respect to Ancient and Classical philosophy, nor from seeking the common beliefs that underlie the different vocabularies of Ancient Greek, Latin, Modern French, and English. The desire to explore the interconnection between body and soul, or mind, seems perennial, and arguably even more urgent in the modern age, as advances in science enable progressively greater understanding of the relationship between mind and brain. Descartes is of course a vital figure in this history for, although the exact nature of his metaphysical dualism is a contentious issue, his conception of man as made up of two substances, *res cogitans* (the rational soul, or mind) and *res extensa* (corporeal substance), and his attempts to explain their interaction still remain a common philosophical reference point. If we are seeking similarities beneath the differences, we will note that Aristotle considered the heart to be the centre of the soul, whereas Descartes located the central link between body and soul in the pineal gland in the brain, and we nowadays consider the brain to be the physical origin of mind. But, despite these attempts at precise location, both Descartes and Aristotle connect the soul with the body as a whole as well as recognizing its special relationship to a central organ. Indeed, Descartes makes clear that the soul cannot be located 'in one bodily part to the exclusion of the others', though its principal seat in the centre of the brain is the only 'part of the body in which the soul exercises its functions immediately'.[17]

But Descartes and Aristotle none the less have quite different views of the role the soul plays with respect to the body, since for Aristotle it is the source of life, whereas Descartes explicitly refuses such a notion and insists, in a reversal of scholastic natural philosophy, that the life of the body is entirely self-sufficient, arising from the heat in our heart, so that death does not occur when the soul leaves the body, but rather the soul leaves the body because death has occurred (naturally) and the body has become cold and corruptible.[18] Soul then, for Descartes, is the principle not of life but of thought.

Furthermore, Aristotle and Descartes react in very different ways to the ancient, physical conceptions of the soul as fire, water, blood, sperm etc., whose substantialism Aristotle mocks in the first section of *De Anima*, before making explicit his own view of soul as the animating *form* of the body. Descartes on the other hand confesses to having himself previously imagined the soul as 'something tenuous, like a wind or fire or ether',[19] and he is considered by many to have retained a substantialist view of the soul, albeit as a non-material thinking substance. What is certain, in any case, is that Descartes identifies his self primarily with his soul rather than with his body, as the Sixth Meditation makes clear: 'It is certain that I [that is my soul, by which I am what I am] am really distinct from my body, and can exist without it',[20] though he does also refer to himself as 'a being composed of mind and body' or of 'body and soul', and maintains that he forms a single unity with his body:

> Nature also teaches me by these sensations of pain, hunger, thirst and so on, that I am not only present in my body as a sailor is present in a ship,[21] but that I am very closely joined and, as it were, intermingled with it, so that I and the body form a unit.... For these sensations of hunger, thirst, pain and so on are nothing but confused modes of thinking which arise from the union and, as it were, intermingling of the mind with the body.[22]

We notice here the shifts between 'soul' (*âme, anima*) and 'mind' (*esprit, mens*) and the apparent interchangeability of the two terms, which is made explicit later in the same Meditation when, speaking of the divisibility of the body and the indivisibility of the mind, Descartes concludes: 'This would be enough to show me that the mind [*esprit*] or soul [*âme*] of man is entirely different from the body, if I had not already learned it from other sources'.[23] Such an identification through apposition of course coheres fully with Descartes's repeated description of the soul as 'nothing but a thing which thinks'.[24] None the less, Descartes is very willing to discuss the consequences of the embodiment of the soul:

> I do not see any difficulty in allowing on the one hand that the faculties of imagination and sensation belong to the soul, because they are species of thoughts, and on the other hand that they

belong to the soul only as joined to the body, because they are the kinds of thoughts without which one can conceive the soul entirely pure.[25]

Descartes's contention that the 'esprits animaux' ('vital spirits' – tiny, rarified corpuscles carried by nerves and blood) mediate between body and soul via the brain[26] may seem to some commentators[27] to anticipate contemporary neurological theories of psychosomatic interaction, as for example when he argues that 'when a mind joined to a body thinks of a corporeal thing, certain particles in the brain are set in motion',[28] or that 'there is no doubt that the soul has great power over the body, as is shown by the great bodily changes produced by anger, fear, and the other passions'.[29] Indeed, he recognizes that the process is a two-way affair:

> In man the brain is also acted on by the soul which has some power to change cerebral impressions just as those impressions in their turn have the power to arouse thoughts which do not depend on the will.[30]

Or again:

> The principal seat of the passions in so far as they are corporeal, is the heart, since that is principally affected by them; but in so far as they affect also the mind, their seat is in the brain, since only the brain can act directly upon the mind.[31]

And Descartes is even willing to speak of the soul itself as material or corporeal in so far as it is united to the body[32] But more interesting for our purposes is the role played by love in the mysterious union of body and soul, for Descartes considers joy and love to have been the soul's first passionate reactions to its own embodiment.[33] And of course passionate love itself necessarily depends on body as much as on soul, for soul on its own would be capable only of intellectual or rational love whereas the sensuous element arises from the fact that the soul is joined to the body.[34] And if Descartes is inclined at times to belittle such passion as 'nothing but a confused thought, aroused in the soul by some motion of the nerves', his rhetoric betrays his own attraction to, and perhaps knowledge of, such an experience:

So, in love, a mysterious heat is felt around the heart, and a great abundance of blood in the lungs, which makes us open our arms as if to embrace something, and this makes the soul join to itself in volition the object presented to it.[35]

Usually, Descartes maintains, rational and sensuous love combine in human passion, though they can of course be separated:

Commonly, however, these two loves occur together; because the two are so linked that when the soul judges an object to be worthy of it, this immediately disposes the heart to the motions which excite the passion of love; and when the heart is similarly disposed by other causes, that makes the soul imagine loveable qualities in objects in which, at another time, it would see nothing but faults.[36]

This understanding of passion creates an intriguing dilemma for Descartes where love of God is concerned, because, logically, love of God can only be rational or intellectual, since in Descartes's view 'nothing about God can be visualized by the imagination'[37] which would be necessary for love to be sensuous or passionate. However, he claims to understand those philosophers who consider that it is only through the Christian religion and the mystery of the Incarnation that we can truly love God. Furthermore, he even suggests that the only possible way for us to love God passionately is via imagination, not of God because that is impossible, but, indirectly (and one might even say deviously) through imagination of love itself and of the union it affords, since 'the idea of such a union by itself is sufficient to produce heat around the heart and cause a violent passion'.[38] We may perhaps think in this context of the sheer sensuality and mystical lyricism of the biblical *Song of Solomon* to which we will return later in the context of Kristeva's analyses of religious love.

It is clear from the convoluted nature of Descartes's argument that he finds himself with a logical conclusion from which he is attempting strenuously to escape, even at the cost of partial self-contradiction. For even if the soul is the highest part of the human being it might still seem an impoverishment if love of God were to be restricted to the purely rational realm, whereas love of other men and women could be passionate, that is both rational and sensuous. Descartes's contention that the source of life is purely bodily, and independent of the soul, also creates potential problems where the death of a loved one is concerned; for the body may be a mere machine, functioning through the heat of the heart and blood, and the self may, as we have seen, be identified primarily with the mind, but where does this leave the passions of the soul which arise from the interaction of body and mind and which give human love its sensuous, bodily aspect? If love for another is passionate, that is to say sensuous as well as rational, where does this leave it at the moment of death, when the separation of body and soul is definitive? Its rational aspect can of course continue, in a love for the eternal soul that survives death, but its sensuous dimension is doomed to mourn a mere machine or corrupt corpse. A less radical separation of body and soul is needed if mourning is to avoid abjection.

Socrates, we remember, forbade his friends to mourn him at his death, since he would not himself be dying – only his body would decay. Such dualistic Platonism is hard for the bereaved, and inimical to the human experience of love. What is more, and necessarily more speculative, what does this separation mean for the soul which experienced, Descartes suggested, joy and love at the moment of its embodiment? Disembodied, it can no longer experience passion in the full sense, but a form of intellectual sadness at its loss might perhaps be expected at the dissolution of a union necessarily more powerful and intimate than that between any human couple.[39]

Since Descartes, philosophical attempts to understand the mind–body relationship have almost all started from Cartesian dualism, whether to deepen its foundations or attempt to contradict it. Descartes's own view is that the senses and 'the ordinary course of life' and experience lead us to view ourselves as a single unity of soul and body, and that only abstract metaphysical reflection can make us question this and query just how 'the soul moves the body and the body acts on the soul'.[40] Be this as it may, much post-Cartesian philosophy and thought seems, on the contrary, to take the separation rather than the unity of body and mind for granted and to expend a great deal of its effort in trying, like Descartes himself, to understand their apparent interaction.

There are however some notable exceptions to this. Already in the immediate wake of Descartes, Spinoza rejects out of hand all attempts to explain mind–body interaction, maintaining the very notion to be unintelligible, and proposing rather a theory of a single substance (*Deus sive natura*) expressed as two attributes: 'mind and body are one and the same thing, conceived now under the attribute of Thought, now under the attribute of Extension',[41] both of which are subject to causality rather than freely self-determining.[42] In this way, Spinoza attempts to refute Descartes's substance dualism and, a fortiori, his contention that reason can control passion, or mind direct the body. In Part V of the *Ethics*, he takes 'this illustrious person' directly to task for what he describes as his 'occult' theory of mind–body union passing through the pineal gland, and argues that the Cartesian conception involves such a radical initial distinction as to render any subsequent interaction incomprehensible. The power of the mind, in Spinoza's view, lies not in the will but rather in the understanding and, since mind and body are two ways of envisaging the same substance, all understanding, be it ostensibly of mind or body, is necessarily a form of self-understanding and not therefore in need of a third element to explain it. Indeed, Spinoza defines a 'passion' precisely as an emotion that has not been adequately understood, and before which we are therefore passive and reactive. It is self-knowledge, not the will, that enables us to be agents, and thus self-knowledge that makes us free, or at least relatively free.

Like Descartes, Spinoza makes special room for love in his epistemology and ethics: he conceives it as an affect or emotion that involves knowledge, for love is defined as 'joy accompanied by an idea of its cause', and he contends that it involves contentment in the presence of its object.[43] And again like Descartes, Spinoza envisages the union of body and mind in human embodiment as a source of joy, grounded in love, ('What a union! What a love!'),[44] but since, in his conception, the body and mind that are 'united' are also already one, their union is inextricable. None the less, Spinoza does seem, perhaps unwittingly, to allow for an implicit separation between body and mind in so far as he argues that the mind is subject to passive emotions 'only while the body endures', and that therefore only intellectual love is eternal. All this leads ultimately to a position where God's self-love is perfect and infinite, and the mind's (intellectual) love is subsumed within God's love (218–19). Once again, it is unclear where this leaves the very human – and cherished – aspect of physical love, which appears, in the last analysis, to be dispensable. But apart from this enduring problem, what we might call Spinoza's early compatibilism arguably constitutes a convincing early attempt to resolve some of the thornier aspects of the mind–body problem raised by the Cartesian position.

Later in the century, Malebranche's contribution to the mind–body debate radicalizes the dualist position, as he proposes a form of parallelism, or occasionalism, according to which we are composed of two substances which work together but with no causal or necessary relationship between them.[45] Leibniz's alternative to this occasionalism is that of a pre-established harmony, probably most familiar through the memorable image of two clocks keeping time with each other with no need for any mutual interaction[46] which he uses to express his hypothesis of 'the perfect agreement of all the substances'.[47] Indeed, Leibniz argues against Descartes that it is 'inconceivable' that the soul and body should have any influence on one another and that such an interaction would be incompatible with the laws of nature.[48]

Furthermore, unlike Descartes and Malebranche, Leibniz considers that the true reality is in fact mind, and that matter is merely phenomenal, the visible face of an invisible reality. And against Spinoza, Leibniz maintains that rather than being 'free only in appearance', we are, on the contrary, 'determined in appearance only . . . and are perfectly independent'.[49] These various and complex interpretations of mind and body mean that human self-understanding is bound to be problematic, to say the least, and Malebranche for example reverses Descartes's contention that our minds are necessarily much easier to understand than our bodies,[50] claiming repeatedly that we are mere shadows for ourselves.[51] Indeed, Descartes's optimism about the possibility of self-understanding seems to have been the aspect of his philosophy that found least favour with his successors. Hume famously goes so far as to contest the very idea of a self-identical 'me', arguing that the mind is no more than a bundle or collection of different perceptions in constant flux, though he still maintains that experience shows that the mind can voluntarily influence the body despite the fact that we do not understand how it does so.[52]

Later in the eighteenth century, Kant argues powerfully that the Cartesian proofs of the simplicity and unity of the soul are untenable because they depend on paralogisms of reason: it is not possible, he insists, to move from the *cogito* to the *res cogitans*, that is, from my awareness of thinking to the assertion that 'I am a thinking thing.' Ultimately, Kant argues, in his defence of transcendental idealism, I can have no possible knowledge of my self or my soul, only of their phenomenal appearances; nor, a fortiori, can I have any knowledge of how 'communion between thinking beings and extended beings' is possible, nor any knowledge of how or whether 'the soul after the cessation of all communion with the corporeal world could still continue to think'.[53]

Dualism has not, of course, had total dominance in the human attempt at self-understanding, as is evidenced by the early materialism of philosophers such as Democritus and Epicurus who maintained that the soul was a body composed of very fine particles. And, following Spinoza, materialism was further explored by eighteenth-century sensualist (or 'sensationalist') philosophers such as Hobbes, D'Holbach, and La Mettrie, who saw matter as active and sensitive, not inert, and by ideologues such as Cabanis in the nineteenth century whose radical materialism led him to compare the brain's production of thought to the liver's secretion of bile, and to argue that 'all moral affections and intellectual faculties reside in the nerves'.[54] La Mettrie is a particularly interesting case in the context of a discussion of passion, as he focused particularly on sensual pleasure, and considered love a test-case in so far as 'all the passions are eclipsed by the passion of loving'.[55] In his version of materialism, erotic love involves what we usually refer to as body and soul, sensory feeling, and imaginative anticipation, and recollection, so that the highest form of pleasure produces a kind of (psychosomatic) ecstasy, or *volupté*, of the heart as much as of the body.[56] Indeed, in 'L'Art de Jouir' ['*The Art of Enjoyment*'] he writes, 'It is not the *jouissance* of bodies but rather that of souls that I need.'[57] Passion may ultimately be a matter of nervous excitation, tension, and disturbance of the blood, but our experience of it is in no way diminished by its corporeal underpinning.

Mind and body: some twentieth-century attempts

Twentieth-century philosophers too have found a wide variety of ways of opposing or bypassing dualism. Before we turn to our central concern with French philosophy, we will look finally, and briefly, at a few of the alternative strands of thought, focusing in particular on those where questions of passion or death are primary issues. Wittgenstein famously criticized dualism as a deeply damaging way of imagining the human; however, he is arguably not the anti-mentalist he has sometimes been seen as, but rather, like many of his predecessors, someone who is interested in 'soul' and 'body' as different ways of referring to the human being; indeed he frequently refers to the 'soul', describing for example the face as 'the soul of the body', or discussing the look of enchantment exchanged between lovers. Indeed, he claimed in a memorable phrase that 'the human body is the best picture of the human soul'.[58]

Gilbert Ryle also dismissed what he called the 'official doctrine' of the mind–body relationship as absurd, describing it as 'the dogma of the Ghost in the Machine' and arguing that it results from the Cartesian 'category mistake' of conceiving mind and matter as similar kinds of entity, whereas in fact there are no distinct mental and physical worlds, but rather mental processes *are* intelligent acts and are not distinguishable from them.[59] In a sense, Ryle, like Spinoza, 'solves' the mind–body problem at a stroke by denying that it exists.

None the less, the human need to understand what, at the very least, *seems* to be a dualism between mind and body at the heart of experience never really disappears, though it changes in nature in accordance, at least in part, with the progress of science and in particular biology. Many twentieth-century philosophers including Quine[60] subscribe to the views of neuroscientists such as J-P Changeux[61] that emotions, for example, simply *are* microphysical changes in the brain. There are, of course, more or less subtle versions of this view, ranging from Identity Theory which considers mental states to be identical to brain processes, through Epiphenomenalism which maintains that mental states are passive effects of brain activity and that there is a causal link between them, to the Eliminative Materialism propounded by Paul and Patricia

Churchland[62] who dismiss all psychological descriptions and explanations as quite simply false and misleading. The drawback of these reductionist theories is perhaps self-evident: they take no real account of human experience and seek to deny, often dogmatically, what seems transparently obvious in the natural attitude (Descartes's 'ordinary course of life').

And objections to contemporary reductionism come from a variety of eminent sources such as Paul Ricœur in his dialogues with Changeux, for example;[63] or Popper,[64] who is prepared to accept parallelism between body and mind, and perhaps even identity, but who considers that cause and interaction between them occurs sometimes in one direction, sometimes in another (which was, we remember, Descartes's view also); or indeed David Chalmers, an anti-materialist philosopher of Mind who conceives consciousness as an irreducible dimension of nature, like gravity or electromagnetism.[65] A further possible position is represented by John Searle who, like Ryle, considers the mind–body problem to be a false one, and who attempts to achieve a non-reductionist materialism. Searle maintains an unusual position as a biological naturalist who insists on the irreducibility of consciousness, and on subjectivity as one of its fundamental characteristics. He accepts that conscious states are caused by low-level neurobiological processes in the brain, but insists that neither behaviourism nor the computationalism of cognitive science can adequately account for them and that consciousness, subjectivity, and intentionality all need further extensive philosophical and scientific investigation.[66] Given the state of neuro-science today and its ability to recognize the brain activity and patterns which accompany mental states and activities but not to read from the brain to the mind, there is probably no compelling reason to accept more than a very limited materialism which recognizes the necessary connection between mind and brain but eschews a premature and perhaps ultimately unwarranted reduction of the former to the latter.[67]

Once again, passion and death seem to provide test cases for contemporary materialism. It is easy to see how philosophies inspired by current neuroscience may relegate love to being a mere by-product of the chemical changes in the brain caused by neuro-transmitters carrying endorphins, serotonin, oxytocin, and dopamine etc. which have undeniably been observed to

accompany and perhaps even cause the experience commonly
referred to as 'falling in love'. Indeed, this is one of the aspects of
neuroscience which has most captured the popular imagination,
and is arguably most dangerous in its simplifications which leap
from brain imagery to subjective representations in a move which
is unsupported by current science.[68]

Death too may seem unproblematic if there is no room for
mind, spirit or soul beyond the epiphenomenal effects of activity
in the brain. Death of the brain will automatically entail death of
all aspects of the person, including those we might usually consider to be mental, emotional or even spiritual. Radical materialism can certainly de-dramatize our experiences of passion and
mortality. None the less, a desire for a more human and humane
understanding of such fundamental experiences as love and death
is often manifest between the lines of even the most apparently
reductionist thinkers. Quine, for example, despite his espousal of
the discoveries of neuroscience, always insisted on the irreducibility of the mental and claimed never to have denied the existence of consciousness, arguing rather that 'consciousness is . . . a
mystery, and not one to be dismissed'.[69]

Again, neurobiologist Francis Crick actively encourages work
towards an explanation of consciousness in his collaborative work
with Kristof Koch.[70] And J-P Changeux himself shows in *Raison
et Plaisir* (2002),[71] as well as in his willingness to work with the
Christian philosopher Paul Ricœur[72] in a text which claims Spinoza
as a conceptual precursor, that he wants to understand the origin
of emotions such as love rather than simply dismiss them. This
scientific humanism is also evident in his work as President of a
French consultative committee on ethics and in his insistence on
the need for further reflection on issues such as consciousness,
truth, beauty, and goodness.[73]

Similarly, neurophysiologist Marc Jeannerod has collaborated
with psychoanalyst and psychiatrist Jacques Hochman in a
joint attempt to understand the nature of mind,[74] as well as in
his own explorations of human emotions, thought, consciousness,
and memory in *Le Cerveau intime*[75] and *La Nature de l'esprit*,[76]
Again, another contemporary biologist, Jean-Didier Vincent,
has also worked closely in recent years with the philosopher
Luc Ferry[77] on the question of human freedom, as well as inves-
tigating the nature of passion in single-authored texts including

Biologie des passions[78] and *Le Cœur des autres: une biologie de la compassion.*[79]

Neuroscience and materialism are then often very far from evacuating human subjectivity and passion or dissolving them in the neurological tangle of synapses, neurons, and neurotransmitters. And indeed, some neurologists go even further and explore the interconnection and interdependence between subjectivity and emotion in a way that bears witness to the persistent deep complexity of the human, even in an age of radical demystification. Neurologist Antonio Damasio has made an exceptional contribution to this question in his integration of emotions into the mainstream explanatory schema of neuroscience.[80] Damasio has developed a theory of the three-fold emergence of the conscious self from the body, involving first a 'proto-self' which regulates the homeostasis of the body; secondly the development of self-awareness in the 'I'; and finally the 'autobiographical self' which recounts its own narrative history.

It is the second stage that is of most interest here, for it places emotion at the core of subjectivity. Consciousness is a physical/emotional reaction to a stimulus, it is self-generated and self-aware, it is the very act of relating; there is no 'clever homunculus . . . You are the music while the music lasts'.[81] Physical emotions do not manifest feelings, they generate them: 'There is no central feeling state before the respective emotion occurs, that expression (emotion) precedes feeling'.[82]

Emotion is the body's response to powerful stimuli that might harm or help us and, in Damasio's terms, 'feeling' is our conscious awareness of (physical) emotion, and is the source of our sense of self and subjectivity. Not only can mind not exist or operate without body, so that 'pure rational thought' is impossible, but when we approximate to it – as in the case of patients who have suffered damage to the frontal regions of the brain and who are unable to respond emotionally to graphic images of sex and violence – we are, in Daniel Dennett's terms, 'pathetically ill-equipped . . . for the real world'.[83] The 'cool-headed, passionless thinkers philosophy has tended to encourage as the ideal'[84] are in fact unable to respond appropriately or, indeed, make decisions under pressure, since they lack the necessary emotional responses to enable social cognition and decision-making. Damasio could not be further from reducing human reason, art, and morality to

chemicals and neural pathways: on the contrary he is trying rather
to understand the highest of human activities, which can never
be 'pure' reason. As Dennett points out, such ideas are not entirely
new: they are to be found in Aristotle, in Nietzsche, and more
recently in psychologist Nicholas Humphrey[85] who himself quotes
Zarathustra's comments 'on the despisers of the body': 'Behind
your thoughts and feelings, my brother, there stands a mighty
ruler, an unknown sage – whose name is self. In your body he
dwells; he is your body. There is more reason in your body than
in your best wisdom'.[86]

So, human passion is still clearly at the centre of even the most
radically materialist philosophical theories, just as the nature of
death necessarily continues to fascinate contemporary investiga-
tors of human life, such as biologists and neurologists, whatever
their attitudes to the spiritual and metaphysical. None the less,
passion and death are not usually discussed together in modern
philosophy or science, despite their intimate proximity in psychoanalysis, any more than are mortality and subjectivity, despite their
necessary alliance in the constitution of the human. Having
explored very briefly some of the main strands of philosophical
enquiry into the nature of the human – body and soul, heart and
mind, brain and consciousness – we can now turn to the core of
our discussion, that is to say, the intertwining themes of mortality
and subjectivity, love and death, in (late) twentieth-century French
philosophy.

Death and the subject in recent French philosophy

Despite their intimate imbrication, then, mortality and subjectivity are not often analysed in conjunction with one another. Modern
philosophy has produced a vast range of theories of subjectivity,
from the Cartesian *cogito* through Kant's unity of apperception,
Husserl's transcendental ego, Sartre's non-self-identical subject, to
the fragmented and decentred subject of post-structuralism and
deconstruction. But what is generally explored in the theorization
of subjectivity is its genesis, its constitution, its essence (or lack of
essence), its identity, and its relation to otherness, not its disintegration, weakness, and ultimate dissolution in the radical alterity
of death. Critiques of the subject tend to assume its coherence,

independence, and voluntarism: they set up the subject as a straw man whose overweening pretensions to unity and autonomy are all the easier to demolish; they rarely allow for conceptions of subjectivity which already manifest the vulnerability and fragility which they claim characterize the subject as it should be understood. But the link between subjectivity and mortality lies at the heart of this study: what happens to the subject in death? What does the embodiment of subjectivity mean for the subject at the point of death? And how do these fundamental questions relate to the 'death of the subject' as it was understood in the second half of the twentieth century?

When we reflect on human mortality, we are usually light years away from the so-called 'death of the subject', where death is used as a metaphor – and on this occasion I would wish to say a *mere* metaphor – to refer to a complex epistemological change in which one conception is gradually, or even suddenly, replaced by another. We have not been able, of course, really to *think* the death of the Subject, or the death of Man, or even the death of God. The Subject, Man, and God are still with us in diverse guises. And the phrases themselves imply on some level an aggression: the death of God, or the subject, is not something we are encouraged to mourn (though some may), it is rather held up before us as a kind of challenge, a challenge to assist in the declared demise, or at least to celebrate it. Here, of course, positions have changed over time.

Derrida's appeal in 'Structure, sign, and play' of 1966 to the joyous Nietzschean affirmation of a 'world of signs [. . .] without truth or origin'[87] perhaps needs to be compared to what he later calls the 'jubilatory' phase of mourning,[88] and contrasts sharply with his rebuke to Jean-Luc Nancy in 1989 when the latter asks him to comment on the 'liquidation' of the subject.[89] For, as he is quick to remind Nancy, he never spoke of the liquidation of the subject, any more than did Lacan, Foucault, Althusser or Philippe Lacoue-Labarthe among others. The very term 'liquidate', Derrida remarks, has no philosophical meaning: it comes rather from the register of finance, terrorism, and banditry. It implies something negative that calls out for redress. The post Freudian, post Marxian, post Nietzschean reinterpretation of a decentred subject is, Derrida argues, a very different matter. This is probably, perhaps certainly, true. But the tone of some of Derrida's early writings is arguably less measured, and Foucault's proclamation of the 'disappearance of man' may have been simplified and misrepresented, but its connotations are undeniably celebratory.[90]

But mortality itself is a very different matter. The term has not yet, to my knowledge, been hijacked by the anti-humanist lobby. Nor is it usually associated with a concept: the death of Man, the mortality of man, have a very different sense, the former describes the end of an outmoded notion, the latter an inevitable and inescapable part of the human condition. I want now to try to think about human mortality in the light of the death of Man. It is a task I have been drawn to by personal circumstances, but then, these are precisely the circumstances of us all: those we love most will die, we ourselves will die. What is singular for me is thereby also universal. Auden was wrong, as well as right, when he said 'We must love one another or die'. We must love one another *and* die.[91]

And what does death mean for our understanding of the subject? I do not intend at this point to enter the debates around the merits or demerits of the Heideggerian notion of 'being-for-death' and its opposition by Sartre among others. Nor do I wish to remain on the level of bodily mortality, that undeniable disintegration of our physical selves. My purpose is somewhat different. It is to offer a reflection on the implications of human mortality for our understanding of the human subject and, perhaps more uncertainly, to try to begin thinking about the implications for our understanding of human mortality of contemporary meditations on the fragility of the subject. For fragility would seem to be one of the links between the two kinds of death: fragility and vulnerability. If the self-contained, self-sufficient subject of classical humanism never in fact existed, even as a concept, it is none the less true that our contemporary understanding of the human subject stresses fragmentation over totalization, decentring over centredness, difference over identity, absence over presence; all the classical markers, in fact, of death over life. But this is not, none the less, what is usually meant by the 'death of the subject', the replacement of a subject characterized by vitality and growth by a subject marked by the downward path of disintegration and weakness. 'Weak thought' may have entered our conceptual apparatus as an alternative to the thought of so-called 'master thinkers', but the 'weak subject' still tends to sound close to a form of oxymoron, and has yet to find its elegist.

So we rarely, if ever, bring together the two meanings of the death of the subject. Our meditations on subjectivity remain at a level of philosophical abstraction that necessarily excludes individual, personal death. Our contemporary reflections on mortality use the terminology of selfhood, individuality, the body, not that of subjectivity. In a sense, we may be said to be continuing, unwittingly, a form of mind–body dualism, albeit with a different vocabulary that tends to mask the divide more effectively.

Similarly, love, passion, and desire are pervasive preoccupations in recent French philosophy, and not only for psychoanalysts such as Lacan, but also far more widely, for example in Sartre, Jankélévitch, Kristeva, Derrida, and Nancy. But this does not mean that the philosophical analysis of passion and desire has necessarily managed to avoid dualism either, or to find a way of speaking about the body that is non-reductive. Given the way that passion is inextricably rooted in embodiment, and that the erotic permeates our relations with others more powerfully than any other human drive, except perhaps its inverse, aggression, we might expect twentieth-century French philosophy – post-Freudian as well as post-Kantian – to place it at the very heart of the human. Indeed, passion is the place where love and death, mortality and subjectivity, body and soul, collide in a conflagration that philosophy may find it hard to contain or indeed explain. It is human embodiment that makes us mortal and makes us passionate; in turn, our mortality deepens our passion because it ensures the ultimate loss and destruction of all we love. Passion and death are intimately involved in subjectivity; it is our mortality that makes us free subjects, able to love, to give, indeed to die for others. We are mortal because we live in time not eternity, and this constitutes also our singularity as subjects. Subject to time, subject to death, subject to passion. These themes lie at the heart of the work of all the twentieth-century French philosophers of paradox and finitude we are about to explore.

2

Phenomenology of Emotion and Forgetfulness of Death

Jean-Paul Sartre, Maurice Merleau-Ponty, Simone de Beauvoir

Sartre, Merleau-Ponty, and Beauvoir form a phenomenological trio whose philosophical explorations of subjectivity, passion, and death share the same existential focus and the same radical opposition to all forms of mind–body dualism. What is more, the three philosophers formulate and develop their theories in conjunction with, and sometimes in opposition to each other, through explicit interaction and response as well as through common preoccupations in ontology, psychology, and politics. Many of the most important texts we will examine in this chapter were written in the 1940s (Sartre's *L'Etre et le Néant*, 1943, Merleau-Ponty's *Phénoménologie de la perception*, 1945, and Beauvoir's *Le Deuxième sexe*, 1949, for example), but they build on texts by Sartre from the 1930s and go forward to the 1960s, by which time there was less agreement between the three thinkers, but more mutual refutation and at times hostility which arguably spilled over from the political into the philosophical arena.

It is probably fair to say that, initially at least, both Merleau-Ponty and Beauvoir are responding to Sartre, whose first philosophical considerations of issues of subjectivity and mortality come several years before the published works of his two friends and sparring partners. But quickly the lines of response and reaction become more complex and interwoven, so that Beauvoir, for example, reacts vigorously at one stage to Merleau-Ponty's critique of Sartre, though Sartre himself does not respond explicitly, at least in print. What will emerge, I believe, throughout this chapter is that, in their various different ways, none of the three philosophers is able to maintain a consistent position in the face of the challenges posed by the contemplation of human mortality. Death seems to be the reality which brings most pressure to bear on their shared anti-dualist ontology, as well as being the existential touchstone which reveals most starkly the unintended ambiguities and conflicts of their common phenomenology. The reasons for this will, I hope, become progressively clearer.

Jean-Paul Sartre

Desiring the impossible

Sartre's best-known comment on passion is probably the provocative 'Man is a useless passion' from *L'Etre et le Néant* (EN, 708/615), which forms part of his discussion of our futile yearning to achieve simultaneous freedom and identity in an impossible self-coincidence (of 'in-itself-for-itself' ['*en-soi-pour-soi*'] which only God could attain. But this is not the usual sense of 'passion' for Sartre, for whom it refers rather to a form of emotional response and behaviour in which an affective state – of love, joy, fear or hatred, for example – seems to be 'caused' by its object. For Sartre, emotions originate in consciousness as a response to the world about us and are never literally *caused* by the world; but he is well aware that this is not how we usually experience them and that they appear to us, at least unreflectively, as reactions which we may be able partially to control but which we do not choose. Indeed, emotions that are consciously chosen, or acted out, are deemed to be insincere by Sartre, just as they are in everyday experience.

But the notion of man as a 'useless passion' provides an intriguing way into an exploration of Sartre's phenomenology of emotion as well as to his understanding of the role of the body in passion and his conception of human mortality. Our passionate desire to achieve self-coincidence while remaining free is useless only in the sense that it is impossible to achieve: Sartre's ontology demonstrates that freedom is an unavoidable aspect of consciousness in so far as it can imagine and that

self-coincidence would entail 'the death of consciousness' by
eradicating that freedom. But our desire to achieve the impossible is not itself useless; it is what drives us onwards in a never-
ending quest for a fulfilment that is always deferred; in the
terms of Wordsworth's Prelude:

> Effort, and expectation, and desire,
> And something evermore about to be.

The ambiguity of our position, always yearning for an identity that
would end both our anguish and our freedom, is reflected in our
ambiguous status as embodied consciousness, evocatively described
by Simone de Beauvoir as 'the passion of incarnate consciousness'.[1] Consciousness cannot exist except as embodied, but the
relationship between consciousness and body is just as complex
for an existentialist philosopher as it was for Aristotle or Descartes.
The body represents the condition of consciousness, that is to say
what roots us in the world, what enables us to have a situation,
what makes us human rather than ethereal. It is the body that
enables us to act, to carry out our projects, to express our desires,
to communicate with others, to know the world; but it is also the
body that marks the limits of our strength, that insists we rest
when we are tired, that keeps us rooted in time and space, and
that sometimes reacts in ways we have not chosen and do not
welcome: sneezing, vomiting, sleeping, becoming ill, ageing, and
eventually dying.

Sartre's discussion of the mind–body relationship is both resolutely anti-dualist and also fully cognisant of the aporias and
dilemmas that arise from our reluctance to accept all the implications of our embodiment. But, as we shall see, Sartre is himself
arguably unable to accept all the implications of human embodiment either, at least where mortality is concerned. We will look
first at his conception of embodied subjectivity, especially with
respect to emotion and desire, before exploring his theorization
of human mortality.

In *L'Etre et le Néant* Sartre lays out very clearly his conception
of the radical inseparability of body and consciousness:

> Being-for-itself must be wholly body and it must be wholly con-
> sciousness; it cannot be *united* with a body. Similarly being-for-

others is wholly body; [...] But the body is wholly 'psychic'. (EN, 368/305)

The body is part of the 'facticity of the pour-soi' (371/308), 'it is nothing other than the pour-soi' (371/308), 'as such, the body cannot be distinguished from the *situation* of the pour-soi' (372/309).

> The body is a necessary characteristic of the for-itself [...]. Yet in another sense the body manifests my contingency [...]. And Plato was not wrong either in taking the body as that which individuates the soul. Yet it would be in vain to suppose that the soul can detach itself from this individuation by separating itself from the body at death or by pure thought, for the soul is the body insofar as the for-itself *is* its own individuation. (372/309–10)

It is impossible then for the *pour-soi* to escape its individuation by the body, impossible for the soul to be separated from the body, even in death. But 'the body is perpetually the surpassed' (390/326), both point of view and starting point. This means that I both am and am not my body: 'I am my body to the extent that I *am*; *I am* not my body to the extent that I am not what I am' (391/326). As 'facticity of the pour-soi' the body is not 'a contingent addition to my soul; on the contrary, it is a permanent structure of my being' (392/328). And Sartre reminds us of the characteristics of this facticity: my birth, my race, my class, my nationality, my physiological structure, my character, my past... 'All this... is my body... the body is the contingent form that the necessity of my contingency takes' (393/328).

Emotion and embodiment

Sartre's conception of the intimacy and inextricability of the relationship between body and consciousness is evident in his study of emotions. His earliest analyses of emotions are to be found in *La Transcendance de l'ego* of 1936 and *Esquisse d'une théorie des émotions* in 1938. In *La Transcendance de l'ego*, Sartre discusses the way in which reflection 'poisons' unreflective affective responses and desires by making them self-conscious and thereby

transforming them from simple, instantaneous emotional reactions such as repulsion into permanent states such as hatred (TE,
45–7/21–3). These states are conceived as passive, that is to say
that I experience them as emanating from the outside world and
affecting me in ways that are beyond my control; they are also
transcendent, that is to say that I endow them with permanence
and objectivity. In other words, by reflection I transform the spontaneous reactions of consciousness into inert and durable psychic
states (TE, 51/26). This is also the process that transforms impersonal, spontaneous consciousness into a transcendent, permanent
self or ego with which I identify.

In *L'Esquisse d'une théorie des émotions*, Sartre explains further
how he understands the phenomenology of emotion, and how
consciousness and body are inextricably intertwined in all emotional reactions. The bodily changes we experience during
emotion represent what Sartre calls 'le sérieux de l'émotion'
(ETE, 52/50), that is to say the inimitable bodily phenomena
that accompany, and often prolong, conscious emotional
responses. Sartre situates himself very carefully with respect to
the varying theories about the role of the body in emotion: he
refuses the reductive theory which would identify emotion with
its bodily manifestations, or even view the bodily response as
causing the emotion, for in his view it is the particular emotion
experienced that enables us to make sense of our bodily reactions. Trembling and weeping, for example, might be signs of
fear or sadness or even joy. Rapid heart beat or pulse are not
identical with emotion, then, for their meaning depends on the
emotion experienced, and much physiological change is common
to several different emotions. It is the emotion that determines
the interpretation, not the bodily change that determines the
emotion.

Sartre none the less recognizes the way in which bodily
changes may prolong, deepen, and enforce emotional response,
possibly transforming it into a more durable state. In fear, for
example, 'One can stop oneself from running away, but not
from trembling' (ETE, 52/50). Sartre is interested in the function of emotion in our projects: emotions transform the way we
view the world, and they can also act as a means of escape from
difficult or impossible situations, as when I faint in the face of

danger, or become angry when I am losing the argument (ETE, 30/27). Indeed, this seems to be the aspect of his discussion that has most intrigued commentators, but it is in fact only a relatively small element of his overall theory and is deemed by Sartre himself to be insufficient on its own in so far as it does not take the role of consciousness sufficiently into account (ETE, 32/28).

Sartre's own interpretation of emotion is of course phenomenological: emotion is intentional (always directed towards an object), and it is initially unreflective. There is no sense in which we *decide* to have a particular emotional reaction, or if we do, it is necessarily insincere or exaggerated. Emotion feels passive, though we may prolong it actively through will and reflection. Emotion transforms the world in our eyes, and our body changes along with the world, in such a way that our physiological reactions are a means of distinguishing between genuine and feigned emotion (44/41). I can jump for joy at receiving a present, or run away from a problem, but I cannot raise my blood pressure, heart beat or pulse rate, any more than I can lower them, voluntarily, or indeed stop trembling if I am truly afraid. It is through my body that the genuineness of my emotion is demonstrated (54/52). I cannot escape emotion at will, though purifying reflection can sometimes help me understand and control it (55/53).

Indeed, Sartre seems, particularly in his concluding pages, to envisage us as having little control over our emotions: we cannot escape the horror of a frightening face, or the disquiet caused by an inexplicable and disturbing impression. Our consciousness experiences such disturbances with a real degree of passivity, and it carries our body along with it in its fear: in true emotion we are thus returned to a primitive, magical view of the world, which can be modified by purifying reflection, but rarely is. On the contrary, we usually use reflection to entrench us deeper into our magical view of the world and other people, saying to ourselves not the liberating message 'I hate him because I am angry', but rather the self-perpetuating 'I hate him because he is hateful', or, indeed, 'I love her because she is loveable'.[2] And it is this perpetuation, in Sartre's account, that shifts us from emotion into full-blown passion.[3]

Love and desire

In emotion, then, the body represents, enacts, and prolongs the spontaneous responses of consciousness in a way that is largely beyond our conscious control; and reflection on emotion tends to transform spontaneous responses into more permanent 'states'. How does this fit with the radical philosophy of freedom to be found in *L'Etre et le Néant?* We have already seen that Sartre describes the body as 'a necessary characteristic of the pour-soi', the essential condition for consciousness to exist; furthermore, it represents 'the facticity of the pour-soi', that is to say the situation from and in which consciousness makes its free choices. Like emotion, desire provides a test-case for the limits of embodied consciousness, and for the complex relationship between human freedom and facticity. Sartre's discussion of the inescapable tourniquets of love and desire in *L'Etre et le Néant* is well known.[4]

Love is analysed primarily in terms of the Hegelian struggle between consciousnesses, of a fight for supremacy in which seduction and fascination are the tools of conquest. The satisfaction of love is ontologically as well as psychologically impossible, because the longed-for unity with the other is doomed to fail in face of the threat it poses to my liberty. In love, I am at the mercy of the loved one; rather than grounding myself in freedom, I lose my freedom in alienation to another subject. Love is an attempt to assimilate the alterity of the other, to possess the other *as* free, to be both self and other, to be like God. This is an impossible ideal. Love fails me by reducing me to an object. Desire, Sartre argues, arises from the failure of love, and vice versa. In desire I assert my subject-hood and attempt to meet the other on an equal basis, as a free being. But this self-assertion inevitably reduces the other to the status of object. Like love, desire is bound to fail, and for similar reasons: if my desire to possess the other were to be realized she would no longer be free, but her freedom is essential to the satisfaction of my desire.

Sartre's analyses of love and desire focus on the impossible quest for a relationship with the other which does not annihilate the liberty of either, a quest described in terms of a futile struggle to reconcile subject and object. These analyses are primarily ontological, but he also provides a phenomenological description of the transformation of consciousness in desire. Here of course the body plays a very significant role, and the descriptions of desiring consciousness seem loaded with negative connotations: desire compromises the *pour-soi*, and is a fall into complicity with the body; in desire, consciousness becomes *empâtée*, opaque, *pâteux*, heavy, swooning (*pâmée*), and vertiginous. In a word, consciousness becomes bodily.

However, further examination of Sartre's discussion reveals a much more complex attitude towards the embodiment of consciousness in desire. Desire, for Sartre, is of course intentional: it is a mode of consciousness, like imagination or perception, directed towards an object. Indeed, it is a primary [*'originelle'*] mode (EN, 451/382), fundamental not contingent. Sartre is taking a stand here against the opposed camps of empirical psychologists, on the one hand, and 'existential philosophers' such as Heidegger on the other. Both camps conspire to reduce desire to a matter of physiology – to mere 'instinct', which falls within the realm of biology rather than philosophy. Notably, Sartre criticizes Heidegger for excluding sexuality from his existential analytic, so that Dasein appears asexual (EN, 451/383). In Sartre's own account, man is not a sexual being because he possesses sexual organs, but rather the opposite: man possesses sexual organs 'because he is originally and fundamentally a sexual being' (452/383). In describing desire as a mode of consciousness, he is also implicitly rejecting the Freudian model of desire as emanating from the unconscious. 'Who desires?' he asks. I do: 'C'est moi' (455/386). And in sexual desire the profound unity of the *pour-soi* is evident, for there is no possible division between body and consciousness for a *pour-soi* who desires. Desire is a privileged locus where the embodiment of consciousness is clearly manifest.

Again, desire may be defined by its transcendent object. Desire is not desire for pleasure, for sexual intercourse, or for orgasm. These are its end but not its aim. They are secondary objects that habit, convention, or fatigue may cause us to confuse with the primary object of desire – the other. And desire pursues not simply the body of the other, but the 'body and soul', the conscious, corporeal being, the spirit incarnate: 'We do not desire the body as a purely material object . . . Consciousness remains . . . always at the horizon of the desired body' (455/386). In desire, consciousness and body are transformed: desire is *trouble*, it disturbs both body and consciousness. This is clear if we look more closely at one of Sartre's descriptions:

> Consciousness almost becomes heavy in sexual desire; it seems that one is invaded by facticity, that one ceases to flee it and that one slides toward a *passive* consent to desire [...] even the weakest desire is already overwhelming [...]. The heavy, fainting consciousness slides toward a languor comparable to sleep. The man who desires becomes heavily and frighteningly tranquil; his eyes are fixed and appear half-closed, his movements are stamped with a heavy and sticky sweetness [...]. In this sense desire is not only the revelation of the Other's body but the revelation of my own body [...]. The for-itself suffers the vertigo of its own body ... Thus the final state of desire can be swooning as the final stage of consent to the body [...]. The being that desires is consciousness making itself body. (457–8/388–9)

In desire, the other too is made incarnate in his (or her) consciousness through the caress, through contact with my body: 'the revelation of the Other's flesh is made through my own flesh [...]. And so possession truly appears as a *double reciprocal incarnation*. Thus in desire there is an attempt at the incarnation of consciousness' (460/391).

Sartre insists in this section of *L'Etre et le Néant* on the difference and specificity of sexual desire, which he places in a different category from all other desires, and which tends to overwhelm consciousness even when it is relatively weak. This specificity is something he seems to believe is self-evident: 'Now everyone knows that there is an abyss between sexual desire and other appetites' (456/387). It is in this context that Sartre recognizes, as if in passing, a relationship between desire and death:

> From this point of view, desire is not only the clogging of consciousness by its facticity; it is correlatively the ensnarement of a body by the world [...] that is why sensual pleasure is so often linked with death – which is also a metamorphosis or 'being-in-the-midst-of-the-world'. We are familiar with the theme of the 'pseudo-death' ['*fausse morte*']⁵ so abundantly developed across all literatures. (461–2/392)

But Sartre does not pursue the link between desire and death, neither of which can be reduced to 'a physiological accident' (466/393), but which are both rather an integral part of the facticity and incarnation of the *pour-soi*. One of my aims in this chapter is to show that the failure to pursue the implications of this relationship is more than a mere oversight on Sartre's part.

Sartre's ontology of desire shows then a further way in which we can understand his claim that 'man is a useless passion'. And his phenomenology of desire shows again how impossible it is to disentangle body and consciousness at the heart of the human. Indeed, Sartre's descriptions of the complexity of desire and the way in which it can overwhelm consciousness and transform our relation to the world, to the other and indeed to ourselves reveal a deep knowledge and understanding of the processes of desire. Although some aspects of his descriptions may seem predominantly negative, he does seem to be an expert in the field and to give an account of desire as lived from the inside.

The body in pain[6]

But desire is only one of several discussions in *L'Etre et le Néant* which deal with embodied consciousness. Hunger and thirst, and pain and illness are other examples, though they receive a very different treatment from that of sexual desire. Indeed, they are not envisaged as overwhelming, or even significantly affecting, consciousness, but rather as experiences towards which consciousness remains free to choose what attitude it will adopt. Hunger, for example, is quickly transcended towards something beyond itself: 'hunger is a pure surpassing of corporeal facticity', though Sartre does recognize that starvation would lead to a rather different experience in which hunger could not simply be transcended at will, as an insignificant, 'clear and distinct' desire. Most of his analysis of hunger concentrates however on the way in which it is not experienced as an intrinsic element of the *pour-soi*:

> Hunger [. . .] *does not compromise* the very nature of the For-itself, for the For-itself immediately flees it toward its possibles, that is, toward a certain state of satisfied-hunger. (456/387)

Pain and illness represent a further area where the relation between psyche and soma might be thought to be at its most acute and significant. But as in the case of hunger and thirst, Sartre does not see illness as 'overwhelming' ['submergeant]' for consciousness, on the contrary he envisages the sick subject as rather 'choosing' the attitude he will take towards his illness:

> By the very fact that I live, I have assumed even the disability from which I suffer; I surpass it toward my own projects, I make of it the necessary project for my being, and I cannot be infirm without choosing myself as infirm. This means that I choose the way in which I constitute my disability (as 'unbearable', 'humiliating', 'to be concealed', 'to be revealed to all', 'an object of pride', 'the justification for my failures', and so on). (395/328)

Like illness, pain ('what we call "physical" pain' 396/331) is also usually something to be transcended by consciousness, though Sartre does select it as an example of coenaesthesic 'privileged experiences' which can be examined in their own right and not simply as part of the texture of consciousness transcended by our project. And in his analysis of painful vision for example, Sartre seems to accept that it can entail not only a choice of attitude towards the pain itself but also more fundamental changes in my way of experiencing the world. In reading, for instance, eye pain may alter the very way I see and understand the words on the page in front of me:

> It is with much difficulty that the words are detached from the undifferentiated ground that they constitute; they may tremble, quiver [...] their sense can be given two or three times without being understood, as 'to be reread'. (397/332)

Our consciousness of pain may be unreflective, in this case pain is identified with the body; or it may be reflective, in which case pain seems to be distinct from the body. Again, it is the attitude of consciousness that seems to determine precisely how pain is experienced. Sartre's analyses conclude with an identification of the body and the 'psychic' ('the body is the psychic object *par excellence, the only psychic object*' 347/414), which leads him to argue, but without explanation, that it is the body that ultimately explains theories such as that of the unconscious, or indeed memory:

> It is the body that motivates and to some degree justifies psychological theories like that of the unconscious, problems like that of the conservation of memories. (404/338)

It would seem that the body is envisaged by Sartre as conserving memories and therefore as providing a way in which the past is retained within the present, despite the translucidity of consciousness. This is then another way of understanding what he means when he refers to the body as the 'facticity of the pour-soi'.

Apart from desire, then, Sartre's phenomenological descriptions of the relationship between body and consciousness seem to belie the intimacy, and indeed identity, of the two aspects of the *pour-soi* outlined in his ontology where we saw strong statements of their total interdependence: 'Being-for-itself must be wholly body and it must be wholly consciousness' (368/305), 'the soul is the body insofar as the pour-soi *is* its own individuation' (372/309–10). If it remains true that the body 'is nothing other than the pour-soi' (371/309), Sartre seems arguably more interested in the other side of the coin whereby the body is transcended by consciousness: 'the body is perpetually the surpassed' (390/326). We will turn now to human mortality, test case par excellence of the inextricability of body and consciousness, or body and soul.

Mortality and facticity

Sartre's first discussion of death in *L'Etre et le Néant* comes in part two, where he concentrates specifically on the way death reduces the *pour-soi* to something fixed and reabsorbed into the self-identity of the *en-soi*:

> Death reduces the for-itself-for-others to the state of simple for-others (156/112)

> At the limit, at that infinitesimal instant of my death, I shall be no more than my past. [...] At the moment of death, we *are*. (158–9/115)

> Thus the past is a For-itself reapprehended and inundated by the In-itself. (164/120)

These comments all occur in the context of his ontology and would not therefore be expected to contain the phenomenological descriptions of incarnate consciousness which do not enter Sartre's text before part three where the *pour-autrui* reveals our embodiment. In his later analyses of our facticity, Sartre insists that although there are innumerable ways of experiencing the body, ('there are as many ways of existing one's body as there are For-itselfs'), none the less there are certain invariables: 'certain original structures are invariable and in each For-itself constitute human reality' (533/456). One of these invariable structures is certainly human mortality. In his discussion of embodiment in the third part of *L'Etre et le Néant* (Being For-others), Sartre lists six elements of my facticity: my birth, class, nationality, physiology, character, and past, which together constitute my body: 'All that is my body [...] conditions consciousness' (393/328). Birth is included here, but death is not. However, in the first chapter of the fourth part, in the section entitled 'Freedom and Facticity: The Situation', five elements of facticity are analysed: my place, my past, my surroundings, my neighbour, and finally my death. This is undoubtedly the point at which we might expect Sartre to offer an extended presentation of his own existential understanding of the significance of mortality for the human subject.

Sartre's objections to previous attempts to deal with the subject of death are well known. He criticizes a variety of philosophical and religious interpretations of the meaning of death: death is neither 'pre-eminently non-human' [*'l'inhumain par excellence'*] (the realist conception), nor 'an event of human life' (the idealist, humanist conception) (615/531). Sartre claims to understand the desire to recuperate death to be found in poets such as Rilke, novelists such as Malraux, and philosophers such as Heidegger, but he rejects it. Heidegger's conception of 'Sein zum Tode' [being for/towards death], in which death becomes 'mine', is attractive, Sartre argues, because it enables us to internalize death and connect it to human freedom; indeed, it contains an element of truth, but ultimately it deceives us by a concealed circular argument (617/533–4): that is to say it individualizes death on the basis of Dasein, at the same time as it individualizes Dasein starting from death. We are not going to spend long now on the details of this debate between Sartre and Heidegger which has been discussed by others many times before,[7] but must none the less look briefly at Sartre's ontological analysis before considering what has been most strikingly omitted: that is to say a truly phenomenological account.

For Sartre, death is merely an aspect of my facticity, as contingent as my birth. It does not found my facticity, and nor does it found my finitude: I am finite in so far as I make choices, and immortality would not remove this finitude. Death marks the end of my world-view: in death I become finally subject to the other whose point of view dominates mine. But death is not part of the ontological structure of my being, at least as *pour-soi*:[8] it is the other who is mortal in his being.[9] I am mortal for others. I am not free *for* death, rather I am a free mortal. Death poses a real limit to my projects and my freedom, but my freedom remains none the less total and infinite because death is not its end or aim, but rather the reverse of it. Death is not part of my subjectivity which is necessarily independent of it.

Death, in the description Sartre proffers in opposition to Heidegger, 'is not my possibility of no longer realizing a presence in the world, but an always possible nihilation of my possibles' (620/537).[10] Life is perpetual waiting, Sartre believes, but this is not a contingent defect in human nature, a form of nervousness, for example; it is rather a structural element of the human subject, which he describes as 'the very structure of ipseity: to be oneself is to come to oneself' (622/538). However, Sartre will not accept that death should form an integral part of this waiting. Even if we agree with Sartre that death does not give meaning to our lives, we need not agree with what he sees as the corollary of this – that death necessarily removes all meaning from life (623/539). In Sartre's eyes, death represents the triumph of the point of view of the other on my life: 'the characteristic of a dead life is that it is the life of which the Other makes itself the guardian' (626/541).

Sartre does not seem able to envisage my own relationship to my future death: he passes directly from his refutation of Heidegger to an analysis of the *pour-autrui* of death. It seems as if he fears that his rejection of Heidegger's position would be threatened if he acknowledged the perspective of the *pour-soi* on its own death. Indeed, he even comments that 'there is no place for death in the being that it is for-itself'. But this is so clearly at odds with lived experience that Sartre seems to be driven to conduct his argument in abstract terms which mask its implausibility, as in phrases such as 'when the pour-soi "stops living"' (625/540), which arguably confuses two different levels of analysis. It is true that there are moments when Sartre seems about to change course and to give us a phenomenological account of our relationship to death, as, for example, when he discusses the difference between sudden death and death in old age:

> There is a considerable difference in quality between death at the limit of old age and sudden death that eliminates us in our prime or in youth. To await the former is to accept that life is a limited enterprise, one way among others of choosing finitude and electing our ends on the foundation of finitude. Awaiting the latter would be to wait for my life to be a failed endeavour. (EN, 620/536)

Here Sartre initially appears to be accepting that we can authentically wait for death in old age, however this is quickly retracted when he goes on to explain that since we may well die before, or indeed after, we have finished our life's task, awaiting death in old age necessarily involves moral blindness or bad faith.

This refusal to accept any form of waiting for death, even in its most familiar forms, might seem to represent a fear of death, or an inability to face mortality. But it is not appropriate here to undertake a psychoanalysis, or even an analysis, of Sartre's attitude, though we might suspect that the war perhaps contributed to his resolute, determined stance. What is more interesting in this context is the consequences of Sartre's attitude, for he seems to miss a perfect opportunity for an existential analysis of death that might have rivalled Heidegger's own, but that he seems obdurately to avoid, particularly in his repeated insistence on the bad faith inherent in any attempt to confront one's own death. What Sartre seems to be lacking here is imagination, for his extraordinary descriptions of desire – which he clearly has experienced, and evokes with real conviction – bear witness to his powers of phenomenological evocation, whereas he has, necessarily, no personal experience of death, and the externality of his analyses suggest that he also has little or no experience of watching another person die. Of course, in the midst of war, one might argue that Sartre's determination to envisage death as something external that does not concern me personally was highly appropriate. None the less, it remains, I believe, a limited attitude that seriously impoverishes his analysis.

Death, then, is for Sartre an integral part of human facticity. But if this facticity includes our body, or our 'physiological structure', it does not do so simply when we are in the flower of youth, it also includes our illnesses, our wounds, and especially our continuing ageing, for, if illness is rare and intermittent, ageing begins at birth and cannot be overlooked. Eye pain and stomach ache, which are Sartre's chosen examples in *L'Etre et le Néant*, are far from exhausting the range of illnesses and are indeed among the least significant. AIDS, of course, did not exist in 1943, but cancer, TB, and all the other devastating terminal illnesses were as prevalent sixty years ago as they are now. The slow weakening of the body, the inexorable descent into incapacity, be it visual, auditory, motor or cerebral, constituted, even in the midst of war, the most usual path towards death. And this downward path does not only affect the body, it also concerns consciousness, the body as *pour-soi* as well as the body as *en-soi*.

It is certainly true, as Sartre maintains, that it is up to us to choose the attitude we will take towards disease, ageing and, in the case of terminal illness, death itself, but this does not take into account what one might call the psycho-somatic dialectic, the dialectic between soul and body, liberty and facticity, life and death. It does not recognize that severe illness and ageing do not affect only the body; all my capacities are thereby weakened and lessened, including my ability to choose, to face what is happening to me, and even the lucidity of my consciousness. It is not only sexual desire that disturbs consciousness, muddies it, and brings it close to fainting; pain and illness can have the same effect. But in this case, it is not simply a matter of a temporary state of which orgasm will rid me, and that I may even cherish as a sign of my successful relations with a loved one.

On the contrary, the torpor of my limbs, the weakening of my vision and hearing, the confusion of my mind, and the heaviness of my consciousness are rather signs of approaching death, from which I cannot escape in either pleasure or distraction. The more the body diminishes and weakens, the harder it is for the *pour-soi* to identify with it, and the more it may seem like a prison where consciousness languishes and itself grows weak. Sartre's analyses of death in *L'Etre et le Néant* correspond perfectly to his remarks on torture in the 1940s: his insistence that it is I who choose the moment at which I will speak under torture seems to demonstrate an almost complete lack of understanding of the effect on consciousness of extreme pain,[11] which it weakens and even annihilates.

Indeed, Sartre himself was later highly critical of his own position, commenting in an interview in 1970: 'It's incredible: I really believed it.'[12] Similarly, to maintain that I am in full control of the attitude I take towards illness, pain or death reveals the same wilful forgetfulness of the psycho-somatic body and, ultimately, the same dualism that elsewhere Sartre tries so strenuously to avoid. Sartre's discussions of death ignore the body as resolutely as his discussions of love – only desire seems truly incarnate in Sartre's phenomenology.

Maurice Merleau-Ponty

> La morsure du monde telle que je la sens sur mon corps est blessure.

These weaknesses in Sartre's account have been commented on and analysed by many critics over the years,[13] and among the first and most significant of these is the uncompromising phenomenological critique by Sartre's fellow philosopher and one-time friend, Maurice Merleau-Ponty. Merleau-Ponty himself consistently gave a primary role to the body in the constitution of subjectivity, from his early work on *La Structure du comportement* (1942) in which he expresses his opposition to the reductivism of empirical psychology, through his extensive elaboration of the body-subject in *La Phénoménologie de la perception* (1945) to his ultimate refutation of realism, intellectualism, and ontological dualism in *Le Visible et l'Invisible* (1964).

Mind–body dualism: the case against Sartre

In *La Structure du comportement*, first published in 1942, Merleau-Ponty could of course respond only to those works of Sartre which preceded *L'Etre et le Néant*, in particular *L'Esquisse d'une théorie des émotions* and *La Transcendance de l'ego*. This means that when Merleau-Ponty argues that my behaviour necessarily goes beyond the *en-soi pour-soi* opposition ('in the experience of behaviour, I effectively surpass the alternative of the for-itself (*pour-soi*) and the in-itself (*en-soi*)', SC, 137/126) he cannot be referring to *L'Etre et le Néant*, though this is certainly one of the objections which he will later level at Sartre also. He is objecting rather to all philosophies which, in his view, depend on what he sees as a radical and unwarranted dualism.

According to Merleau-Ponty, if a proper perspective is taken, which envisages matter, life, and spirit not as three orders of reality but rather as three dialectical 'levels of signification' or indeed three 'forms of unity' (SC, 217/201), then the problems of understanding interaction between body and consciousness, or body and soul, disappear. There is no question of causal interaction, which Merleau-Ponty rejects as vigorously as Sartre, precisely because the body is not a closed mechanism on which the soul might, or might not, be able to act. Man's body and soul are integrated at a higher, dialectical level, at which 'his soul and body are no longer distinguished' (SC, 219/203).

In this sense, the accidents of our bodily constitution do not impede our perception of the world, they rather permit and indeed enable that perception, so that El Greco's astigmatism, for example, is one with his artistic vision, and questions of cause and effect are irrelevant as well as unanswerable. (This perspective allows Merleau-Ponty to account convincingly also for phenomena such as hallucinations or simply errors, 237/220.) And Merleau-Ponty insists that his argument is not concealing an empiricist agenda which would attempt to account for experience without recourse to consciousness; on the contrary, his aim, he says, is to expand the domain of consciousness from a potentially exclusive translucence to the whole of experience: 'we want to gather into consciousness for-itself (*pour-soi*) all the life of consciousness in-itself (*en-soi*)' (SC, 240/223).

By the time of *Phénoménologie de la perception* however, Merleau-Ponty had *L'Etre et le Néant* to respond to as well as Sartre's
earlier works. And we know from his review, 'La querelle de
l'existentialisme', published in *Les Temps modernes* in 1945, the
extent of both his admiration for and his reservations about that
text. Here once again Merleau-Ponty reiterates his objection to
the presentation of the relationship between *en-soi* and *pour-soi* as
one of antithesis rather than communicative bond, which is, in his
view, one of the major weaknesses of *L'Etre et le Néant*, along with
the identification of the subject with 'nothingness', to be thought
of merely against a background of the world.

None the less, in his defence of Sartre against Catholic critics
such as Gabriel Marcel and Madame Mercier, Merleau-Ponty
seems to get closer to a recognition of the true complexity of
Sartre's position for, in refusing to accept that Sartre's philosophy
'starts by putting out the light of the spirit', he goes on to argue
that 'it makes it shine because we are not body *and* spirit or consciousness *confronting* the world but spirit incarnate, being-in-the-
world' (*Sense and Non-Sense*, pp. 74–5). Indeed, in this review
essay Merleau-Ponty defends Sartre not only against Catholic
accusations of materialism but also against Marxist accusations of
idealism, whereas, in Merleau-Ponty's view, Sartre understands the
relationship between subject and object as one of *being* rather than
of *knowledge*, 'in which, paradoxically, the subject *is* his body, his
world, and his situation, by a sort of exchange' (*Sense*, p. 72). And
even though Merleau-Ponty does not consider that *L'Etre et le
Néant* makes this paradox entirely clear, and argues that it remains
'too exclusively antithetical', his review arguably gives a fairer
presentation of Sartre's position than many of Merleau-Ponty's
later accounts. None the less, even here Merleau-Ponty can be seen
to simplify Sartre's position and push him towards the very
dualism he is striving so strenuously to avoid.

So, whereas we must recognize that Merleau-Ponty is right to
claim that *L'Etre et le Néant* does not offer any social theory – and
Sartre was later to acknowledge fully Merleau-Ponty's role in
leading him in that direction – we do not need to concede that
Sartre's view of freedom lacks a 'theory of passivity' (77). Indeed,
we have already seen that Sartre's account of emotions describes
our experience of them precisely as passive: 'in the majority of
cases, we are struggling [...] against the development of

emotional manifestations: we are trying to master our fear, to calm our anger, to restrain our weeping' (TE, 29/33–4).[14]

Merleau-Ponty would then seem to be attributing to Sartre a mind–body dualism that he is very far from espousing. And we might well ask why. *Phénoménologie de la perception* will throw light on this problem. Here Merleau-Ponty sets out clearly his own conception of the relationship between body and consciousness, or body and soul, and between freedom and situation. He describes 'the facticity of the cogito' as not an imperfection but rather as what assures me of my existence (PP, 17/xix). He seeks to describe what are traditionally envisaged as oppositions in terms of inter-dependence and interaction, referring, for example, to 'the fusion of soul and body in the act' (PP, 97/114).

What is more, he emphasizes precisely those aspects of existence that he believes Sartre puts in question, arguing that habit and sedimented structures are what enable us to function in the world and to see it clearly: 'Thus it is by giving up part of his spontaneity, by becoming involved in the world through stable organs and pre-established circuits that man can acquire the mental and practical space which will theoretically free him from his environment and allow him to *see* it' (PP, 117/100). And it is this which allows him to link the physiological and the psychic, which, once 'reintegrated into existence [...] are no longer distinguishable respectively as the order of the in-itself and that of the for-itself' (PP, 118/101), and to argue that mental disturbances cannot be clearly categorized as either psychic or somatic (118/102). In short, for Merleau-Ponty, the subject is bodily, 'I am therefore my body' (PP, 240/231), and the body represents what he calls the 'natural ego' (PP, 209/198) or the 'natural subject' (PP, 240/231).

> In so far as, when I reflect on the essence of subjectivity, I find it bound up with that of the body and that of the world, this is because my existence as subjectivity is merely one with my existence as a body and with the existence of the world, and because the subject that I am, when taken concretely, is inseparable from this body and this world. (PP, 470/475)

The heart of the disagreement seems to lie here: despite Sartre's insistence that the body represents the situation and the *soi* of the *pour-soi* ('Being-for-itself must be wholly body and it must be wholly consciousness' EN 368/305, 'I *am* my body to the extent that I *am*' EN 391/326, etc.), Merleau-Ponty cannot accept that this is even really thinkable for Sartre, given his description of the *pour-soi* as a *néant*. Indeed, Merleau-Ponty starts his section on freedom in *Phénoménologie de la perception* with a deliberately unacknowledged summary of what he sees as Sartre's position, maintaining that freedom is an all-or-nothing affair, and that it cannot be attenuated or limited, only to lead us inexorably to an apparent volte-face when he argues that such a conception of freedom would be meaningless since it would make it impossible to discriminate between free and unfree acts (PP, 499/510).

Similarly, having taken Sartre's example of a steep rock being 'unclimbable' precisely because of my desire to climb it, Merleau-Ponty argues that, on the contrary, the world has intrinsic structures to which I can respond but cannot change and do not create. However, to anyone familiar with *L'Etre et le Néant*, these arguments will seem, to say the least, puzzling. Despite Merleau-Ponty's insistence, none of this is in fact incompatible with Sartre's own position. Sartre does not imagine that I in any way constitute the physical size or steepness of the rock – that depends on 'an unnameable and unthinkable *residuum* that belongs to the in-itself' (EN, 562/482) – simply that my perception of this as an obstacle will depend on my project to climb the rock.

Again, Merleau-Ponty may claim that Sartre's conception of freedom is idealist and voluntarist, but in fact, as we have already seen, Sartre always maintains that I am free starting from my situation in the world and my facticity and that, in some circumstances, these may constitute a 'permanent *alienation*' (EN, 614/530). When Merleau-Ponty discusses Sartre's account (in *L'Etre et le Néant*) of the hiker who gives up because he is 'too tired', it is particularly evident that his account does not do justice to Sartre's position. It is true that Sartre maintains that the hiker who gives up demonstrates a project in which fatigue and physical discomfort are unwelcome and to be avoided. But this does not mean that he believes that the hiker could simply have chosen to continue: on the contrary, this example is part of his discussion of how difficult we find it to change once we are embarked on a particular course. Change is not impossible, but it is certainly very hard: 'I could have done otherwise, but at what price?' (EN, 531/464). So when Merleau-Ponty stresses the need to recognize 'a sort of sedimentation of our life' (PP, 505/513), he may be using a different vocabulary from Sartre but he is making the same point: personal transformation is not easy, most of the time we choose to persevere in our project and continue along the track we have already mapped out for ourselves. As Sartre argues:

> The free perseverance in one and the same project does not imply any permanence; quite the contrary, it's a perpetual renewal of my engagement – as we have seen. But the realities enveloped and illuminated by a project that develops itself present, on the contrary, the permanence of the in-itself; and to the extent that they refer our image to us, they support us with their perennity; in fact it frequently happens that we take their permanence for our own. [...] In this sense, there is no character – there is only the project of one's self. But we must, however, understand the 'given' aspect of character. [...] character is often what the Pour-soi tries to recuperate in order to become the In-itself-for-itself that it projects itself to be. (EN, 636–7/551–2)

Or, in Merleau-Ponty's terms: 'this past, though not a fate, has at least a specific weight [...]. Our freedom does not destroy our situation, but is enmeshed in it: our situation, in so far as we live it, is open' (PP, 506/514).

> What then is freedom? [...] The world is already constituted, but also never completely constituted. [...] There is therefore never determinism and never absolute choice, I am never a thing and never bare consciousness. [...] In this exchange between the situation and the one who takes it upon himself, it is impossible to determine precisely the 'part of situation' and the 'part of freedom'. [...] The idea of situation excludes absolute freedom from the origin of our engagements. [...] Nothing determines me from outside [...]. We need have no fear that our choices or actions restrict our liberty, since choice and action alone cut us loose from our anchorage. (PP, 517–20/527–30)

This is the conclusion to *Phénoménologie de la perception*, it could equally well be part of *L'Etre et le Néant*.

The body-subject

But if I am insisting that Merleau-Ponty misrepresents Sartre by simplifying his arguments and failing (or refusing) to acknowledge the importance of situation and facticity in Sartre's account of human existence, this is certainly not to say that Merleau-Ponty is doing no more than take over Sartre's own positions. On the contrary, there are clear differences between Merleau-Ponty and Sartre, especially with respect to the role of the body, but Merleau-Ponty unintentionally masks these in his desire to mark himself off from Sartre and demonstrate his own originality. For in fact Merleau-Ponty's position is subtle and complex and does not depend for its originality on a contrast with an over-simplified version of Sartre's thinking which in the end is no more than a distraction.[15] His phenomenology aims to overcome mind–body dualism through his conception of the body-subject which implies that it is impossible to explore the structures of consciousness without at the same time analysing the role of the body. Sartre on the other hand does not introduce the body in *L'Etre et le Néant* until Section Three where he discusses the *pour-autrui*. Even his initial discussion of the facticity of the *pour-soi* (EN, 121–7/79–83) does not refer to the body.

For Merleau-Ponty the body is an intrinsic element in the activities of consciousness and its imbrication with consciousness is therefore stressed from the outset. In the case of illness, for example, or indeed madness, Merleau-Ponty envisages the world-view of the sick man as irremediably affected by his physical condition. Whereas Sartre argues that we are free to take whatever attitude we choose towards our illness, for Merleau-Ponty it is only through that illness that we exist at all, and it cannot be viewed as something extraneous that we can simply transcend. His examples of phantom limb pain and of brain damage (in the case of Schneider) rather than stomach ache and eye strain are themselves indicative of the seriousness with which he takes the body:

> After all, Schneider's trouble was not initially metaphysical, for it was a shell splinter that wounded him in the occipital region. The damage to his sight was serious, it would be ridiculous, as we have said, to explain all the other deficiencies in terms of the visual one

as their cause, but no less ridiculous to think that the shell splinter struck symbolic consciousness.

It is through his sight that Mind [*l'Esprit*] has been wounded [*atteint*]. (PP, 158/145).

Sartre might perhaps agree with this, but he certainly never said anything like it, and in his exploration of the relationship between body and consciousness he never tried, as Merleau-Ponty did, to understand the relationship of identity and difference between brain and mind. So that whereas Sartre would have no problem acceding to Merleau-Ponty's claim that 'psychic illness' may be linked to 'some bodily accident' (PP, 171/158), it seems unthinkable that he could himself write, as Merleau-Ponty did, 'consciousness can be ill' (PP, 171/158).

Another way of looking at this question might be to say that whereas for Sartre the effect of the embodiment of consciousness is not usually apparent or significant unless something has gone wrong, for Merleau-Ponty it is not only always apparent but also genuinely constitutive. For Merleau-Ponty, the physically aberrant is just a modality of the normal, which is to say that *all* bodily phenomena contribute to the perspective consciousness has of the world. And this difference of emphasis would also explain why Sartre elects to discuss eye strain which can (almost) be ignored by consciousness, whereas Merleau-Ponty chooses more extreme illnesses such as brain damage which serve to demonstrate the inescapability and generality of embodiment. However, while recognizing that Merleau-Ponty has a far more developed view of the body and its relationship to consciousness, it none the less remains true that what Merleau-Ponty says is largely compatible with Sartre's own position, and that it is only Merleau-Ponty's wilful blindness that prevents him from recognizing this. In part, as I have suggested, this is in order to emphasize his own originality, but also, I believe, because of a genuine hostility to the radical way in which Sartre likes to talk about the freedom of consciousness.

Merleau-Ponty's most aggressive critique of Sartre's philosophy is to be found in *Les Aventures de la dialectique* of 1955, in which he responds to two of Sartre's political articles, 'Les Communistes et la paix' and 'Réponse à Claude Lefort'. Merleau-Ponty has by the mid 1950s drawn back from the Communist Party whereas

Sartre has moved closer to it – too close, in Merleau-Ponty's opinion. His essay is of course primarily political, but this is not the aspect that will concern us here. Rather we need to notice that Merleau-Ponty attributes what he sees as Sartre's political errors to the errors of his ontology: once again he attacks the excessive purity and disembodiment of the Sartrean *cogito* which he associates with the violent purity of communism; secondly he criticizes Sartre's conception of freedom and commitment which he considers insufficiently rooted in the world to lead to a real theory of action; and finally he argues that Sartre's notion of relations with others as essentially conflictual renders any resolution of the class struggle ontologically impossible.

All of these criticisms depend on a simplification and misrepresentation of Sartre's philosophy, as many critics have observed, though many others have simply accepted Merleau-Ponty's account without observing its distortions.[16] In particular, Merleau-Ponty refuses to recognize in Sartre any real conception of being-in-the-world or intersubjectivity, and together with his ignoring of the importance of facticity and situation, this produces what is close to a polemical parody of Sartre's real position. What is more, it pays no attention at all to the development of Sartre's thought, both philosophically and politically, since *L'Etre et le Néant*. We shall examine shortly Simone de Beauvoir's reaction to what she sees as a travesty of Sartre's philosophy.

Merleau-Ponty's last major response to Sartre is to be found in *Le Visible et l'invisible*, and this holds what is arguably the key to Merleau-Ponty's ambivalent attitude to Sartre. In this work Merleau-Ponty reflects on the implications of his own ontology and finds it severely wanting. In his later view, all his early attempts to understand the relationship between mind and body in his notion of the body-subject were critically undermined by the failure of his ontology to overcome the dualism he so strenuously rejected. He now considers that his early texts did no more than state his opposition to dualism without ever really tackling the problem at its root. This meant that dualism kept reasserting itself precisely because he had not done the hard ontological work necessary to tackle it head on: 'the problems posed in *The Phenomenology of Perception* are insoluble because I start there from the 'consciousness–"object" distinction' (VI, 253/200).

In the light of this late self-criticism the increasing vigour of his critique of what he sees as Sartrean dualism becomes much more comprehensible. As he explains, his initial attraction to Sartre's work was precisely because his ontology of being and nothingness attempted to overcome dualism by establishing a fundamental relationship between them in which consciousness was nothing except in relation to Being: 'We have therefore asked ourselves if a philosophy of the negative would not restore us to the brute being of the unreflected without compromising our capacity for reflection' (VI, 104/74).

However, Merleau-Ponty became progressively more critical of Sartre, and came to consider that he never in fact managed to escape from dualism even when he was most concerned to do so. In other words, Merleau-Ponty sensed in Sartre the failures of his own philosophy, laid bare, as it were, precisely because Sartre did carry out the explicit ontological work that Merleau-Ponty realizes he never himself engaged in. It is then his own dualist errors that he is sensing and rejecting so vehemently in Sartre, but it is not until the end of his career that he manages to turn the spotlight on himself and recognize this. Of course, he also has other objections to Sartre's philosophy, concerning for example his conception of the pre-reflective *cogito*, and the implications of his distinction between *conscience* and *connaissance*, as well as what Merleau-Ponty considers to be his excessively distant *pensée de survol*, but opinions differ on the validity of his objections and they need not concern us here. It is perhaps ironic that the title of this late work of Merleau-Ponty refers back, perhaps unwittingly, to a phrase of Sartre's in *L'Etre et le Néant*, which, in its affirmation of the imbrication of human subjectivity in the world, gives the lie to the accusations of idealism and dualism which Merleau-Ponty is levelling at him.

Like Merleau-Ponty, Sartre too maintains that 'structure of the world implies that we can *see* without being *visible*' (EN, 381/317). But Merleau-Ponty does not believe that this assertion is ultimately compatible with Sartre's ontology and argues that, for Sartre, being-seen is not an intrinsic aspect of being-in-the-world and being-with-others but is rather an ontological disaster: 'Pure seer, he becomes a thing seen through an ontological catastrophe, through a pure event that is for him the impossible' (VI, 115/83). As Margaret Whitford explains so clearly,[17] Merleau-Ponty considers that Sartre's ontology is incompatible with both his epistemology and his phenomenology, and this leads him to take issue with his epistemology and, broadly speaking, to overlook his phenomenology almost entirely.

Passion and death

But where does all this leave Merleau-Ponty with respect to the central questions that concern us here, that is to say, emotion, passion, and death? His notion of the body-subject and his resolutely phenomenological approach to philosophy should enable him to establish a convincing and potentially moving account of what happens to the subject in the throes of passion and, a fortiori, in the throes of death. For Merleau-Ponty, embodiment is not merely acknowledged as part of the unavoidable situation of consciousness, it is rather an intrinsic part of consciousness, an incarnation to be celebrated rather than just accepted. We have already seen how this allows him to give a more satisfactory account than Sartre's of illness, both physical and mental, but it is difficult to say the same for passion and death. One of his most interesting discussions comes early on in *La Structure du comportement*, when he uses passion and death as test cases for his view of the simultaneous identity and difference of body and soul. The physical movements of a dying man may no longer be meaningful – and Merleau-Ponty uses Proust's account of the death of Marcel's grandmother to illustrate this – just as our thoughts may not always manage to find full bodily expression, in cases of extreme shyness for example. Such an apparent lack of correlation between mind and body might seem to demonstrate an underlying distinction and thereby support dualism. But Merleau-Ponty takes a more complex view, and argues that in both cases the disintegration is not simply restricted to body or soul alone:

> In these cases of disintegration, the soul and the body are apparently distinct: that is the truth of dualism. But the soul, if it possesses no means of expression – one should rather say: no means of actualizing itself – soon ceases to be *anything whatsoever* and in particular ceases to be the soul, as the thought of the aphasic

weakens and is dissolved; the body that loses its meaning soon ceases to be a living body and falls back into the state of a physico-chemical mass; it arrives at non-sense only by dying. The two terms can never be distinguished absolutely without ceasing to be; thus their empirical connection is based on the original operation that establishes a meaning in a fragment of matter and makes that meaning inhabit it, appear and be. In returning to this *structure* as we return to fundamental reality, we render comprehensible both the distinction and the union of the soul and the body. There is always a duality that reappears at one level or another: hunger or thirst prevents thought or feelings; the properly sexual dialectic reveals itself ordinarily through passion; integration is never absolute and it always fails – at a higher level in the writer, a lower one in the aphasic. There always comes a moment when we divest ourselves of passion because of fatigue or self-respect. (SC, 226/209–10)

It is interesting to note here that passion is placed on the side of the soul and sex, like fatigue, on the side of the body. As Merleau-Ponty himself observes, it is impossible to speak of these questions without to some extent using the language of dualism, and in any case, as he goes on to explain, what really matters is that the apparent duality is not a question of substances but of levels of complexity. So passion and death are indeed used as test-cases, in both cases as testing the limits of body–soul identification in the face of apparent disintegration. The *experiences* of passion and death are not themselves described.

Sexuality and love

Perhaps Merleau-Ponty's later works will make good this arguably surprising lacuna? In *Phénoménologie de la perception*, Merleau-Ponty's discussion of 'the body as sexed being' again takes sexuality as a kind of test-case of the identity of mind and body. Affectivity is described as 'an original mode of consciousness' (PP, 192/179), and sexuality or eroticism as an attitude of consciousness, that is to say, not a particular, self-contained bodily state but rather 'coextensive with life' (207/197). And Merleau-Ponty is very clear and convincing in his discussion of the way in which the body does not simply 'express' or manifest' the feelings and experiences of consciousness: it *is* those experiences, so that an inability to speak following a trauma, or generalized hysteria ['pithiatisme'] are envisaged as 'an illness of the *cogito*' (199/187) at the same time as being physical states which cannot be cast off by an act of will. Indeed, the longer they last the harder it becomes to overcome them: 'Sulking or loss of voice, for the period that they endure, become consistent like things'; 'with every moment that passes, freedom is depreciated and becomes less probable' (PP, 201/189); 'the role of the body is to ensure this metamorphosis. [...] If the body can symbolize existence, it is because it realizes it and is its actuality' (202/190). So in sexual desire, it is not just the body that is desired, but rather 'a body brought to life by a consciousness' (205/194). This may sound reminiscent of what Sartre had to say about sexuality, and indeed it is but, unlike Sartre, Merleau-Ponty tends to take examples of the failure of normal functioning to illustrate his theories, as in the case of Schneider's loss of eroticism. Here too then, Merleau-Ponty's analysis of sexuality does not constitute an elaborated phenomenological account but rather an examination of its implications.

Similarly, Merleau-Ponty discusses love in *Phénoménologie de la perception* in the context of his distinction between true and false sentiments and in his discussion of jealousy in Proust (PP, 486/494), but the discussion remains at a fairly abstract level. Again, he takes the example of a dying man to illustrate the way in which we take for granted all the imperfections and weaknesses of our body as the price we pay, quite unreflectingly, for being in the world. Indeed, the dying man is described, much as Sartre describes him, as retaining his consciousness up until the last moment: 'Until the moment of coma, the dying man is inhabited by a consciousness, he is all that he sees, and enjoys this means of escape' (PP, 496/504). None of this engages very powerfully with what must surely be recognized as two of the most significant experiences of any human life. It seems as though Merleau-Ponty, despite his insistence on embodied subjectivity, is even less able than Sartre to express within his philosophy itself the full implications of human incarnation at its most radical moments.

We may regret this when we look at a couple of instances in Merleau-Ponty's later texts when, in the context of art, the power of literature and of painting respectively, we get a glimpse of what a more evocatively phenomenological description could have brought to the relative (and paradoxical) abstraction of Merleau-Ponty's more theoretical philosophy. In *La Prose du monde*, for example, in his discussion of incarnation and the simultaneous intimacy and distance of our knowledge of other people, Merleau-Ponty writes of the experience of watching another person waking up in the hot sunshine after a sleep and reaching for his hat:

> The moment the man wakes up in the sun and reaches for his hat, between the sun that burns *me* and makes *my* eyes squint and the gesture that from a distance *over there* brings relief to my fatigue. [. . .] A bond is tied without my needing to decide anything, and if I am forever incapable of effectively living the experience of the scorching the other suffers, the bite of the world as I feel it upon my body is an injury for anyone exposed to it as I am – and especially for this body that begins to defend itself against it. (*La Prose du monde*, 190/137)

This brief passage arguably does more to help us understand what Merleau-Ponty believes is involved in genuine intersubjectivity than several pages of more theoretical discussion, and phrases like 'la morsure du monde' may lead us to regret that a real phenomenology of passion was never attempted. Similarly, in Merleau-Ponty's discussion of painting in *L'Œil et l'esprit*, his evocation of bodily life and death may make us regret its brevity:

> There is a human body when, between seeing and the seen, between touching and the touched, between one eye and the other, between hand and hand, a blending of some sort takes place – when the spark is lit between sensing and sensible, lighting the fire that will not stop burning, until some bodily accident undoes what no accident would have sufficed to do. (OE, 21/125)

And the last words of his text, concerning the inevitable incompleteness and failure of all works of art, as of all science, philosophy, and indeed all human endeavours, including love (Merleau-Ponty quotes Lamiel's famous 'n'est-ce que cela?') seem strangely prescient given the imminence of his own death:

> If no painting attains the completion of painting, if no work even attains its own completion absolutely, each creation changes, alters,

enlightens, deepens, confirms exalts, re-creates or creates in advance all the others. If the creations are not to be taken for granted, it is not only because, like all things, they pass, it is also because they have nearly all their life ahead of them. (OE, 93/194)

It seems then, as though Merleau-Ponty may disappoint us if we seek in his philosophical works a phenomenology of human emotion, passion, and death. Perhaps the fact that, unlike Sartre, he did not write fiction or drama, meant that he had, as it were, no practice in the evocation, rather than the analysis, of the experience of mortal subjects, and he needed the stimulation of other artists (Proust, Cezanne et al.) to allow him to bring his writing itself a little closer to the human ambiguity, complexity, and depth that he was analysing.

Simone de Beauvoir

The two sexes are [. . .] eaten away by time, stalked by death.

Simone de Beauvoir, on the other hand, produced a considerable amount of literary autobiography, fiction, and drama, and she is arguably more successful in her discussion of mortality and passion than either Sartre or Merleau-Ponty. But before we explore what she has to say on these fundamental existential questions, we will look first briefly at her intervention in the debate between Sartre and Merleau-Ponty about the relationship between body and consciousness, facticity and freedom.

Beauvoir and the debate on embodiment

Beauvoir's first response to *Phénoménologie de la perception* came in a review article in *Les Temps modernes* where she compared Merleau-Ponty's conception of the relationship between consciousness and body with that of Sartre and argued, with apparently objectivity, that Merleau-Ponty had a considerably stronger notion of embodiment.[18] Ten years later, her response to Merleau-Ponty's attack on Sartre in *Les Aventures de la dialectique* is unsurprisingly far more polemical. Entitled 'Merleau-Ponty et le pseudo-sartrisme'[19] it takes the form of a scathing critique of Merleau-Ponty's account of Sartre's philosophy. Basically, Beauvoir contends that Merleau-Ponty's criticisms of Sartre as giving insufficient importance to the body, as an idealist who does not recognize himself as such, and as holding a false view of the human subject, are all based on the same, fundamental misreading. In her view, Merleau-Ponty has failed to distinguish between consciousness, subject, and self, and between *pour-soi* and ego, and therefore misunderstands Sartre's philosophy at a most basic level.

By conflating what Sartre has to say about consciousness and what he has to say about the subject, Merleau-Ponty creates a 'pseudo-sartrisme' which functions as a philosophical straw man that he then proceeds to knock down. And Beauvoir is certainly right on this issue: Sartrean consciousness may be translucent, but Sartrean subjectivity is complex and indirect, and arises from the 'circuit of ipseity' in which the self-reflexivity of the *pour-soi* personalizes it. Merleau-Ponty has, wittingly or unwittingly, conflated the subject indiscriminately with 'consciousness, the Ego, man' (*Privilèges*, 205).

Beauvoir quotes tellingly from *L'Etre et le Néant* to prove her point, and shows Sartre discriminating clearly between consciousness and subject: 'On the contrary, we have shown that the self on principle cannot inhabit consciousness' (EN, 148/102), 'The Ego appears to consciousness as a transcendent in itself' (EN, 147/103), and finally 'It is as the *Ego* that we are subjects' (EN, 209/162). Indeed, all this section of *L'Etre et le Néant* is concerned to discuss precisely the difference between consciousness and any kind of self-hood. And Beauvoir insists that many of Merleau-Ponty's supposed corrections to Sartre, as for example when he objects to what he sees as the lack of mediations in Sartre's philosophy, are in fact to be found explicitly formulated by Sartre himself in his account of the reciprocal conditioning between the world and the self: 'Without world, there is no ipseity, no person; without ipseity, there is no person, no world' (EN, 149/104).

Beauvoir in fact makes several other major criticisms of Merleau-Ponty's misrepresentation of Sartre, such as his mistaken view that Sartre cannot distinguish between true and imaginary love, his conflation of choice and decision, and his assertion that Sartre lacks a notion of inter-subjectivity, but their detail need not concern us here. What matters is that Beauvoir's account of Sartre is clearly far more detailed and accurate than Merleau-Ponty's and, even though both may be suspected of having an axe to grind, Beauvoir's *parti pris* seems to have led her to a refined and complex understanding, whereas Merleau-Ponty's has encouraged him to construct a rather crude argument which belies his own very genuine intelligence and philosophical acumen.

Subjectivity and situation

Beauvoir is of course also concerned to give her own account of the vital existential questions such as the relationship between mind and body, consciousness and facticity. In *La Force de l'Age*, she describes her own resistance to what she saw as the excesses of Sartre's radical view of liberty in *L'Etre et le Néant*, and recounts how, as early as 1940, they disagreed on the question of the relation of situation to freedom. Beauvoir is more sensitive than Sartre to the intolerable pressures some situations may exercise (her example is a woman in a harem), and questions whether active transcendence is always possible.

This is of course the problem that I have been highlighting in the case of illness, for example, and of which Merleau-Ponty was more aggressively critical in his later attacks on Sartre. Beauvoir is certainly not denying the human capacity for transcendence, as we see for example throughout *Pyrrhus et Cinéas* of 1944 where she argues that 'Freedom is the only reality that I cannot transcend' (293), and again in *Pour une morale de l'ambiguïté* of 1947 where she sets out to show the way in which human beings cannot be bound by their facticity and situation since one is always 'at a distance from oneself' (16/33). None the less, in this later text she goes on to insist that situations are not all equally easy to transcend, and that in some cases oppression has rendered transcendence practically impossible and reduced consciousness to a state of near-passivity: a position that Sartre would ultimately concede but which he does not himself emphasize until much later.

Sexual difference

Embodiment similarly has a greater place in Beauvoir's philosophy than in Sartre's, and especially the question of sexual difference. Some critics describe this as an attempt to radicalize the Sartrean programme, or to 'take him at his non-Cartesian best'.[20] Beauvoir certainly wishes to take fully into account the ambiguity of the human situation as both body and consciousness, but she does not attempt a thorough-going philosophical and ontological account of how materiality and consciousness might be related, though what she means in practical terms is very clear as we see from several accounts of arguments with Sartre in her autobiography:

> I reproached Sartre with regarding his body as a bundle of striated muscles and with having cut it off from his sympathetic nervous system. If you gave in to tears, to hysteria, to seasickness, he said, you were willingly complying with it. I claimed that the stomach, the tear ducts, even the head itself sometimes were obeying irresistible forces (FA, 134–5/154).

In *Le Deuxième sexe* Beauvoir perhaps comes closest to a philosophical theorization of her own position when she argues that 'the body is never the *cause* of subjective experiences, since it is the subject itself in its objective form' (DS, II, 586/754), which closely resembles Merleau-Ponty's own conception of the 'body-subject'. Indeed, in her discussion of women's relations to their bodies she contends that 'Woman, like man, *is* her body: but her body is something other than herself' (DS, 67/41), and refers in a footnote to Merleau-Ponty's *Phénoménologie de la perception*. She explicitly assimilates her conception of the body to that of other existentialist philosophers such as Heidegger, Sartre, and Merleau-Ponty, who view the body not as an object but rather as a situation (DS, 73/46). None the less, she does seem to hesitate over the extent to which we are determined by our physical make-up, arguing both that we are free with respect to our bodies but also that they provide a kind of destiny, albeit one which is imposed as much by others as by biology (DS, II, 29/294).

It might be thought that this is not a matter so much of ambiguity as of inconsistency, and that paradoxically one of the reasons

Beauvoir resists Sartre's insistence that we can transcend all situations and all facticity is because she lacks a firm grip on the basic philosophical decision that has to be made between freedom and determinism. To some extent this may be true, and we remember that a lack of a rigorous ontological foundation also formed part of the basis for Merleau-Ponty's own self-criticism in *Le Visible et l'Invisible*, but it does not render her phenomenological analysis any less interesting, any more than it did Merleau-Ponty's. Beauvoir talks in terms of the way in which 'transcendence falls back into immanence', and of the 'degradation of existence into *en soi*, and of freedom into facticity' (DS, 33/16). These transformations are arguably difficult to defend from a philosophical point of view, but their practical significance in situations of alienation and oppression is undeniable.

None the less, Beauvoir's understanding of women's existence does seem to be from a remarkably male perspective, and she notoriously undervalues all specifically female bodily activities, ranging from menstruation which we might indeed acknowledge as passively undergone, to orgasm, pregnancy, and childbirth which are understood as equally passive, if not thoroughly alienating and undesirable. What is more, there is no recognition of the value of any kind of passive experience, so that Beauvoir's privileging of what she sees as 'masculine' values may seem exhaustingly active to the contemporary reader.

However, her attempt to recognize the incarnate nature of the human subject is obviously desirable, and it is only her association of embodiment primarily (though obviously not theoretically) with women that is inimical. Toril Moi refers to her 'idealization of the phallus' and her 'mindless admiration of masculinity',[21] which she sets against her view of the female body as ineradicably alienated, especially during menstruation when apparently 85 per cent of women experience problems such as period pains, high blood pressure, constipation, and diarrhoea, problems of the throat, liver, pituitary gland, vision, and hearing, not to mention unpleasant odours (DS, 66/41). Childbirth involves an even worse alienation: tiring, sacrificial, and entailing a multiplicity of different forms of physical degradation, quickly followed by the 'exhausting servitude' of breast-feeding, and ultimately leading to premature deformation and ageing (DS, 68/42). No wonder Beauvoir did not choose to try it for herself.

All this evidently seems unattractive and unconvincing in the twenty-first century, especially after the rise of 'difference feminism' and its celebration of the female body. But what is important here is rather Beauvoir's attempt to deal with what she saw as the unwelcome and unfair double alienation undergone by women, alienated not only in the same way as men, to the Other, but also by their own bodily inferiority. One of the problems seems to lie with Beauvoir's ambivalence as to what is inevitable and unchanging in women's lives and what is part of female oppression, and with her hesitation concerning the responsibility women carry for their own alienation. At times she describes the alienation she is depicting as a scandalous part of social conditions, at others she seems to subscribe to the view that women are complicit in their own oppression. And of course the latter view is wholly compatible with her argument that beyond a certain point it becomes impossible actively to resist alienation, and that this is not a moral fault but a fact of human existence, but it still sits uneasily with her emphasis on human freedom and transcendence, at least where men are concerned.

Paradoxically then, it seems as though Beauvoir's determination to deal seriously with human, and especially female, embodiment, has led to a position which is arguably incompatible with a radical philosophy of freedom and, perhaps more surprisingly, inimical to contemporary women for whom the basic tenets of feminism are now taken for granted. In some ways Beauvoir does not seem unequivocally to represent what we now call 'equality feminism' since in practice women are described as far more in thrall to their bodies than men, and nor does she benefit from the appeal of 'difference feminism', since all the major differences she describes are negative. It is as if, rather than being what marks Beauvoir off positively from Sartre, her stress on embodiment has led her inexorably into a kind of impasse where biology is destiny despite her denials (DS, II, 29/294).

Sexual desire

Unsurprisingly, Beauvoir's ambivalence about the female body is carried over into her discussions of sexual desire. Erotic desire is clearly an area where the identity and difference between consciousness and body can be most acutely experienced, as Beauvoir is well aware:

> The erotic experience is one that most poignantly discloses to human beings the ambiguity of their condition; they experience it as flesh and spirit, as the other and as subject. (DS, II, 190/416)

But this is not an aspect which Beauvoir dwells on at any length, and she seems more concerned to give a physiological rather than a metaphysical description of female desire. According to Beauvoir, women experience arousal and desire as shameful (DS, II, 82/335) and profoundly alienating (DS, II, 183/410). They are taken over by their desire throughout their whole bodies in a way that men are not, and have to accept passivity if they are to experience physical pleasure (DS, II, 400/577). Beauvoir's lengthy description is full of physiological detail, and makes the experience of female sexual desire sound both frustrating and unpleasant (like a bog, a leech etc. DS, II, 167/398). It is of course true that she has warned us that she is describing the 'traditional destiny' of women, and that she argues that true reciprocity can save women from the negative aspect of this experience and make intercourse into a means of mutual recognition (DS, II, 189/415).

None the less, the descriptions of female sexuality as it is usually experienced are deeply unattractive and disturbing, and it is hard not to ascribe them to Beauvoir herself, especially in the light of similar analyses in her fiction. Moi shows convincingly how Beauvoir simultaneously demonstrates the way in which 'patriarchal ideology is internalized by its victims', and also becomes herself 'ensnared in the very patriarchal categories she sets out to describe'.[22] This analysis sums up admirably, I think, the ambivalence and tension underlying the whole of *Le Deuxième sexe*.

Beauvoir does not however stop at these descriptions of passive, distasteful female sexuality. Some of her discussions, for example of lesbianism, seem to offer a more positive conception of equally shared sexual encounters ('more equal, more continuous', DS, II, 213/433); and there is a moving evocation of spontaneous fidelity in which 'the magic of eroticism' ensures that 'to each lover is delivered, in the instant and in their carnal presence, a being whose existence is an unlimited transcendence' (DS, II, 256/467). Ultimately, she is of course well aware that what applies to women applies to men also with respect to love, desire, and the relationship between body and mind in sexual relations, and her last few pages paint a utopian picture of possible egalitarian relations between men and women, based on exchange and reciprocity rather than power and oppression:

> The same drama of flesh and spirit, and of finitude and transcendence, plays itself out in both sexes; both are eaten away by time, stalked by death; they have the same essential need of the other [...]. It is absurd to contend that orgies, vice, ecstasy, and passion would become impossible if man and woman were concretely similar; the contradictions opposing flesh to spirit, the instant to time, absolute pleasure to the nothingness of oblivion will never be lifted; tension, being torn apart, joy and the failure and triumph of existence will always be materialized in sexuality. [...] New carnal and affective relations that we cannot conceive will be born between the sexes. [...] The reciprocity of their relations will not do away with the miracles that the division of human beings into two separate categories engenders: desire, possession, love, dreams, adventures; and the words that move us − 'give', 'conquer', 'unite' − will retain their meaning. [...] And the human couple will discover its true form. (DS, II, 659–662/763–6)

It is clear from these poignant and evocative pages that ultimately Beauvoir does not hold the view that female biology is destiny, and we may perhaps regret that so much of *Le Deuxième sexe* reads as though she did. Her description of the nature of truly reciprocal erotic relations is certainly more attractive, and indeed convincing, than anything we find in Sartre − or indeed in Merleau-Ponty who, as we have seen, writes so little about love and passion − and it is extended of course in her fiction and her volumes of autobiography, especially in her account of the early stages of her relationship with her American lover, Nelson Algren. We will look now at what Beauvoir has to say about death to see whether she is equally empathetic and imaginative on this arguably more difficult subject.

Death and finitude

Beauvoir spends considerable time in *Le Deuxième sexe* showing how women represent not only passivity, immanence, and bodily contingency, at least in the male imagination, but thereby also death. It is in our 'carnal contingency' (DS, 249/167), in our involvement in the cyclical patterns of birth, copulation, and death, that we remind men of their inability to maintain their transcendence of their bodies and therefore of their eventual demise. For all but a naive optimist, this reminder might be seen as salutary. And certainly Beauvoir herself seems much more willing to face up to death in both its physical and metaphysical aspects than either of the male philosophers whose work we have examined so far in this chapter. Theoretically, as we see in *Pyrrhus et Cinéas*, she espouses Sartre's position on death, that is to say a rejection of the Heideggerian notion of 'being-for-death' and an insistence that death is not part of life, to be faced and anticipated in advance, but rather the end of life, and a moment with no more true significance than any other.[23]

Moreover, it is our mortality and finitude that enable us to give positive meaning to our lives as well as saving us from sclerotic self-identity: 'In *Pyrrhus et Cinéas*, I wanted to demonstrate that without [death] there could be neither projects nor values' (FA, 699/606). But Beauvoir's rhetoric belies her Sartrean arguments; both *Pyrrhus et Cinéas* and *Pour une morale de l'ambiguïté* begin with a story about death, the former with an anecdote about the effect on a child on the death of the concierge's son, the latter with a quotation from Montaigne: 'The continuous work of life is to build death.'[24]. Beauvoir sees the fact that we are born in order to die as the tragic ambivalence of life that plants and animals also undergo but of which only human beings are conscious. This is the 'tragic ambiguity' (12/7) that underlies the ambiguity of all ethics as she attempts to describe it. And this too is another sense to the Sartrean 'useless passion', which Beauvoir interprets in terms of the necessary failure inherent in all human action, the failure which makes morality possible because it enables us to escape the ossification of fixed identity and the *esprit de sérieux*: 'without failure, no ethics' (15/10).

Throughout these texts Beauvoir's thought reveals a tension between her acceptance of the Sartrean paradoxes about death and failure and what we may suspect to be her own deep feelings about the subject. A similar ambivalence seems to me to underlie her over-rational comments about the appalling choices faced by so many in war time, the bargaining of one death against several, for example, or the terrible decisions faced by some in the war camps when they were asked to choose the day's victims of the gas chambers. She defends, for example, the Communist Party's consistent saving of their own members on grounds of the rational nature of their choice: they believed they had 'a valid principle of selection', and in any case the deaths were inevitable: 'Since one could in no way escape the atrocity of these massacres, the only thing to do was to try, as far as possible, to rationalize it' (142/114–15). Of course, 1944 and 1947 were not dates when it can have been easy to get the right balance (if such exists) between human emotion and reason.

In any case, Beauvoir's own tendency is clearly to give a very large place to death and its implications in her thinking about life. Not only do *Pyrrhus* and *Pour une morale* both start with stories about death, but death is arguably the major preoccupation of many other of Beauvoir's texts, from her account in *Mémoires d'une jeune fille rangée* of the death of her friend Zaza, through *Une Mort très douce*, which recounts the death of her mother, *La Vieillesse* where death underlies every line of her vivid and disturbing account of old age, to *La Cérémonie des adieux* which recounts in unexpurgated physical detail the last days and weeks leading up to Sartre's own death. *Le Deuxième sexe* ends with the acknowledgement that both men and women live out their days 'eaten away by time, stalked by death' (DS, II 658–9/763) which sits somewhat uneasily with her earlier rejection of Heidegger's being-for-death.

It is of course true that Beauvoir can always claim that at times she is describing things as they are, in their inauthenticity and alienation, and at others she is describing how they could or should be, but, even allowing for this, her obsession with ageing and death would seem to indicate a preoccupation with mortality that goes far beyond her theoretical position. Oliver Davis's recent study of Beauvoir's conception of ageing reveals how neglected an area it is, despite its pre-eminence in Beauvoir's writings. Davis

singles out Penelope Deutscher as an exception to this neglect, as
she reads *La Vieillesse*, for example, as Beauvoir's response to
certain assumptions in early Sartrean ontology of the subject:

> Sartre's subject is embodied, sometimes sick and fatigued, but
> patently a young adult body. Beauvoir's response is that an exces-
> sive weighting of ontological freedom generalizes and neutralizes
> those lived and embodied differences that should also hold our
> theoretical attention.[25]

But there are still many paradoxes in Beauvoir's own position as
she describes old age as an inevitable alienation that contains 'an
insurmountable contradiction'.[26] Although Beauvoir, like Sartre
and Merleau-Ponty, likes to claim that 'I am my body', this does
not mean that I am willing to accept that identification when my
body is ill, old or, a fortiori, dying. Although Beauvoir advises that
we stop cheating, and stop pretending to ourselves that we are
not 'this old woman', for example, she also seems to suggest that
such self-recognition is humanly impossible. Once again, Beauvoir's determination to espouse the radical existential position
which insists that we are free to take up our chosen attitude with
respect to our own ageing, comes up against her awareness of the
difficulty we experience in identifying with our body's deterioration and decline. As Davis notes, this means that *La Vieillesse* tends
to lurch from one side of the opposition to another with disconcerting suddenness, as it bears witness to the 'clash between the
elderly subject's ageless self-perception and the fact of old age'
(42) in what he calls an intense form of 'the Cartesian delusion
of the self's independence from the failing body' (46).

What is more, *La Vieillesse* does not take further the specific
analysis of the ageing of women, started in *Le Deuxième sexe*,
perhaps because the female body has always been seen as alienating by Beauvoir, 'alienated, opaque thing' (DS, 67/41), whereas
she considers that this alienation applies to men only when
they encounter obstacles, are old or ill. *La Vieillesse* concentrates
primarily on the experience of men as they lose their accustomed
transcendence, start to experience their bodies as obstacle
rather than instrument, and are reduced to frustration and suffering. It is clear, I think, that there is a large gulf between (existential) theory and (phenomenological) practice in Beauvoir's

understanding of our embodiment, whether we are men or women, and we will look now at the implications of this for her theorization and description of death itself.

It is already clear that Beauvoir's most enduring understanding of ageing is that it is an ineradicable form of physical and psychological alienation, both in the sense that age and illness prevent us from the easy transcendence of our bodies that (paradoxically perhaps) enables us best to enjoy our embodiment, and also in the sense that we find it difficult or impossible to identify with our ageing or sick bodies. Ageing is also a one-way street, a path that leads in only one direction, that is, towards death. Beauvoir's accounts of the illness and death of first her mother in *Une Mort très douce* and later Sartre in *La Cérémonie des Adieux* are remarkable for their plethora of detail of physical and mental deterioration and for their unsparing lucidity. There is however a sense in which the reader may feel that Beauvoir forces herself to be scrupulously truthful about the dying, but does not necessarily succeed in being as perspicacious in her analysis of her own reactions.

Beauvoir's autobiography makes clear the extent to which she was tormented from a relatively early age by the idea of death. In *Mémoires d'une jeune fille rangée*, she recounts her distraught reaction at the age of fourteen to her realization of her own mortality: 'I realized that I was condemned to death. [...] I screamed and tore at the red carpet. It seemed to me impossible that I could live my whole life with such horror gnawing at my heart' (MJFR, 194/138), and a year later she is once again unable to cope with the anguish she feels at the thought of death (288–9/206–7). On the other hand, her fictional and philosophical works clearly attempt not only to understand death as an inevitable part of all human experience but also to interpret it as necessary for a purposeful and enjoyable life, as we see in *Tous les hommes sont mortels* (1946) for example, in which immortality is presented as a curse which renders life meaningless for the protagonist Fosca who has drunk an elixir. Mortality and transience are precisely what enables human passion: it is finitude, risk, and temporality that permit intensity and desire.

There is of course no insuperable philosophical problem in Beauvoir's ambivalence towards death: the problem arises only when the philosophical argument itself seems ambiguous or self-contradictory. Similarly we may feel uneasy when Beauvoir's acceptance of death seems to be of the death of another person, rather than of her own future demise, especially in the light of Heidegger's contention that contemplating the death of others is precisely a way of avoiding facing our own death authentically.

Beauvoir's initial reaction to the news that her mother's illness may be fatal is one of rational resignation: 'after all, she was at the age for dying' (*Une Mort*, 51–2), but the sight of her mother's diminished, shaven body in the hospital arouses much more visceral feelings of pity, disgust, and disorientation. The *récit* purports to narrate the story of her mother's death, in the process it also narrates Beauvoir's eventual coming to terms with her mother and their difficult relationship, and with her own ambivalence about death. Indeed, the text ends with an open admission of what she has come to see as the impossibility of taking a rational attitude towards the reality of death, a retraction of her own earlier stance of stoical acceptance, and a recognition of her own fragility and vulnerability:

'Useless to claim to integrate death into life and to behave in a rational manner when faced with a thing that is not rational: in the confusion of feelings, we can all but cope in our own way' (122). Critics have found much to dislike in Beauvoir's account: in the first place what she describes as her own 'betrayal', that is, her decision not to tell her mother that she was suffering from cancer, which may seem disempowering and patronizing to an English readership which does not share the French medical habit of concealing terminal illness from its victims. Beauvoir tries to account for the deception as the triumph of hope and kindness over brutal truth, but not all readers will agree. Again, the degree of physical detail in the account of her mother's degeneration over the month of her death has been found severely distasteful and even sensationalist by some readers.

And finally, she has been criticized for failing to record any real sense of loss when her mother eventually dies.[27] But these are all, I would contend, matters of opinion: one could equally well admire her acknowledgement of the difficulty of deciding between honesty and reassurance, as well as her refusal to shun the distasteful and disturbing physical deterioration of the dying body, and finally her rejection of the temptation to present a more emotional or sentimental account of her feelings at her mother's death. In any case, the emotion comes through strongly enough for most tastes in lines such as: 'my despair eluded my control: someone other than me was crying within me [. . .] compassion tore me apart' (67), and she concludes with a thoroughgoing rejection of her initial rational response to the news of her mother's illness which she has come to view as a cliché, and which she has long since abandoned. In the end, she is asleep when her mother dies, and arrives at the hospital to find a 'corpse lying on the bed instead of my mother' (112). Her comment encapsulates precisely the ambivalence experienced by those who look on the face of the dead: 'It was still her, and forever her absence' (112). Like illness, death puts our rejection of Cartesian dualism sorely to the test.

Similarly, *La Cérémonie des Adieux* aroused even more severe criticism as Beauvoir was seen to transgress the bounds of decency and dignity in describing the incontinence, addictions, weaknesses, evasions, and pathos of Sartre's last days. It is true that the text does not make easy reading, but Beauvoir's apparent conviction of her own self-righteousness has arguably a bigger role to play here than our natural, if philosophically indefensible, distaste for the evocation of the sights and smells of the death bed. As Sartre's friends and lovers smuggle him in cigarettes and whisky Beauvoir is inevitably forced into *le mauvais rôle*, the role, we might think, of her own mother as she struggles to maintain discipline and hygiene against the transgressive forces of life and liberality. Of course, Beauvoir's strict discipline is enforced out of love, and for Sartre's own good, but is this not the claim of mothers also when they try to shield their children from the harmful friends, substances, and situations that they crave? And Sartre too, even more inexplicably, is shielded, as her own mother was, from the full truth of the gravity of his terminal illness.

In these texts on death and dying, the scale of Beauvoir's ambivalence becomes increasingly clear: however radical the claims of her existential philosophy, these fall away as useless in the face of the most extreme situations she has to face. However strong her allegiance to truth, her desire to protect those she loves from the bitterness of that truth is even stronger; however convinced she claims to be that death is no more than the end of life, this conviction proves ultimately unequal to the physical reality of death.

But perhaps this is in the end Beauvoir's strength; in a kind of 'qui perd gagne' reversal we can perhaps see that it is in revealing herself 'all too human' that she shows herself at her best, her most intelligent and her most passionate. 'Without failure, no morality', as both she and Sartre were acutely aware. It may be in her failure to be philosophically consistent, her failure to live up to the existential tenets she wants to espouse, her failure to deal with death as calmly and stoically as Sartre or Merleau-Ponty, that she shows her true understanding of the complexity, the ambiguity, and the intolerable and contradictory richness of human life.

3

Religious Philosophy: Keeping Body and Soul Together

Gabriel Marcel, Paul Ricœur, Vladimir Jankélévitch, Emmanuel Levinas

Religious philosophers might seem at first sight likely to take a very different view of the body–soul relationship from phenomenologists and existentialists. But such a preconception would be naive: in the first place because, of course, many religious philosophers are themselves existentialists and phenomenologists as well as Christians or Jews; and secondly because the relationship between body and soul is far less simple for religious thinkers than we often tend to assume. The religious conception of the immortality of the soul is well known: what is less well understood is the companion notion of bodily resurrection. The orthodox Catholic position, for example, insists on the resurrection of the body that will take place at the end of the world, restoring an essential unity which death temporarily put asunder. This is very far from the popular but essentially parodic conception of the Christian position which assumes that the body can be no more than an encumbrance to the soul, an empty shell to be joyfully discarded at death.

On the contrary, it is only when the body is resurrected that full human integrity will be finally achieved. Similarly, Orthodox Judaism also refuses to separate the body and soul, although Jewish conceptions of resurrection vary throughout history and in different groups. At the time of Christ, the Sadducees, for example, denied the resurrection of the body, whereas the Pharisees and Essenes believed in it, though there was some disagreement as to whether it was universal, or simply for the righteous, or indeed restricted to the Jewish people themselves. Of course, opposition to any notion of bodily resurrection comes from all sides: from the Platonic tradition which envisages the body as a prison for the immortal soul; from the gnostic tradition according to which all matter is essentially evil; and finally of course and more recently, from rationalist and materialist positions which deny all notion of life after death. Indeed, if the doctrine of the resurrection of the body is not immediately associated with religious thought today, this is arguably due to the strength of opposition to the notion which has led contemporary churches to downplay its significance and sometimes to deny it altogether.[1]

Gabriel Marcel (1889–1973)

This wound that I carry within me, *which is me*.

Gabriel Marcel, who converted to Catholicism in 1929 at the age of forty, shares with the Existentialists of Chapter 1 the same preoccupation with the question of the body, its relationship to the person, to the soul, to 'me'. Indeed his meditations on these topics frequently anticipate by one or two decades the reflections of Sartre and Merleau-Ponty, whose views are considerably better known. From his earliest philosophical publications, such as *Journal Métaphysique* in 1927, and most clearly *Etre et Avoir* of 1935, he opposes the instrumentalist view of the body and the idealist view of the self. He rejects the notion that I *have* a body and insists rather that I *am* my body in the sense that I act and see the world through my body, and cannot envisage anything without my embodiment. But the relationship between self and body is complex and can be properly conceived neither in terms of being nor of having: 'Corporeity as the frontier zone between being and having' (*Etre et Avoir*, p. 119/82). The knowing subject is not independent of its bodily incarnation through which it knows the world: 'Incarnation – the central "given" of metaphysics ... opposition to the cogito' (EA, 11/11), and Marcel argues that, in starting from consciousness, the Cartesian *cogito* presents an inescapable trap, 'no longer a way out' (EA, 150/104).

Indeed, like recent post-structuralist thinkers, Marcel prefers an impersonal construction: 'One cannot overly stress how much preferable the formula *es denkt in mir* is to the *cogito*, which exposes us to pure subjectivism' (EA, 35/27). None the less, I am not 'nothing but my body'; Marcel insists on the unity but not the identity of self and body: 'Of this body, I can neither say that it is I, nor that it is not I, nor that its is *for me* (object). The opposition between subject and object finds itself transcended from the start' (EA, 11/12). 'To be incarnated is to appear to oneself as body, as this particular body, while being neither identifiable with it nor distinguishable from it' ('L'Etre incarné', in *Essai de philosophie concrète*, p. 35/20). Moreover, although Marcel prefers the question 'am I my life?' to 'am I my body?' (EA, 126/87), he none the less maintains that I do not end when my life ends precisely because I am not identical or reducible to my life. I transcend both my body and my life: 'mon être ne se confond pas avec ma vie' (*Remarques sur l'irréligion contemporaine*, p. 291).

Modern philosophy has, in Marcel's view, made the unity of mind and body problematic, and thereby made it almost impossible to understand the relationship between self and world. Against Descartes, Marcel holds that it is sensation that is indubitable, not thought: 'Things exist for me insofar as I regard them as extensions of my body' (*Journal métaphysique*, p. 305, from a journal entry of 1922). 'The subject of the cogito is the epistemological subject' (*Esquisse d'une phénoménologie de l'avoir*, p. 249/ EA Eng. 170). When I act, I destroy the fiction of 'ideal disincarnation' and regain body/self unity. The subject is not a point of departure as Descartes believed, but an achievement and an end, and the body is not separate from but rather a constitutive part of the subject:

There is something in my very structure that forever opposes itself to the effective establishment of this univocal relation between my body and myself, on account of a kind of irrestible encroachment of my body over me, which is at the basis of my condition as man and animal. (EA, 120/82-3)

We must somehow take the notion of the self, of oneself, and recognise that [. . .] the *self* is a thickening, a sclerosis, and, perhaps – who knows? – a kind of apparently spiritualised expression [. . .], not of the body in the objective sense, but of *my body* insofar as it is mine, insofar as my body is something that I have. (*Esquisse*, 243/ EA Eng. 167)

Nor does the self pre-exist my relations with the world and with others: it is not an 'isolable reality' with precise boundaries (*Homo Viator*, p. 18) but rather a vulnerable openness to the other, a wound: 'this wound that I carry within me, *which is me*' (HV, p. 19), which he also describes in terms of 'angoisse' and 'néant'. For Marcel there is a painful contradiction between my desire for self-sufficiency and my awareness of my distance from that state: 'consciousness obscured by this nothing, this nothingness that I am in spite of everything' (HV, p. 20). In case Marcel's vocabulary here should make him sound excessively derivative of Sartre it should be pointed out that the essay in *Homo Viator* (1944) from which these quotations are taken was first given as a lecture in 1941.

Like Sartre, Marcel is vehemently opposed to any notion of autonomous individuality in the sense of essential selfhood; indeed he distinguishes between what he calls 'le moi' and 'la personne'. 'Le moi' is the illusory self, shut in on itself, which I imagine constitutes my essence; 'la personne', on the other hand, is the self I choose to create through my actions and relations with others: 'I affirm myself as a person [*comme personne*] to the extent that I assume responsibility for what I say and what I do' (HV, p. 26), 'the person [*la personne*] is realized only in the act through which it tends to be incarnated [...] but [...] at the same time, it is part of its essence never to become fixed or definitively crystallized in this particular incarnation', 'its currency is not *sum*, mais *sursum*' (32). However, unlike Sartre, Marcel rejects the notion that I am the centre of my universe and that others are obstacles to my projects; he refers to this as the illusion of 'moral egocentrism', as 'egolatry', and 'idolatry of the ego [*le moi*]' (HV, p. 24). The 'person', in Marcel's sense, confronts her/his situation and commits herself in it. And such personal engagement is necessarily not only to oneself but also to the other ('before myself and before another', 26). For Marcel, the person is 'available' ['*disponible*'], open to others, self-giving, and able to respond to the call of the other:

> In fact it depends on the ego [*moi*] whether this call is recognised as a call and, in this sense, however singular this call may be, it is true to say that it emanates simultaneously from me [*moi*] and

from elsewhere; or rather, we grasp in it the most intimate connection between that which comes from me [*moi*] and that which comes from the other, a nourishing and constructive connection that cannot be relaxed without the ego [*le moi*] becoming anaemic and tilting towards death. (HV, 29)

It is clear that despite the similarities between Sartre's and Marcel's existential conceptions of the self as vulnerable, in flux, and always in the process of creation, Marcel has a very different view from Sartre of relations with others, and this is one of the aspects of his thought which makes it potentially more congenial than Sartre's to contemporary thinkers. Rather than envisaging the other as an inevitable source of conflict, Marcel describes him as enabling the very existence of the self-conscious self: 'the impossibility of clinging to the fiction of a transcendental I' (EA, 159/110):

The self, insofar as self-consciousness, is only *subexistent*, it exists only insofar as it treats itself as being for another, in relation to the other; to the extent, consequently, that it recognises that it eludes itself. (EA, 151/105)

Like Levinas, and for similar reasons, Marcel's conception of the imbrication of self and other avoids, and indeed shuns, what now may seem like a tendentious and ill-conceived view of personal independence. In both cases, the religious nature of their philosophy has arguably preserved them from the potential excesses of modern forms of individualism.

Embodiment and subjectivity

Marcel also seems to have a more acceptable view than Sartre's of the real implications of human embodiment: 'this need for embodiment [*incarnation*] that the person [*la personne*] cannot escape without betraying its true purpose, without losing itself in the mirages of abstraction, without reducing itself paradoxically to an impoverished determination of that very self [*moi*] it was attempting vainly in all ways to exceed' (HV, 35). And indeed in Marcel's essay on *L'Etre et le Néant*, which appeared in November 1943, it is Sartre's conception of the body which is most severely criticized. Marcel's response appears initially extremely favourable: he embraces Sartre's account of the *en-soi–pour-soi* division, his analysis of the non-self-coincidence of consciousness, and his description of the relationship between human freedom and facticity. His early criticisms are directed mainly to what he calls Sartre's solecisms and 'galimatias', which he proceeds to interpret and explain. But reservations appear towards the end of his essay when he discusses Sartre's accounts of love and desire and argues, as I did myself in Chapter 1, that the poverty of the former is matched by the richness of the latter. Sartre's conception of the body seems to allow him an admirable understanding of human sexuality, and Marcel gives an excellent brief account of the way in which, no more than consciousness, is the Sartrean body self-identical or merely *en-soi* (HV, 247–8). None the less, despite this sympathetic understanding, it is Sartre's view of the body that Marcel ultimately rejects, for he interprets Sartre's claim that body and soul are inseparable even at death, and that 'the soul *is* the body in so far as the for-itself *is* its own individuation' (EN, 372/310) as a form of crude materialism emanating, paradoxically, from apparently idealist premises (HV, 248–9).[2]

It seems to me however that Marcel has probably reacted to the form rather than the content of Sartre's account, for no more than Marcel does Sartre identify soul and body in any simple sense: both philosophers are, as we have seen, acutely aware of the complexities and ambiguities of the relationship between them. Sartre, like Marcel, I would maintain, is simply emphasizing the impossibility of envisaging disembodied or disincarnate human existence.

None the less, Marcel arguably has a more convincing and secure conception than Sartre of the inextricable imbrication of body and soul, at least during life. We can see this for example in his understanding of human illness. We will remember that Sartre seemed in *L'Etre et le Néant*, to have an untenably weak view of the effect of human illness on consciousness and selfhood, in so far as he envisaged it as an extraneous event to which consciousness was free to respond as it chose, and I pointed out that whereas such a conception might be applicable to his selected examples such as eye strain it could hardly be said to apply to more debilitating illnesses such as cancer or TB where consciousness and the capacity to think and choose are themselves put at risk.

Marcel, on the other hand, seems to have a more realistic and more humane conception of illness and ultimately death, and recognizes the degree to which pain and suffering impede the freedom of consciousness. Indeed, he considers that the very desire to transcend illness and to dissociate from the sick body might contribute to its negative effects (EA, 121/78). For Marcel, serious illness and suffering are inseparable from my self and cannot truly be envisaged as external or accidental events:

> The more completely this suffering invades my being, the greater the sharpness with which the problem is posed, and yet, on the other hand, the more that this is so, the less I can split it off from myself, as it were, and take up my position before it. It is embodied in me; it *is* me. (EA, 166–7/115)

Death and love

For Marcel, it is I who am sick, and not merely my body. But this union of body and soul does not extend beyond life, as we just saw in Marcel's criticism of Sartre's claim that body and soul remain inseparable even at the point of death. Death is a very powerful element in Marcel's philosophy, and his approach to it is somewhat unusual and might even be described by sceptics as a form of denial. It is of course easy to understand his point of view when he maintains that my embodiment means that I cannot truly think of, or anticipate, my own death, for I cannot imagine myself as separate from my body. And here he may even seem closer to Sartre than to Heidegger, although he criticizes Spinoza for denying the value of meditating on death (EA, 180/124).

But it is the question of death that seems to trigger the most forceful of Marcel's objections to Sartre, for he rejects out of hand the apparently innocuous comment that people can be present to us (when we think lovingly about them) even when they are physically absent, until the moment of their death. Marcel describes this as revealing a 'disastrous confusion' between *en-soi* and *pour-soi* (HV, 248–9) and insists that the dead can be just as present to us as the living. In fact, I believe, it is rather the nature of the *pour-autrui* that is at stake and, *pace* Marcel, Sartre in fact also argues that survival after death depends on our continuing presence in the minds of others. What is more, Sartre argues explicitly that this posthumous existence is not merely a matter of mental images and memories:

> If we share the realist views that we presented in Part Three, we must recognize that my *existence after death* is not a simple spectral survival 'in the Other's consciousness' of simple representations (images, memories, etc.) concerning me. My being-for-others is a real being. If it remains in the hands of the Other like a coat I leave to him after my disappearance, this is by virtue of a real dimension of my being – a dimension that has become my unique dimension – and not an insubstantial specter. (EN, 628–9/544).

But, whereas for Sartre such survival is simply an inevitable consequence of intersubjective human relations, for Marcel it is a fundamental duty and an inalienable aspect of human love, for it is love that saves us from death: 'To love a being is to say to it: You will not die.'[3] Indeed, he describes love as the 'ontological counterweight' to death.[4]

But just as Marcel accuses Sartre of confusing *en-soi* and *pour-soi*, so might we consider that Marcel himself is confusing levels here. Surely the question he really needs to tackle is not so much that of our life after death in the hearts and minds of those who love us, but rather the far more problematic issue of the implications of the body–soul union at the point of death. Already in his *Notes sur le problème de l'immortalité* in 1913, Marcel maintains that the problem of immortality in the religious sense has to be distinguished from the problem of the survival of the soul which may turn out to be a question that physics will ultimately be able to solve.[5] And he argues here too that love conquers death in the sense of denying it, and that this kind of survival in thought and memory is the psychological transposition of a real survival which transcends verification because it transcends experience. But we may well consider that Marcel's position is ultimately more equivocal than that of Sartre: like Sartre, Marcel makes individual immortality depend on the love and thoughts of others, but whereas Sartre makes no metaphysical claims beyond the after-life of the *pour-autrui*, Marcel uses the idea to identify faith, love and freedom, and to justify my immortality by affirming that I will always exist as loved by God.

When we look back at Marcel's early, pre-conversion writings, and forward to the essays he writes after his conversion and after his reading of the later and better-known French Existentialists, we will find surprisingly little change in his understanding and analysis of the fundamental issues of the body–soul relationship and the questions of love and death. Whether we consider this as consistency or stagnation will perhaps depend on our appraisal of his ideas: it seems to me that Marcel has achieved by solitary reflection and intuition some admirable insights into the most elusive and important of philosophical questions. But his unsystematic method means that he repeatedly reiterates the same set of ideas in similar and sometimes identical formulations.

The technique of writing a Metaphysical Journal rather than attempting to construct a philosophical system has the undeniable advantage of showing reflective philosophy in the very process of being made; but it has the equally undeniable drawback of making it impossible to see clearly when any progress has been made because questions are constantly raised but definitive answers are never given, and no real attempt seems to be made to get any closer to formulating any. So whereas Marcel appears initially to offer a great deal of promise for reflection on the topic of mortality and subjectivity, and although he does without question anticipate some of the ideas of Sartre as well as, as we shall see shortly, Levinas, and gives us a very attractive way of exploring the area, we must in the end conclude that he evades the hard questions and retreats into a mode of meditative reflection which allows him to dissolve issues into ambiguity and equivocation. The appearance his writings give of having gone straight to the heart of the issues is then a mixed blessing, for his lack of rigour is not just a matter of philosophical mode, it is, I would argue, an unavowed abdication of responsibility for drawing conclusions, making decisions, and contributing to real philosophical progress.

Paul Ricœur (1913–2005)

Passivity becomes the very attestation of alterity.

Paul Ricœur was a pupil of Marcel's in the late 1930s and he remained very close to him, as a commentator, critic, and interlocutor. His first single-authored book, published in 1948, was a comparison of the work of Karl Jaspers and Marcel, centred on the distinction between Jaspers's conception of paradox and Marcel's of mystery.[6] In 1968 he published a series of six interviews (*Entretiens*) with Marcel, then aged seventy-nine, in which he encouraged him to review his philosophical positions in the light of the developments of the past fifty years. And Marcel continued to figure as a positive reference point in all his writings, up to and including the posthumously published *Vivant jusqu'à la mort* which appeared in March 2007.

Although a committed Protestant, Ricœur is even more wary than his (Catholic) mentor of the title Christian philosopher: just as Marcel refused the title Christian Existentialist and preferred to be called a Socratic, so Ricœur insists on separating his religious beliefs from his philosophical argumentation, with possibly unexpected consequences that will become progressively clearer.

Embodiment and subjectivity

As he explains in the *Entretiens*, Ricœur sees Marcel's major contribution to philosophy as lying in his conceptions of embodiment, intersubjectivity, and interrogation. Indeed, he introduces the conversations by crediting Marcel with prefiguring the contemporary understanding of the lived body, and with paving the way for Merleau-Ponty's investigations of the phenomenology of perception (EGM, 22–3). Marcel's awareness of the philosophical importance of illness and death for the human subject is recognized as constituting a significant theme in his plays, but he is shown to be a more positive and optimistic thinker than either Jaspers, with his emphasis on failure and solitude, or indeed Heidegger, with his emphasis on the anguish of being-towards-death.

The interviews end with Ricœur's reiteration of Marcel's deep understanding of the unity of the 'carnal' and the 'spiritual'. His early study of Marcel and Jaspers focuses on Marcel's conception of relations with the Other which break the otherwise closed (and potentially vicious) circle of selfhood ('egolâtrie'), and elaborates on Marcel's notions of openness to the call ('appel') of the Other in hospitality and *disponibilité*. Ricœur also stresses Marcel's conception of incarnation and historical situation as forming part of selfhood, so that we can no more speculate seriously on what it might mean to be born into another culture than into another body: my situation and bodily facticity literally constitute me, so that it makes no sense to ask what 'I' might otherwise be, since that person would no longer be 'me'.

To anyone familiar with Ricœur's work it will already be apparent that he has taken a great deal from Marcel, but his treatment and elaboration of the material is far more systematic, detailed and, to the contemporary eye, more properly philosophical than Marcel's. It is probably the case that Ricœur is best known for the work of his 'middle-period', that is to say his hermeneutic theorizations, but of course his philosophical career starts and finishes with questions of ethics and personal identity, in which problems of narrativity remain relevant but arguably subordinate. And, as we shall see, his later writings also engage in a dialogue with British analytic philosophers such as Strawson and Parfit in a way that gives his work a scope and ambition far beyond that of Marcel and perhaps analogous to Merleau-Ponty's engagement with scientific psychologists and neurologists in his early writings.

One of the areas in the *Entretiens* where Ricœur encourages Marcel to reconsider his earlier positions concerns the Cartesian *cogito* which he believes was originally misconceived by Marcel as excessively abstract and closer to the transcendental ego of Kant or Husserl than to Descartes's own conception. He sees Marcel's 'correction' of Descartes as in fact a return to Descartes who himself viewed the *cogito* as an indication of being ('je suis') rather than as having the purely epistemological function Marcel attributed to it (see above, p. [71]). Marcel's positive reponse is a tribute both to Ricœur's tact and to the quality and precision of his scholarship:

I think you are probably right when you say that I had too much of a tendency to read Descartes in Kantian terms. Moreover, it is probable that it is much more the idea of the transcendental ego correlative to the Kantian object that is at the heart of all my reflections. In any case, I am sure that your reservations are, from the historical point of view, absolutely justified. (EGM, 40–1/227)

And it is Ricœur's own work on personal identity which is of most significance for the present study. Like Marcel, Ricœur refuses dualism and sees the subject as irremediably incarnate. Like Marcel too, he rejects any notion of the self as separable from the Other, and reflects at length in *Soi-même comme un autre* (1990) on the manner in which alterity is actually constitutive of identity. He situates himself here in relation to Levinas on the one hand and Husserl on the other (SMA, 382/331), just as he also situates himself between what he calls the philosophers of the 'exalted subject' such as Kant and Fichte and those of the 'humiliated subject' or the 'broken cogito' (SMA, 22/16) such as Nietzsche.

Ricœur's own 'hermeneutics of the self' is deliberately positioned between the two extremes (SMA, 35/23). His major contribution to the theorization of subjectivity is probably the distinction he draws between what he describes as two very different senses of identity which are often conflated: identity as *idem* and identity as *ipse*. Identity as *idem* is an identity of sameness, of 'mêmeté', self-same over time; identity as *ipseity*, on the other hand, does not imply any such stasis: 'Our thesis throughout will be that identity in the sense of *ipse* implies no assertion concerning some supposedly unchanging kernel of personality' (SMA, 13/2).

Indeed, Ricœur came to consider his own earlier conception of human character as too immutable: described as 'involuntary' in *Le Volontaire et l'Involontaire* of 1950 and as 'finite' in *L'Homme faillible* of 1960, indeed as a 'immutable and inherited nature' (SMA, 145/120). Ricœur's later reflections on selfhood led him to a more nuanced and arguably uncertain position with respect to questions of continuity of identity over time, the relationship between mind and body, and even more basic questions of individual autonomy and independence in which he considers character in terms of durable dispositions and habits, and what he describes as a dialectic of innovation and sedimentation (150/122).

A response to analytic philosophy

From his own account in *Soi-même comme un autre*, it would appear to be in large part an engagement with analytic philosophy that brought Ricœur to his later, less dogmatic view of the self. Ricœur considers at some length a variety of different accounts of personal identity and evaluates their merits and drawbacks. Strawson, for example, in *Individuals* (1959), is praised for his conception of personal ascription, according to which there is only one referent, the person, to whom we may ascribe different sets of predicates. In other words, 'we ascribe to ourselves certain things' which may be physical or mental: 'One's states of consciousness, one's thoughts and sensations are ascribed *to the very same thing* to which these physical characteristics, this physical situation, is ascribed' (SMA, 49–50/36, quoting *Individuals*, p. 89).

One major advantage of such an account, in Ricœur's view, is its avoidance of dualism, its bypassing of any notion of a separate soul and body: 'It is the same thing that weighs sixty kilograms and that has this or that thought' (SMA, 50/36). It also makes a significant contribution to solving the problems of solipsism or other minds by taking the same attitude towards others as towards myself, and by refusing to prioritize my personal experiences of consciousness; in Strawson's words:

> To put it briefly, one can ascribe states of consciousness to oneself only if one can ascribe them to others. One can ascribe them to others only if one can identify other subjects of experience. And one cannot identify others, if one can identify them *only* as subjects of experience, possessors of states of consciousness. (*Individuals*, p. 100, quoted SMA, 52/38)

The drawback of Strawson's account, however, is three-fold in Ricœur's view: it privileges sameness over a more sophisticated version of identity (idem v. ipse); it gives an inadequate account of questions concerning 'le corps propre' or 'this body as mine' (*Individuals*, p. 103), that is to say not merely an object in the world but constituting my own point of view on the world; and it fails to take sufficiently into account the dissymmetry between any account of my experiences and those of others. In other words, it occludes problems of alterity by too great an insistence on the equivalence between self and other. Strawson, in Ricœur's assessment, has made a very real contribution, but one that needs completing by a more nuanced account of my relations with the Other and with myself (SMA, 53–4/39).

But Strawson's resolute refusal of dualism has not of course dissolved the mind–body problem, which is still a crucial issue in contemporary debate. Before engaging with more recent arguments, Ricœur gives a brief critique of Locke's use of memory as the criterion of identity which he considers slippery in so far as it slides unacknowledged from a notion of 'sameness with itself' to one of reflection over time, or in other words from identity as *idem* to identity as *ipseity*. So, while claiming to treat personal identity according to the same criteria as objects such as ships, oak trees, and animals, Locke in fact smuggles in a new concept which undermines the strength of his argument for similarity of criteria.

What is more, Locke's major criterion for personal identity is psychic, and this opens the flood gates for arguments as to whether mental or physical identity should be key to the self-identity of human beings. Locke's consistency on this issue is evidenced by his treatment of problems such as the transplantation of memory: if the memory of a prince is transplanted into a cobbler, will the cobbler become the prince? Locke's answer is yes, but, as we shall see shortly, Ricœur will use Parfit to challenge the excessive simplicity of such a response.

Hume too is praised for his introduction of the notion of degrees of identity, but criticized for his conception of personal identity as pure illusion: the diversity Hume finds in the experiences of consciousness does indeed militate against any notion of identity as sameness but does not, in Ricœur's view, disqualify a conception of identity in terms of ipseity (153/126). In this connection, Ricœur is keen to forestall any equation of physical identity with sameness and psychological identity with ipseity: on the contrary, both body and mind bear witness to both kinds of sameness and difference, whether this be in terms of undeniable elements of physical change as well as continuity on the one hand, or in terms of the fragility of memory and the relative permanence of character on the other.

But Ricœur's major interlocutor from the analytic tradition is undoubtedly Derek Parfit and in particular his work on *Reasons and Persons* (1986). Ricœur seems to relish Parfit's 'puzzling cases' which take imaginary examples, similar to Locke's memory transplant, and explore their implications for our conception of identity. By evoking extreme cases Parfit is able to force us beyond our common-sense responses and to test our unacknowledged preconceptions. Ricœur describes him as demonstrating the paradoxes beloved by Locke as well as Hume's scepticism, and as an ideal interlocutor because of his radical reductionism which refuses to recognize any difference between sameness and ipseity: for Parfit identity is simply a matter of self-sameness. And Ricœur maintains that it is precisely the terminology of Parfit's reductionist view (the person is not a separate further fact beyond his physical or psychic continuity), when used to describe the views he opposes, that elides and neutralizes the very aspects of difference he is denying, such as lived experience and the lived body.

For Parfit, my personal experience is merely an example of what can equally well be described impersonally. And this view is what underlies the selection of the puzzling cases he explores so intriguingly, and which Ricœur places in the historical lineage of other explorations of the paradoxes and aporias of identity. As Ricœur remarks, beliefs such as the transmigration of souls, personal immortality, and the resurrection of the body have always aroused speculation and debate (SMA, 161/134).[7] But Parfit's conclusion about the puzzling cases he describes such as teletransportation, exact copies of my brain etc., is that the question of identity is an empty one; his purpose in evoking them is precisely to focus attention on our unquestioned assumptions and to force us to dissociate elements which we generally consider indissociable. In Parfit's view 'Identity is not what matters' (163), and indeed his ultimate aim is to make a moral point: the major flaw in self-interest theory is precisely that the 'self' is never examined, so that our preoccupation with our own selves, our lives, and indeed our deaths, is based on a misconceived view of selfhood. Ricœur takes up this claim in order to explore further its ethical implications.

Parfit's rejection of the specificity of personal experience has been described as having links to Buddhism – 'identity is not what matters' – and this is an aspect which intrigues and attracts Ricœur for its potential to loosen the self-centredness of selfhood. But he believes, to put it simply, that Parfit has thrown the baby out with the bathwater. For Ricœur, the specificity of selfhood cannot simply be evacuated, not only because such an evacuation would involve a severe misrepresentation of experience, but also because selfhood is necessary precisely for self-giving, or, in Ricœur's terms (taken from Marcel) for 'availability' ['*disponibil-ité*'] to the other (SMA, 168/138, 198/168). If the self-centred-ness of the self is to be challenged, the challenge must come from an other who is not merely a repetition of the self-same, and this kind of alterity is not available within a conception of selves as broadly interchangeable. For Ricœur, we are precisely constituted by our relations to and implication with the Other, who cannot therefore be another me.

Ipseity, alterity, and passivity

We are close now to the point where we can put flesh on the rather abstract notion of *ipseity*, which has so far only been defined negatively in opposition to the self-sameness of identity as *idem*. Ipseity is the kind of selfhood which is neither self-same nor self-contained; as we have already seen it is not self-identical over time (as is the case with identity as *idem*), and neither is it independent and autonomous. It is open to the Other who in fact forms part of its very constitution. Ricœur's final chapter, '*Vers quelle ontolo-gie?*' ['What Ontology in View?'], gives the clearest description of what this openness might involve, for in it he attempts to situate his conception of ipseity in relation to alterity as it is understood in particular by Husserl, Heidegger, and Levinas.

It is here too that Ricœur explains the perhaps unanticipated relationship between alterity and passion, or in today's terms, pas-sivity. Passivity, he argues, is the phenomenological counterpart to the ontological notion of alterity. In other words, just as passion is the opposite of action, and passivity the opposite of activity or agency, so it is also the subjective counterpart to alterity which is precisely what affects me from outside, what I undergo or suffer. Passivity is what makes me open to the Other, and ultimately what saves me from being closed in on myself in a vicious circle of self-identity:

> How are we to account for the work of otherness [*altérité*] at the heart of selfhood [*ipséité*]? It is here that the play between the two levels of discourse – phenomenological discourse and ontological discourse – proves to be most fruitful, by virtue of the power of

discovery that this play provokes at the same time on both planes. In order to determine our vocabulary here, let us posit that the *phenomenological* respondant to the metacategory of otherness is the variety of experiences of passivity, intertwined in multiple ways in human action. The term 'otherness' is then reserved for speculative discourse, while passivity becomes *the* attestation of otherness. (SMA, 368/318)

So passivity bears witness to alterity in its different modes, and Ricœur will describe three of these: the body as mine, or the lived body ('le corps propre' or 'le chair'); the alterity of the Other; and the experience of moral conscience.

My experience of my body lies, of course, as Ricœur shows, at the heart of traditional philosophical accounts of the passions, such as those we find in Maine de Biran, Marcel, Merleau-Ponty, and Michel Henry (371/320–1). In accounts such as that of Maine de Biran, experiences of affectivity and auto-affection may be classified according to their degrees of passivity, ranging from the interaction of effort and resistance in the active body, through the susceptibility of my body to moods (a primarily negative passivity), to the resistance of the outside world to my body: in all these ways my body mediates between my inner self and the external world (SMA, 372/320). And here Ricœur assesses the positions of Husserl and Heidegger with respect to the lived body and finds both inadequate.

Husserl's opposition between *Leib* ['*chair*', flesh] and *Körper* ['*corps*', body], although vital for all future phenomenologies of the body, has a fundamental flaw at its core: since Husserl derives knowledge of the other from knowledge of the self, the other is not present at the heart of the constitution of my body as 'flesh', and indeed I can understand the other only starting from myself.[8] This poses evident problems for Ricœur whose conception of ipseity involves the other from the outset, and ultimately makes it impossible, in his view, for Husserl to explain how I can come to know myself as a body among other bodies.

Conversely, Heidegger's conception of being-in-the-world would initially appear to constitute a firm grounding for understanding my body as mine as well as the embodiment of others since both self and other are given together from the outset. Heidegger, however, does not have any real conception of the lived body, or of incarnation, and Ricœur argues that this lacuna may well depend on the absence in his philosophy of any authentic phenomenology of the spatial: authenticity is restricted to the temporal dimension and there is no room for a consideration of the lived body (SMA, 379/326).

When Ricœur turns to his second category of passivity/alterity, that of the alterity of the Other, similar conceptual aporias arise. Here his main reference points are Husserl and Levinas, and their inadequacies are once again seen as complementary. Husserl, as we have just seen, has a conception of the other as an *alter ego*, a secondary concept derived from the ego. Levinas, conversely, privileges the Other over the self to an extent that makes intersubjectivity difficult to conceive:

> Emmanuel Levinas's entire philosophy rests on the initiative of the other in the intersubjective relation. In reality, this initiative establishes no relation at all, to the extent that the other represents absolute exteriority with respect to an ego defined by the condition of separation. The other, in this sense, ab-solves itself of all relation. This irrelation is the very definition of exteriority [*Cette irrélation définit l'extériorité même*]. (SMA, 221/188–9)

Ricœur's own position is dialectical: he aims to establish a new dialectic between Same and Other in which 'the Other is not only the counterpart of the Same but belongs to the intimate constitution of its sense' (SMA, 380/329). Husserl and Levinas, in their very different ways, and contrary to their avowed intentions, both appear to make the establishment of such a reciprocal dialectic theoretically impossible:

> I should like to show essentially that it is impossible to construct this dialectic in a unilateral manner, whether one attempts, with Husserl, to derive the *alter-ego* from the *ego*, or whether, with Levinas, one reserves for the Other the exclusive initiative for assigning responsibility to the self. A two-pronged conception of otherness remains to be constructed here, one that does justice in turn to the primacy of self-esteem and also to the primacy of the convocation by the other to justice. What is at stake here [. . .] is a formulation of otherness that is homogeneous with the fundamental distinction between two ideas of the Same – the Same as *idem* and the Same as *ipse* – a distinction

on which our entire philosophy of selfhood (*ipseity*) is based. (SMA, 382/331)

Ricœur describes Husserl's suspension of all knowledge of the other in the fifth of his *Cartesian Meditations* as a strategy akin to Descartes's hyperbolic doubt, and compares it to the analogous but opposed hyperbole that founds Levinas's notion of radical alterity. However, both strategies have unexpected and possibly paradoxical consequences in Ricœur's view: put simply, in Husserl's case this involves his understanding of the body of the other as 'flesh' by analogy with my own body (SMA, 385–6/336–7); in Levinas's case my separation from the other is so radical that the appearance of the face of the Other to me cannot be understood phenomenologically, but only as an epiphany, resulting ultimately, in Ricœur's account, in a 'reversal of a reversal' which brings back the *Soi* as a necessary witness to the Other (SMA, 392/340). Husserl and Levinas are both seen, then, as having made intersubjective relations initially incomprehensible by their extreme and opposed positions on the priority of self or other, but as having, through the hyperbolic nature of their arguments, been led, paradoxically, to a point where the other (or the self) has resurfaced by sheer logical implication.

This brief summary of a dense and lengthy discussion may none the less give some of the flavour of Ricœur's argument, and it leads us to the third area in which he considers passivity as the counterpart to alterity, and perhaps the least expected, that is to say moral conscience. Ricœur's text is at times less clear here, for he has to explain that he is using the (French) word 'conscience' in the sense of conscience rather than consciousness. This is an ambiguity that does not arise in English or German. Conscience, he argues, is the locus of a third form of dialectic between ipseity and alterity, and it is clearly visible in the metaphor of the voice, be it conceived as the internal voice of conscience or as a call coming from the Other. Ricœur starts by disposing of a wide range of conceptions of conscience from which he wishes to dissociate himself, using Kant, Hegel, and Nietzsche as variously exemplary, before turning finally to Heidegger and Levinas as privileged interlocutors.

Heidegger's conception of conscience as witnessing to an authentic mode of being attracts Ricœur by its notion of a silent call which comes to Dasein from within and yet is undeniably transcendent: 'The call undoubtedly does not come from another who is in the world with me. The call comes to me and yet from beyond me' (SMA, 401/348, quoting Heidegger).[9] However, he considers that Heidegger's refusal to understand conscience as in any way related to guilt or even to admonition, while enabling him to avoid many of the traps attendant on more conventional views, is not ever supplemented by an alternative conception which would allow him to show conscience as ultimately related to the ethical. Even the notions of *attestation* and *resolution* do not satisfy Ricœur's requirement for a link between conscience and morality.

At the other pole, and perhaps symmetrically, Levinas's model of the call that comes from the Other cannot escape from the radical exteriority which he has ascribed to alterity. Ricœur's own position, he insists yet again, is to propose a third mode of alterity that is a constituent element in ipseity. In the case of conscience this involves an attempt to find a way of bringing together 'l'injonction par l'autre' (of Levinas) and the 'attestation de soi' (of Heidegger). To this end Ricœur maintains against Heidegger that if an attestation is not originally an injunction it loses all ethical significance, and against Levinas that if an injunction is not originally an attestation it can never be received or understood:

> The profound unity of self-attestation and of the injunction coming from the other justifies that the modality of *otherness* [altérité] corresponding, on the plane of the 'great kinds', to the *passivity* of consciousness-conscience [*conscience*] on the phenomenological plane, be recognized in its irreducible specificity. (SMA 409/355)

At this point Ricœur seems prepared to describe as 'profound unity' what he has previously termed a 'fragile concordance' and even a 'break at the very heart of commitment' (SMA, 198/168). As he already discussed with respect to the notion of disponibility at the core of Marcel's conception of personal identity, my promise to the other is a response to his call, it is not a binding obligation which would make of my fidelity something rigid and unfree. And Ricœur quotes Marcel's 'All commitment is a response' (SMA, 311/267, EA, 63/46) as manifesting the dialectical openness he is himself striving for in his conception of ipseity. The 'faille' is precisely what saves me from the stasis of self-identity.

This determination to bring the two modes of conscience together – attestation de soi/injonction venue de l'autre – lies at the heart of Ricœur's entire project in *Soi-même comme un autre*, which is fundamentally ethical rather than phenomenological, ontological or hermeneutic. And as a philosopher who is a Christian, rather than a Christian philosopher, Ricœur concludes by proposing to Levinas that, as a philosopher himself, he must ultimately leave open the question as to whether the Other, whose trace we see in the face (*visage*), is to be understood as the absent God, or merely as an empty space (a '*place vide*'): 'With this aporia of the Other, philosophical discourse comes to an end' (SMA, 409/355).

Mortality: self and other

Ricœur's evident sensitivity to questions of embodiment, conscience, alterity, and passivity might seem to put him in a strong position from which to approach issues of personal mortality. But death plays far less of a role in his philosophy than it does in Marcel's for example. It is true that *La Mémoire, l'histoire, l'oubli* of 2000 takes death as a recurrent theme in its discussions of history, and in particular of the degree to which forgetfulness, forgiveness, and amnesty are possible or desirable political or personal choices. And Ricœur uses Freud's considerations on mourning as a pivotal element in his own meditations.

We shall return to this work shortly in our exploration of the ideas of Vladimir Jankélévitch who is a frequent reference point for Ricœur. But the bulk of the text deals with history rather than personal life, and it is only in two very brief sections that the question of death is faced directly: these figure in the section on temporality in Part III of the work, and consider in particular Heidegger's position on the authentic attitude towards death. Ricœur again takes issue with Heidegger's conception of Dasein as being-for (or towards)-death, and as the ownmost possibility of Dasein (MHO, 464–5/356–7), which he criticizes for obliterating Heidegger's celebration, elsewhere in *Being and Time*, of life and the openness of being.

Ricœur sees Heidegger's failure to engage with 'le chair', the body as mine, as lying at the heart of his refusal to consider as authentic any ways of considering death other than his own resolute contemplation. If the body is conceived only from the outside, as an object in the world, then neither its death, nor the death of another, can really touch Dasein at its heart. But if the body is rather my own, my perspective on the world, myself, then its death is necessarily a very different matter, and similarly the death of others may touch me with the very authenticity refused by Heidegger.

So far, Ricœur seems to have a strong and convincing line on Heidegger and death, but when he offers us his own approach we may well be disappointed by its brevity. Death, argues Ricœur, is evident to us both as a scientific, biological fact, and also through the death of others. And it is precisely our sense of ourselves as 'chair' that makes of the biological fact something more intimate, a part of our human condition that we must learn to accept, even though it runs entirely counter to our desire for life. It might well be possible so far to reconcile this position with Heidegger's own. But Ricœur goes on to claim that the real way we learn to understand death is through the death of the other: this is of course anathema to Heidegger who describes our awareness of the death of the other as irremediably inauthentic. And Ricœur acknowledges all the possibilities of inauthenticity that attend our reflections on the death of the other (avoidance strategies etc), but he maintains that it is precisely the loss that we experience at his/her death that teaches us what death really is.

For Ricœur of course, the other is not radically separate from me: through the notion of *ipseity* the other constitutes part of my identity, so my loss of the other inevitably involves a loss of myself. In this sense, our mourning for the other may help us anticipate the mourning others will carry out when we ourselves are dead, and thus help us become reconciled to our own death. And Ricœur goes on to suggest that even the deaths of others we do not know may also teach us something essential and authentic: the violence of death in murder, war, and suicide reveals to us the violence at the heart of all death, which is therefore a necessary rather than contingent aspect of our own death. Here once again Ricœur pits Heidegger against Levinas to whom he attributes the intuition about violence and murder (MHO, 469/360).

La Mémoire, l'histoire, l'oubli does not of course take death as its primary object of reflection, even though death necessarily under-lies much of its discussion, since it is, in a sense, the paradigmatic case of what might be forgotten, remembered or forgiven, whether in personal or public histories.[10] However, a posthumously pub-lished set of meditations reveals that death was a personal and philosophical preoccupation for Ricœur even if it does not feature largely in his published work. *Vivant jusqu'à la mort, suivi de Frag-ments* (2007) consists of a series of reflections written in 1996 when his wife Simone was dying, and a collection of fragments composed in 2004–5 shortly before his own death. The title comes from Spinoza's claim that true wisdom comes from meditating not on death but on life, and from 'living up to death' (*Vivant*, p.12/14).[11] In this way, as we have just seen, Ricœur sides strongly with Levinas against Heidegger: 'Levinas is clear and firm regarding the time before death, which can only be a being-against-death and not a being-towards-death' (MHO, 470/361).

Ricœur is, like Derrida, very concerned by the question of mourning which he considers as the reverse side of, and inextri-cably related to, gaiety. Indeed, as we saw in *Mémoire*, since we can never know or experience our own death it is only through the death of the other that we can really conceive it (V, 36/8). And Ricœur is prepared to consider this question in real physical terms, discussing for example not only the attitude of the dying towards their death (often seeing themselves as 'still alive' rather than as 'dying') but also issues of palliative care and accompani-ment of the dying. He also is clearly aware, unlike Sartre, of the effect of serious illness not only on the body but also on the mind, and he speaks of the 'deteriorating consciousness' of the dying (45/15); just as already in *Soi-même* he spoke of suffering as far more than mere pain that has to be endured, but rather as affect-ing our very selves:

> Suffering is not defined solely by physical pain, nor even by mental pain, but by the diminution, even by the destruction, of the capac-ity for acting, of the ability-to-act, experienced as an attack on the integrity of the self. (SMA, 223/190)

However, he does not develop the reflexions on passivity that we explored in our discussion of *Soi-même comme un autre*, and which might have seemed precisely the conceptual area which would enable a serious discussion of death in its implications for personal identity.

Ricœur's refusal of dualism, his contention that the self is constituted from the outset by alterity, and his understanding of the relationship between alterity and passivity would, I believe, have provided an ideal grounding for a discussion of the way in which passivity (and alterity) take over from activity and selfhood at the time of our death. But this was not to be. Much of the brief text is taken up with discussions of works by Jorge Semprun and Primo Levi, and Ricœur is clearly troubled by the issue of Levi's suicide, which he attempts to understand. But, as we see in the chapter starkly entitled 'La Mort', his major personal preoccupation lies in fact elsewhere, for it is the question of life after death which seems to trouble him most.

Ricœur has always been at pains to keep his Christianity separate from his philosophy, and he reiterates this determination here but, none the less, it is the question of an afterlife which evidently disturbs him, and he considers briefly whether his own notion of identity as ipseity might provide a form of solution, though he does not develop the suggestion (84/48). As a good philosopher, he seems to think that he must not discuss such speculative, metaphysical questions, but as a Christian too it appears that Ricœur envisages the hope for life after death as a temptation to be avoided. In Christian theology, eternal life and the resurrection do not have to be understood as literally implying personal and individual continuation after death; there are many other ways of understanding them, especially in the Protestant tradition, and Ricœur seems attracted by the idea (which he attributes to Whitehead but which is also in Marcel) of personal survival coming through God's eternal memory (V, 78/43). But even this has come to seem to him like a consolation needed by his weakness of spirit, and he remains determined to 'demythologize' the terms of salvation and eternal life, and in particular to reject any notion of physical resurrection (91/53), though he returns to the question at Easter 2005 in what looks like a final attempt to make sense of the question in a structured fashion. Unfortunately the notes are too fragmented to provide any real sense of his last thoughts on the issue, though they appear to follow a fairly traditional Christian line which concludes with the reign of death enduring until the Last Day when victory over death will be proclaimed (133–5/90).

In the last analysis, Ricœur seems to be in an excellent position to discuss the most fundamental questions about death and its implications for notions of selfhood and embodiment, but he does not do so. It is as if his determination not to allow his Christian beliefs to affect his philosophy has provided an ultimate impediment to a discussion which might not have appealed to all his readers but which is so strongly called for by his texts that its absence is arguably a real lacuna. Ultimately, perhaps, we might say that Ricœur has the courage of his philosophical rather than his Christian convictions.

Philosophy and neuroscience

There is one last aspect of Ricœur's varied and determined work on these questions that we must look at briefly, not least because of the evidence it provides of the seriousness with which Ricœur attempted to engage with the science of consciousness. This is his contribution to recent attempts to bring together philosophy and neuroscience. In *Ce qui nous fait penser: la nature et la règle* of 1998, Ricœur and Jean-Pierre Changeux, a neuroscientist, engage in a lengthy series of discussions on the mind–body problem, that is to say on the relationship between the brain and consciousness, between the material and the spiritual, and between causality and ethics (p. 20/10). Both interlocutors are extraordinarily impressive in their knowledge of the other's field, Changeux for example being able to argue happily about quite thorny philosophical questions such as details of the ambiguities or evolution of Descartes's position, or about Aristotle or Spinoza. Ricœur too is clearly extremely well versed in the current scientific literature as well as in the views of philosophers from many different traditions such as Strawson (as we have already seen), Thomas Nagel, or the Churchlands.

The debate therefore looks extremely promising, but in the end its outcome is uncertain. Both thinkers set out to attempt to bridge the epistemological gap between them and to find a third way, which would be neither purely scientific nor purely philosophical, to talk about the vital question of the relationship between mind and brain. But despite all that their discussions may teach us in terms of our knowledge of neurological advances or indeed philosophical nuance (we learn for example that Ricœur entirely rejects the eliminationism of the Churchlands but is more sympathetic to theories of connectionism), there does not seem to have been any substantive progress made in bringing together the two ways of envisaging the human being.

Changeux continues to insist that the progress of neuroscience brings us ever closer to an understanding of the mind and of consciousness, Ricœur's position is always that there is an impassable gulf between the two modes of reflection that no amount of scientific progress could ever bridge. He envisages the question in terms of incompatible discourses or heterogenous perspectives (23/14), and his view seems in the last analysis very close to that of Strawson's conception of ascription in which a single person can be described by different sets of predicates: 'One's states of consciousness, one's thoughts and sensations are ascribed *to the very same thing* to which these physical characteristics, this physical situation, is ascribed'.[12]

Ultimately, Ricœur has replaced a dualism of substance by what he calls a semantic dualism and, although this version of duality does appear considerably more attractive and indeed truer to what we now believe to be the facts of the matter, it seems none the less to have shifted the debate to an equally frustrating and insoluble terrain. What is incontrovertible is that the gap between neuroscience and philosophy of mind is currently too big to be bridged by even the most cooperative and open-minded practitioners of either discipline. Whether Changeux or Ricœur is correct about their ultimate epistemological incompatibility is less easy to decide.

Vladimir Jankélévitch (1903–1985)

On ne peut à la fois aimer et être.

We will turn now to two Jewish philosophers, Vladimir Jankélévitch and Emmanuel Levinas, to see whether they deal any more convincingly with the ultimate questions of subjectivity and mortality.

Both are interlocutors for Ricœur, as we have already seen in the case of Levinas. But it is a quotation from Jankélévitch that Ricœur's *La Mémoire, l'histoire, l'oubli* takes as its Exergue:

> He who has been, henceforth cannot not have been: henceforth this mysterious and profoundly obscure fact of having been is his viaticum for all eternity. (MHO, 631 n.35/602, citing Jankélévitch, p. 275)

The quotation comes from *L'Irréversible et la nostalgie* of 1974, one of the many texts in which Jankélévitch reflects on the double-sided nature of the passing of time, which entails not only a time that can never return, which he calls 'irreversible' and which may be a reason for nostalgia or regret, but also deeds that can never be undone which he calls 'irrevocable' and which may be a reason for remorse.[13] These reflections are important for Ricœur in his own consideration of questions of forgiveness and amnesty, and contribute to his view that whereas forgiveness ('le pardon') is often an appropriate response to a crime – be it personal or political – amnesty never is because it involves an obliteration and enforced forgetting of the crime which is unfair to the victim. Forgetting, like mourning, can never fully efface the irrevocable: there will always be an element that will remain irreparable. Jankélévitch himself, it should be noted, takes a harsher line, at least on political crimes: in his various writings on forgiveness, published between 1948 and 1971, he debates the possibility of forgiving War criminals for the horrors of the Holocaust and argues ultimately that this is both wrong and impossible, not least because forgiveness must be asked for before it can be granted:

> Forgiveness! But did they ever ask us for forgiveness? It is only the distress and dereliction of the guilty that would give meaning and a reason for being to forgiveness.[14]

Jankélévitch is well aware that his position sits ill with various conceptions of love or charity, but he remains resolute:

> Between the absolute of the law of love and the absolute of wicked freedom there exists a tear that cannot be entirely ripped apart.

We have increasingly attempted to reconcile the irrationality of evil
with the omnipotence of love. Foregiveness is as strong as evil, but
evil is as strong as love.[15]

However, it is not these considerations on war and forgiveness that
are most important to us in this context but rather two other
elements of Jankélévitch's philosophy: his meditations on love and
death and his reflections on personal identity.

Ipseity (again)

In the case of personal identity, we should note an unusual phenomenon: Ricœur appears not to acknowledge sufficiently his
debt to Jankélévitch in his analyses of identity in terms of idem
and ipse. This omission is surprising as Ricœur is normally punc-
tilious in his willingness to recognize the way in which his own
thinking engages with and extends that of other philosophers.
Indeed, it is arguably his preferred way of working, as we have
seen in his engagements with Strawson and Parfit for example. But
in the case of the notion of ipseity as a privileged form of human
identity there is little or no acknowledgement of Jankélévitch. Of
course, the term ipseity itself was not coined by Jankélévitch, it
has a long history, and within the immediate context of French
thought which we are exploring it occurs for example in Sartre's
analyses in *L'Etre et le Néant* when he discusses the 'circuit d'ipséité'
which constitutes the *pour-soi*, just as it occurs in Levinas where
it is opposed to 'illeity' or radical alterity.

However, in Sartre's case it is used to describe an aspect of the
reflexivity of consciousness, and in Levinas's case to describe a
self-centred egoity to which he is vehemently opposed, neither of
which bears any real resemblance to Ricœur's own usage, whereas
Jankélévitch seems to employ the very same ipse/idem opposition
as Ricœur but without this similarity being duly recognized and
discussed by Ricœur. One of the clearest accounts is to be found
in Jankélévitch's *Philosophie première* of 1953, in the chapter entitled 'Le pur lui-même' ['*The Pure Itself*']; it comes at the end of
a section called 'Perdre en trouvant' which discusses the way in
which the self can never be captured or pinned down. Like the
present moment, as soon as it seems to be caught it is already past

and lost; 'we have lost it *in finding it*' ['*on l'a perdu* en le trouvant'] (134), it is an 'imperceptible threshold', an 'ungraspable kairos', a 'limit without depth':

> This fleeting Itself [*Lui-même*], melting and fluid, is nothing, not even itself (*soi*): it is *ipse*, itself precisely and in person, it is not *idem*, a self-identical thing. (134–5)

Ipseity can never be grasped, it is always just out of reach:

> *Ipseity* designates a point situated at infinity. [. . .] At this impalpable and fleeting point, [. . .] the subject would truly be itself [. . .], but the subject itself in itself is always *other* and always *beyond* [. . .]. And yet, the inexplicable evidence of the *ipse* is endlessly reconstituted in the very volatility that reveals the inconsistency of the ego-for-itself. (135–6)

It is clear that for Jankélévitch, as for Sartre, and indeed for Ricœur, there can be no substantive self-identical subject; the self is not a mere mirage but nor can it be identified as self-same, it is always other than itself, and always beyond our grasp. And the paradoxes of temporality clearly underpin the paradoxes of ipseity:

> Courageous consciousness on the precipice of its next future, a future that is barely future or already almost present, still present or almost future, becoming or *on the point* of being present; swift consciousness on the threshold of the immediate past, a barely passed present that has *just* become present. (265)

Although Jankélévitch enjoys the paradoxes and reversals of his exploration of non-self-coincidence, and uses poetic metaphors to evoke understanding in his readers ('for one only coincides with a spark [*étincelle*] by becoming a spark oneself', p. 264) in a way that Ricœur's more sober style does not, we can none the less judge that Jankélévitch's distinction between what he calls 'the semelfactivity of the personal *Ipse*' (263) and the *idem*, 'a self-identical thing' (135) is so close to Ricœur's own later *ipse/idem* distinction that it warrants at the very least an acknowledgement and arguably a more extended discussion.[16]

Jankélévitch's subtle analysis of the 'point évanouissant', or vanishing point, of ipseity forms part of his many explorations of the *je ne sais quoi. Philosophie première*, which we have been discussing, is itself subtitled *Introduction à une philosophie du 'presque'*, and in it Jankélévitch analyses for example what he sees as the necessary disjunction between the moment (of, say, joy) and the state (of, say, happiness) (p. 254) arguing that there is an irremediable contradiction between the instantaneous and the continuous, though we always yearn for their resolution. Jankélévitch explores this human inability ever to achieve peaceful self-coincidence outside a kind of undesirable stasis in a wide variety of different areas, especially ethical. The most important for our exploration of mortality and passion are of course those of love and death.

Love and transience

Jankélévitch's discussion of love in *Philosophie première* has much in common with Sartre's in *L'Etre et le Néant* though it is less extended. It is introduced as part of his reflections on the incompatibility of happiness and joy, where love is compared with joy:

> Joy is hope that passes suddenly into regret without having found the time to be happiness: the almost-nothing of joy would be the hinge or fracture in this regret and this hope. [...] Joy resembles love, which is always halfway between the desire for possession and the disappointment of coincidence. (257)

Like Sartre, Jankélévitch opposes love to desire, but in a somewhat different way: for Sartre the two are incompatible because desire depends on turning the Other into an object whereas love puts me at the mercy of the Other and makes me an object in my turn, while for Jankélévitch love hovers between desire on the one hand and the monotony of secure possession on the other. Sartre's analysis is specific to human relations; Jankélévitch's is clearly part of his continuing reflections on the impossibility of reconciling the instantaneousness of the moment with any kind of continuity in time, but both share the conclusion that, in its pure form, love cannot last. Jankélévitch, however, has a further move to make, that of the (Sartrean) *qui perd gagne* which turns failure into success. In this case his argument is that because of its impermanence love can never be happy, but that happiness itself is a lesser mode than joy:

> Joy lies in the flickering of appearance and disappearance. [...] Creatures are made such that they must choose between the chronicity of happiness, which is a 'habitus' without joy, and the instaneousness of joy, which is a short-lived moving fervour without permanence or happiness. (254)

But if there is a choice to be made, Jankélévitch has already made it, for it is clear that in fact his 'happiness' is no more than a stultifying contentment ('it slumbers in the stagnation and siesta of the effective "state" and, consequently, he who is happy is unhappy', 256). So if love is never happy, this is evidently to its credit, it is 'more than happy' ['*plus qu'heureux*'], indeed it has much in common with liberty which is not happy either, though it is a source of joy:

> No-one would think to say that freedom is happy: for the initial instant, or instantaneous initiative, of freedom, is, on the contrary, painful and dizzying and anxiety-inducing; in reality, freedom is beyond the disjunction of happiness and unhappiness, since it is [...] one of the sources of joy. (259)

Jankélévitch's view of freedom as vertiginous and terrifying has further evident similarities with that of Sartre. But his conclusions are more overtly optimistic: love and joy may be essentially evanescent but they are thereby protected from the erosion of time and habit: 'One should neither demand the impossible, nor regret the irreversible, nor seek to perpetuate the instant!' (260). Indeed, in a move that may seem whimsical, he compares them to philosophy itself, which disappears as soon as we try to fix our eyes on it (261). These brief moments of joy, love, and freedom are described in terms that make clear that their value lies precisely in their transience and delicacy: 'vanishing point', 'ineffable', 'fine point and borderline-case', 'almost nothing', 'spark', 'glimpse'. Jankélévitch's poetic conclusion opts decisively for the evanescence of joy over the continuity of happiness:

> One cannot simultaneously love and be; for one must choose between the harsh winter of being without love and the springtime

death of love without being. Now there is an ungraspable point where this tragedy of alternatives becomes a wondrous opportunity. Is it necessary, incidentally, to chase after this highly improbable opportunity? One can, after all, live without the *je-ne-sais-quoi*, as one can live without philosophy, without music, without joy and without love. But not so well. (266)

And it is this preference for mortal joy over a more pragmatic contentment that provides the key to Jankélévitch's fascination with, and extended philosophical analyses of, death.

Embodiment and subjectivity

It will have become clear already that Jankélévitch's discussions of love and desire do not seem to involve a distinction between mind and body or body and soul. In a sense we could argue that this is because he eschews dualism, but we might also wonder if he really gives bodily experience its due. The ethereal nature of his analyses would seem to militate against a sensual account, though this would obviously still be possible. Elsewhere Jankélévitch discusses the body as a deceptive appearance, 'a lie', 'a huge deceit' *(Penser la mort*, 1994, p. 133), which may lead us to trust a hypocrite, or attribute intelligence to a fool who has an interesting face. Socrates, Jankélévitch reminds us, was notoriously ugly (*Méconnaissance*, p. 36). However, this apparent dismissal of the body is itself deceptive, for in his study of *La Méconnaissance: le malentendu* (1980) we see that it is only half the picture: appearances do give some access to truth, if not the whole truth, as we see in particular in the chapter on the 'Ambiguïté de l'apparence'.

In fact Jankélévitch's understanding of the body and its relationship to the mind is both complex and subtle, though his paradoxical and provocative way of writing may sometimes mislead the unwary as he develops certain ideas to a point which goes far beyond what common sense is willing to accept. The body (and indeed its parts) in Jankélévitch's account is an 'organe–obstacle', both organ, in the sense of essential to any action, and obstacle, or impediment to that action. To take a simple example, the eye is both the means of my vision and also what impedes it:

without eyes I could not see at all, but they do not permit me to differentiate the microscopic, distinguish detail in the far distance, or see colours beond the infra-red or the ultra-violet. Similarly, I cannot hear frequencies that are too high or too low for my ear. But the theory of the organe–obstacle goes far beyond the body and applies to a wide variety of aspects of the human condition.

Another example is that of language: the naive view tends to consider language only as 'organe', as enabling me to say what I feel and think; a more sophisticated view, Jankélévitch argues, such as that of the poet or philosopher, can recognize that language is also an 'obstacle', unable to convey everything I might wish to express. This is Jankélévitch's approach to human finitude, and it is analogous to Sartre's in so far as both philosophers emphasize the way in which all aspects of the human are necessarily double-sided: in Sartre's terms, our situation and facticity both enable and impede our activities, in Jankélévitch's terms, this is the role of the organe–obstacle.

Initially we might be tempted to think that Jankélévitch has rejected a mind–body dualism only to replace it by a dualism of organe–obstacle, but this would be unfair. The ambivalence or duality of the organe–obstacle in no way reduplicates the split between mind and body; both terms can apply to the mind just as much as the body, and indeed make it very difficult to draw any kind of line between them: where would we place the limits of memory as organe–obstacle for example? Do these lie in the mind or rather in the neurology of the brain? – we have already seen what thorny territory this leads us to in the debate between Ricœur and Changeux. It is true that Jankélévitch sometimes speaks of 'strangeness' and 'semi-alienation from the body' (*Le Sérieux de l'intention*, 1983, p. 147) in the context of the gap between the way I see myself and the way I appear to others (and we can compare this with the Sartrean *pour-soi* and *pour-autrui*), but this ambiguity/alienation is not limited to the body. Indeed, it applies also to the ego in so far as this is understood as a kind of natural self, and like the body, the ego too has the ambivalence of an organe–obstacle, it forms part of 'the bio-psychological given, corporeality and naturality' (17) that constitutes the unstable and oscillating hybrid of human existence:

It's the same corporeality, the same egoity, that is contradictorily and to the greatest degree simultaneously prevention and instrument: moral man is impeded and weighed down by the lead of egoism; but *because* he is impeded, and even *insofar* as he is impeded, moral man is ipso-facto drawn up to a height: he is drawn up in spite of obstacles, and simultaneously despite and because of his body; he is drawn up although he is impeded ... and at the same time he is drawn up precisely *because* he is impeded: the *despite* is itself paradoxically a *thanks to* [le grâce à]. (19)

And the notion of the ambiguity of egoism serves to demonstrate a further ambiguity inherent in love, for love of the Other ['l'amour 'extatique''] necessarily reduces personal egoism, involving what Jankélévitch refers to as 'the deflation of the substantial subject' (14), but the subject of course remains necessary since there can be no love without a lover, so any 'deflation' is bound to be limited and reveals once again the inherent instability of the human.

Mortality and finitude

It is then human finitude in its multiple and ambivalent forms that lies at the heart of Jankélévitch's analyses of love and, of course, of death. As we have seen, our experiences of love and joy are fragile and ephemeral: their intensity is both what renders them precious and also what prevents us from possessing them in a durable form. Another ambiguity is to be found in temporality itself which is also an organe-obstacle: the passage of time is double-edged, and just as it enables us to pursue our projects so it carries us inexorably towards our death and their extinction. The success of even our most ambitious plans is (just) the positive face of ageing and mortality:

The very instrument of our realisation and our development every day brings us closer to the final non-being: today more than yesterday but less than tomorrow; at whatever moment one contemplates it, the living being will never have been closer to its death. (*La Mort*, p. 105)

But consistent with his conception of the Janus-faced 'organe–obstacle', Jankélévitch sees death and finitude not merely as inevitable limits which can be put to good use, but as essential to all that is positive in human experience. In *Penser la mort* (1994), a collection of interviews from the years following the publication of his magnum opus *La Mort* in 1966, Jankélévitch expresses himself extremely clearly and directly:

> Dying is the very condition of existence. I join with all those who say that it's death that gives meaning to life by withdrawing this meaning from it. Death is the non-sense that gives meaning to life. The non-sense that gives meaning by denying meaning. This is what is shown by the role of death in brief, ardent existences, in short and passionate existences, in which it is death that gives strength and intensity to existence. It is an alternative from which one cannot escape. We would simultaneously like both fervour of life and eternity. But that is impossible, a superhuman outcome, beyond the scope of the human.
>
> The alternative for us is therefore as follows: having a life that is brief but true, a life of love, etc., or rather an indefinite existence without love, which is not really a life and would be a perpetual death. (40)

In this bald form, which opposes the brevity of mortal love to the durability of a life without love he terms a living death, Jankélévitch's ideas may invite all sorts of queries and objections, but this is an inevitable consequence of the interview format. In his written texts, his views are explained and elaborated with immense subtlety, and often seem to forestall and respond to questions even before they can be fully formulated.

Jankélévitch is the only philosopher in this study to devote an entire and lengthy work to the subject of death. *La Mort*, first published in 1966, is an exhaustive exploration of a wide variety of aspects of human mortality. And as we have already sensed, death permeates Jankelevich's work even when its object is ostensibly very different. Death represents all that is unknowable, and it is death that renders precious all that we love and value. It is not the irreversibility of time that is the real cause of human anguish, but rather the finitude of life:

> Irreversibility is anxiety-inducing only when associated with life's finitude, or, to be more precise, the uncertain certainty of death.

[...] Time presses on [...]. Lost time, lost youth, lost life. [...]
The possibility of death is always presupposed in this instant and
irrational clause that is summed up for us in the imperative
of *urgency*. [...] Every hour is precious. (*La Méconnaissance*,
pp. 128–9)

The 'uncertain certainty' is of course our knowledge of our mortality coupled with our ignorance of the hour of our death. Jankélévitch also calls it a 'half-knowing' ['*demi-connaissance*'] and a
'misrecognition' ['*méconnaissance*'] (p. 23). Like Ricœur, he considers that any real understanding we may have of death comes
from our experience of the death of someone close to us [a
'proche']. Our own death is a closed book, the death of the Other
remains a natural, biological phenomenon, it is only the death of
someone we love that might perhaps bring us close to any kind
of understanding of what he calls the mystery of death:

There is only the *death of a loved one* [du proche], which might
perhaps bring together the objective naturality of the death of the
other and the unthinkable tragedy of my own death [*la mort-pro-
pre*]: but it is, on the contrary, neither fully metempirical (since the
loved one is, after all, an other), nor fully natural (since the loved
one is if not myself then at least something of me). One must admit
that the secret is well kept! And one does not scheme against the
impenetrable schemings of death! The experience of death does
not bring us so much as a thousandth of a millimetre closer to
knowing this mystery. (*Philosophie première*, p. 4)

La Mort itself has three major sections, 'La mort en deçà de la
mort' ['*This Side of Death*'], which discusses our awareness of
future death, 'La mort dans l'instant mortel' ['*Death in the
Moment of Death*'], which considers what little we can know of
death itself, and 'La mort au-delà de la mort' ['*Death Beyond
Death*'], which considers the question of life after death. These
sections are lengthy, around 150 pages each, but they all conclude that there is nothing we can ever really know of death:
we know we are mortal but we cannot really internalize (or
'realize') the knowledge; we can observe the death of another
but never know anything of the experience of death itself as
opposed to dying; and despite all our philosophy we can never
have any definitive certainty about questions of mortality and

immortality. Indeed, Jankélévitch refuses to come down even slightly on either side of the debate concerning life after death: one of his chapters is entitled 'Absurdité de survie', but the next is called 'Absurdité de la nihilisation', and both are divided into sub-sections with a series of paradoxical titles such as 'L'Amour, la Liberté, Dieu sont plus forts que la mort. Et réciproquement!'. In a later radio interview Jankélévitch claimed never to think of death:

> I absolutely never think about death. And if you find yourself thinking about it, I recommend you to do the same as me and write a book about death, turn it into a problem. (quoted in *Penser la mort?* p. 9).

At first sight a mere 'boutade', this claim arguably has a deeper meaning: 'Penser la mort?' is a real question, for death is the ultimate unthinkable, not merely because we cannot bear to face our own mortality, or that of those we love, but because once we attempt to think of it we find we are faced with precisely nothing. The 467 pages of *La Mort* attempt to discuss all aspects of the problem, but by the end Jankélévitch still claims to have found nothing at all to say about death itself, merely about a multiplicity of related issues such as terminal illness, capital punishment, mourning, religious belief, theories of metempsychosis and reincarnation, palliative care, and a huge range of writings around (rather than 'on') death by other philosophers and thinkers from Aristotle, Plato, and Marcus Aurelius to Bergson, Jean Wahl, and Maeterlinck.

It is in the last few chapters of *La Mort* that Jankélévitch comes closest to giving us an account of his personal convictions, but these are, as always, paradoxical and undecided, or, in his terms, infinitely ambiguous (p. 384). In 'Absurdité de la survie' [*'The Absurdity of Survival'*], the notion of dualism is analysed, perhaps we might even say deconstructed, in a way that reveals its untenable and self-contradictory assumptions. Dualism, Jankélévitch argues, is a belief that both depends on and attempts to explain death. A living person does not appear to us immediately as a union of body and soul or as a 'psychosomatic composite'; the idea of such a union is one way of dealing with the gap between the lifeless body and the person we knew. But Jankélévitch denies that what remains after death is the body deprived of its soul, it is rather a corpse whose decomposition is imminent and has in fact already begun. We never see a soul without a body, but neither do we really witness a body without a soul (395). The whole question of the destiny of the soul after death is a false one: the soul cannot be localized, it goes nowhere for it was nowhere during life, neither a bird in a cage nor a perfume in a bottle.

These metaphors distort rather than illuminate the question, the dualist view cannot ever sustain a convincing argument for the survival of the soul separate from the body, the 'âme-corps' is indivisible and is nihilated in death rather than divided. Just as the body cannot survive without the soul, except as a rotting corpse, nor can the soul survive without the body, except as an 'âme malheureuse', homeless and despairing (401). The logic of dualism proves, in Jankélévitch's account, to be its own undoing, at least in so far as the idea of a spiritual life after death is concerned.

Conversely, there is no more coherence to be found in the belief in total nihilation after death. The very arguments that have just been used against dualism are now turned against its opposite, materialist reductivism:

> The body is, of course, the vital condition of the soul, it is neither the vase, nor the host nor the cockpit; in losing its body, the soul has lost its vital condition and hence cannot survive. For the soul was only the soul through the body. For that reason precisely, the soul is something other [*autre chose*] than its own condition: not just 'another thing', since the soul is not *a thing*, but something other, though I don't know what. Life is only living through its liaisons with an anatomical substrate, tissues and cells; and yet the vitality of this life, though still impalpable, is always beyond that substrate. Under the conditions of human life, memory is possible only in liaison with a brain: no brain, no memory; but by the same measure, at least in principle, memory is something other than the brain on which it depends. [. . .] The brain is ultimately incorporated in a somatic being that is the condition of its personal existence; and yet the soul is always beyond this corporeality. (403–4)

Jankélévitch has moved here, albeit briefly, onto a similar territory to that of Ricœur in his discussions of Strawson and his debates with Changeux; he is considering the relationship between body and mind, or consciousness, or 'soul', and arguing for an 'explanatory gap' that radical materialism can never bridge and indeed often seems philosophically ill-equipped even to recognize. Death annihilates 'a truly unique ipseity in the world' (412) and this is a human scandal and a mystery, a 'mortal truth' that science cannot begin to resolve (414). Perhaps after all death is not the end: 'Who knows whether the consciousness incarnated in an ipseity won't in turn have the last word?' (423). The tourniquets seem unending, and this is indeed Jankélévitch's ultimate position on the issue – one of chosen uncertainty rather than decision:

> The circle of the diallel, ambiguity, which is to say the regime of the double truth of the contradictory, rather suggests to us the following: that death and consciousness will both have the last word, which (and this means much the same) will only ever be penultimate. (423)

None the less, Jankélévitch does make one further attempt to resolve the apparently insoluble dilemma: he turns to love and considers in what ways it might really be said to conquer death. Love is of course opposed to death in many different possible senses: the passionate desire that the loved one should live, a willingness to die for the beloved, the way in which love may continue long after death, and the way in which children carry on the life of their parents. But none of these actually conquers death physically, just symbolically, and what Jankélévitch calls 'pneumatically' (434). So despite love's passionate refusal of death, it cannot ultimately win the battle whose outcome remains uncertain: 'In truth, love is both stronger and weaker than death, and is therefore just as strong as death' (434). Consciousness, liberty, and God are also tested against the nihilating power of death and each time the result is similarly inconclusive: death and immortality are equally inconceivable: 'impossible not to die, impossible to annihilate oneself forever' (440). Jankélévitch compares this stalemate to the antinomies of Pascal's *Deus absconditus* ('as incomprehensible as death may be, it is incomprehensible that it not be', 439), and to Kant's mathematical antinomies in which thesis and antithesis are equally false and equally true.

But the question remains as to how much real progress Janké-lévitch has made in the course of his lengthy discussions and analyses. A sceptic might well argue that his conclusions are not true antinomies at all, and that death comes out clearly victorious over even love, freedom, and consciousness. Even if we allow to Jankélévitch the equipoise he argues for, some may still feel that we are no further advanced in our understanding of death since the poles of the antitheses are so incompatible that they seem to belong to different realms and are not really mutually enlightening.

How then has Jankélévitch contributed to our reflections on mortality, subjectivity, and passion? In his final chapter, Janké-lévitch returns to the notion of the organe–obstacle, and uses it to illuminate the relationship between life and death in a manner so simple that it unquestionably commands our assent. Death, he argues, is both what enables us to live and what stops us living: 'the means of and prevention from living' (448). 'Vital death is what makes mortal life passionate' (450). 'It is ultimately in life itself, in the joy of living and the supernaturality of lived naturality that we find the pledge of an imperishable existence' (453). But as well as this celebration of finitude as essential to a passionate life that is humanly worth living, Jankélévitch also turns to his notions of the irreversible and the irrevocable which we looked at briefly in the context of forgiveness. In that context, the irre-versibility of time and the irrevocability of action was a double-edged cause for nostalgia, regret, and remorse. Now it is the positive aspect that comes to the fore: irreversibilty is what guar-antees a form of immortality beyond death, for what has been cannot be annihilated:

> Death destroys the whole of the living being, but it cannot anni-hilate the fact of having lived. (458)

> Eternal life, which is to say the indelible fact of having been, is a gift made by death to living persons. (459)

> May the mortality of death remain incurable, so that the *quoddity* of having lived it be indestructible! (461)

> *Finitude* is *infinitely* precious! (463)

> The fact of having been, at least, is inalienable [. . .]: materially, one can remove my being from me, but one cannot annihilate my

having-been. [. . .] The irreversible, which prevents its resurrection, prevents its annihilation. (465)

Jankélévitch's conclusion on the subject of death is that there is no enigma, and no secret. Death brings life to an end, but it also gives life its value, and it cannot take away the fact of having lived. He takes the example of the return of the Prodigal Son to illustrate the way in which, even having come full circle, nothing is ever quite the same again. Life is irremediably changed because I have lived it. And in a sense, *La Mort* may be seen as performing what it describes: Jankélévitch has not so much told us anything we did not know before about life and death, but in the course of his analyses he has taken us on an intellectual and emotional journey that will have inevitably changed us to some degree. In a paradoxical manner quite in keeping with his own preferred way of thinking, he takes us closer than anyone else so far to the heart of the question of death. But the heart is not, as we might have expected, the deep heart of darkness. It is rather the fragile, vulnerable, and impalpable heart of joy, love, and passion – all that makes life worth living. Jankélévitch might have chosen the subtitle of this book for one of his own texts: 'passions of the soul' reflects very accurately just how he envisages the human experience of finitude and mortality.

Emmanuel Levinas (1906–1995)

Sensibilité comme la subjectivité du sujet: La Passion de Soi.

Jankélévitch and Levinas knew each other's work extremely well. Together with Jean Wahl, Jankélévitch was one of the examiners for Levinas's doctoral defence in 1961. The third proposed examiner, Merleau-Ponty, had died a recent and early death. And, as we have seen, Jankélévitch acknowledges Levinas as a source of his ideas on alterity, just as Levinas frequently refers to Jankélévitch's magnum opus on death and, in his obituary essay, praises him as an ethical thinker who recognizes that all duties are mine, all rights belong to the other (*Hors Sujet*, 119/87). As Jews of non-French extraction from immigrant families they necessarily had a certain amount in common, though Jankélévitch was born in France of

Russian parents whereas Levinas was born in Lithuania. Jankélévitch had a classic French education at the Ecole normale supéri-
eure, studying under Bergson from 1922 and coming first in the
Agrégation in 1926 before leaving to teach in Prague. Levinas
came to France to study in Strasbourg in 1924, went to Freibourg
in 1928 where he met Husserl and Heidegger, and took French
nationality only in 1930. He was called up for military duties in
1940, captured by the Germans and imprisoned in a prisoner-of-
war camp near Hanover, whereas Jankélévitch took an active part
in the Resistance. Both philosophers taught in a variety of French
universities and ended their careers at the Sorbonne. Levinas is an
explicitly and committedly Jewish thinker, and in his obituary he
refers to Jankélévitch's Judaism as a religion 'without rites, without
worship, without Hebrew', also perhaps 'without God', but this,
he acknowledges, only God will decide (HS, 120–1/88).

At his doctoral defence Levinas reportedly responded to Jankélévitch's questioning about Bergson by replying that whereas
Jankélévitch was a poet, he was himself rather a writer of prose.
Whatever Levinas may have meant by this in the context of a viva,
it is certain that Jankélévitch's writing is evocative and finely
nuanced whereas Levinas's style is both more traditionally philosophical as well as sometimes heavier and more repetitive. Since
the other string to Jankélévitch's bow was musical analysis, whereas
Levinas's non-philosophical publications mainly concern interpretation of the Talmud, such differences are perhaps inevitable. In
his 1979 Preface to the re-edition of *Le Temps et l'Autre*, first published in 1948, Levinas explains his decision to republish the text
without modification as a homage to its time and to the Collège
Philosophique and its immediate post-war members: witnessing as
it did to the inspiration of Jankélévitch's formulations about the
ineffable, to Jean Wahl's praise of 'la philosophie vivante', as well
as to Sartre and Merleau-Ponty in their introduction of Husserlian
phenomenology and Heideggerian ontology to Paris. Gabriel
Marcel is also cited for his attempt to create a non-systematic
philosophy that remained explicitly tentative and exploratory.

Subjectivity and temporality

Levinas's reflections on mortality and subjectivity run as a constant theme throughout his philosophical writings, from the essays

of the 1940s to the late texts and interviews of the 1990s. His ideas are radicalized, but not, I would maintain, fundamentally changed. Already in *Le Temps et l'Autre*, he rejects the Heideggerian notion of Mitsein, which he considers inadequate to account for either the nature or the significance of human relations with others, as well as Heidegger's conception of being-towards-death which he argues misrepresents death and provides a distorted notion of temporality. He rejects too any view of the Other which tends to assimilate him in a kind of primitive 'participation': 'I *am* not the Other' he insists (TA, 21/42). In this essay, Levinas is keen to stress the solitude of the individual, not as a matter of privation or loneliness but as something more fundamental which is masked by the existential stress on despair and abandonment. Later, as we shall see, Levinas will express himself in somewhat different terms, but it is clear from the outset that he does not conceive community or sociability as able to overcome the inherent isolation at the heart of existence (TA, 21/42).

> Solitude is not tragic because it is the privation of the other, but because it is enclosed within the captivity of its identity, because it is matter. To shatter the enchainment of matter is to shatter the finality of hypostasis. It is to be in time. (TA, 38/57)

True temporality is non-substantive and evanescent: the present is described not as a moment in a series but rather as a 'rupture' ['*déchirure*'], a tearing away and a constantly renewed beginning (32/51). The future is not merely a present still to come, as it is for Bergson, Heidegger, and Sartre, but rather something entirely unknown: 'the future is what is not grasped, what befalls us and takes hold of us' (TA, 64/77). The subject similarly does not exist as a substantive, self-identical 'soi', but rather as a 'departure from self', and identity is envisaged not as a simple self-relationship but rather as a limit to freedom (TA, 36/55).

Levinas seems to attempt here at least a partial rejection of dualism, for he insists that I am not a spirit trapped in the tomb or prison of my body, but that my materiality is rather an inherent part of my existence: 'Materiality accompanies – necessarily – the upsurge of the subject in its existent freedom' (TA, 38/56). And just as time, in its evanescence, frees me from my material chains, so my relations with the world around me introduce a further gap into my self-contained solitude and thereby also free me from my self-identity. It is, *pace* Heidegger, precisely my enjoyment of the everyday that enables me to forget myself and escape my identity as an existent:

> In everyday existence, in the world, the material structure of the subject is to some extent overcome: an interval appears between the ego and the self. [. . .] In this sense, our everyday life is already a way of being free from the initial materiality through which the subject is accomplished [*s'accomplit*]. It already contains a forgetting of self. (TA, 45–6/62–4)

However, this kind of self-transcendence is not sufficient to escape entirely the perils of self-identity for the world is never experienced as truly other. Indeed, Levinas refers to this as the truth understood by philosophical idealism. For radical otherness we must turn elsewhere, and Levinas sees death as the source of an alterity that is truly unknowable, 'absolutely unknowable' ['*inconnaissable*'] (TA, 58/71).

Mortality and alterity

Levinas's account of death is very different from any we have seen so far. It is certainly unlike that of Sartre or indeed Heidegger. Death for Levinas is neither a simple end to our lives nor yet an annihilation we should live towards as a source of anguish. Levinas sees suffering, pain, and work as bringing us closer to an understanding of death than Heideggerian notions of lucidity and freedom. In the face of death, the subject is entirely passive, as he is already partially in suffering. My mastery and heroism as subject are of no use at the point of death, which Levinas describes as a time of weeping, 'le pleur et le sanglot', returning us to the irresponsibility of childhood. Whereas for Sartre, illness and suffering are states that we must face as conscious subjects, for Levinas they place limits on my consciousness and mastery: as death approaches we can no longer have a project (62/75) This raises the fundamental question of my survival as a subject in the face of death:

> How can the existent exist as mortal and nonetheless persevere in its 'personality', preserve its conquest over the anonymous 'there

is' ['*il y a*]', its mastery over the subject, its conquest of subjectivity? Can an existent enter into relation with the other without allowing its very self to be crushed by the other? (TA, 65/77)

Death is radical alterity and leaves the subject no initiative (TA, 73/81). But, in what is evidently another example of 'qui perd gagne', it is this disempowerment that ultimately allows me to escape my individual isolation. Death puts me in relation with the radically other and unknowable, and this alienation fractures my self-sufficient solitude. Death does not confirm my solitude but rather breaks it down. This is the moment at which a relationship with an other becomes possible, and in particular, the erotic relationship which is the relationship with the Other par excellence:

> Only a being whose solitude has reached a state of tension through suffering, and who has entered into a relation with death, takes its place on a ground where the relationship with the other becomes possible. The relationship with the other will never be the fact of grasping a possibility. [. . .] I think the erotic relationship furnishes us with a prototype of it. Eros, strong as death, will furnish us with the basis of an analysis of this relationship with mystery. (TA, 64/76)

It is not immediately clear how my relations to death and to the Other are linked, but a patient reading can disentangle the underlying train of thought. Both death and the Other represent absolute alterity, as indeed does the future (TA, 64/77). In a sense, the erotic relationship is taken as paradigmatic of the positive possibilities of an encounter with genuine alterity. In everyday life, claims Levinas, the radical alterity of the Other is masked from me, s/he seems someone like myself, an *alter ego*, in a relationship of potential sympathy and reciprocity (TA, 75/83). But nothing could be further from the truth as Levinas sees it: the Other is not another I, he or she is a Mystery whose alterity I will never fathom. Taking the erotic as the paradigmatic human relationship, Levinas opposes the common notion of sexual complementarity and fusion with one of insurmountable duality. The pathos of erotic passion lies, he maintains, precisely in its inability to overcome the inalienable alterity and difference of the beloved, described by Levinas as the Feminine in a move to which we will return later. We are alienated to the Other whom we can never possess: 'Love is not a possibility, is not due to our initiative, it is without reason; it invades and wounds us and, nevertheless, the *I* survives in it' (TA, 82/88–9).

However, the erotic relationship is not thereby a failure, on the contrary, just as (for Levinas as for Sartre) I am saved from sclerosis by my inability to achieve peaceful self-identity, so my inability to know the Other and my passivity in the face of erotic love constitute precisely its strength and value; once again we have a case of 'qui perd gagne': 'There where all possibilities are impossible, where one can no longer be able, the subject is still a subject through Eros' (81–2/88).

> Can this relationship with the Other through Eros be characterized as a failure? Once again, the answer is yes, if one adopts the terminology of current descriptions, if one wants to characterize the erotic by 'grasping', 'possessing' or 'knowing' ['*connaître*']. There is nothing of all this, nor of the failure of all this, in Eros. If one could possess, grasp and know the other, it would not be other. Possessing, grasping and knowing are synonyms of power. [...] What one presents as the failure of communication in love precisely constitutes the positivity of the relationship; this absence of the other is precisely its presence as other. (TA, 83/90, 89/94).

And Levinas concludes with a brief reference to paternity as the closest kind of relationship between self and other, in which the self precisely becomes other while remaining himself (TA, 85/91–2). Later, Levinas will argue that paternity is not necessarily a biological relationship and will also consider the nature of maternity, just as he will be led, in part by fierce criticisms from feminist thinkers (despite his acknowledgement of the legitimate claims of feminism, TA, 79/86), to reassess his account of the feminine. For the time being, these elements are proffered with tantalizing brevity.

Totality and infinity: desire and *jouissance*

Totalité et Infini of 1961 develops further the ideas of alterity, erotic love, desire, death, and paternity expressed schematically in

Le Temps et l'Autre. Desire is described as for the 'absolutely other', which is, as we have seen, to be found in *Autrui* (the Other) rather than in the world. Unlike Sartre, Levinas does not envisage human relations in terms of power and domination but rather as ethical and generous, described as 'a non-allergic relation with alterity' (TI, 18/47). Relations with the Other do in one sense put my freedom in question, but paradoxically the Other does not threaten my freedom, he rather invests it: 'The Other [*Autrui*] does not affect us as what must be surmounted, enveloped, dominated' (TI, 61/89), 'the Other does not threaten me with death' (TI, 56/84). On its own, my freedom is arbitrary and unjustified, 'egoist'; in the service of the Other it becomes moral and the 'for-itself' is no longer trapped in its hateful self-containment: 'I have access to the alterity of the Other [*Autrui*] through the society that I maintain with it. [...] Sexuality supplies the example of this relation' (TI, 94/121).

The body has a far greater presence in *Totalité et Infini* than in *Le Temps et l'Autre*, and Levinas claims 'I exist as a body' (TI, 90/117). The body is precisely what gives me my separate individuality and selfhood: 'the body is in fact the *mode* in which a being [...] exists separately. It is the regime of separation' (TI, 142/168). Like the organe–obstacle of Jankélévitch, my embodiment is double-edged and equivocal, health can become sickness, the 'body-master' can at any moment become 'body-slave' (TI, 138/164): through the materiality of my body and its needs I am dependent, but it is also through the body that I can work, possess the world, experience temporality, and relate to the Other in a way that frees me from the limits of my self-identity:

> To be a body is to have time in the midst of facts, to be *me* though living in the *other*.
>
> The revelation of distance is an ambiguous revelation, for time both destroys the security of instantaneous happiness, and permits the fragility thus discovered to be overcome. And it is this relation with the other, inscribed in the body as its elevation, that makes possible the transformation of enjoyment [*jouissance*] into consciousness and labor. (TI, 90/117)

To understand the last sentence quoted we should bear in mind that, in *Totalité et Infini*, *jouissance* is not so much an experience

of ecstatic self-transcendence but rather one which keeps me
trapped within my self: 'In jouissance, I am absolutely for myself.
Egoist without reference to the other [*autrui*]' (TI, 107/134).
Later, Levinas will associate *jouissance* with vulnerability and the
term will lose much of its negative dimension.[17] None the less,
even at this stage, *jouissance* also has a strongly positive sense, for
it is my means of access to the world about me via my sensibility.
But it is clearly limited, not only by its tendency to enclose the
self in its self-sufficiency, but also by its very uncertainty and
evanescence:

> The freedom of *jouissance* is thus experienced as limited [. . .] the
> plenitude of the instant of *jouissance* is not insured against the
> unknown of the very element it enjoys [*dont il jouit*], [. . .] joy
> remains a chance and happy encounter. [. . .] *Jouissance* reaches a
> world that has neither secrecy nor veritable strangeness. (TI,
> 117–19/144–5)

Again, it is this limitation on *jouissance* that provides an opening
to genuine otherness, it is the insecurity and 'inquiétude' of
jouissance that leave room for something less self-centred, 'a
delightful "failure" of the ontological order' that allows me to
welcome the radical alterity of Autrui (TI, 124/150). Like Jankélévitch, Levinas embraces the uncertainty and ambiguity of my
embodiment as a matter not of duality but rather of simultaneity:
the 'encumbered' nature of my body is itself a source of happiness
(TI, 138/164).

My body then provides my access to the Other and to the
world, it also makes me vulnerable to sickness and death. But
death in Levinas's account is not my master, that is the role of the
Other. Indeed, it is only through the other that I can start to
understand death: 'Death is not this master. [. . .] Death, source
of all myths, is *present* only in the Other' (TI, 153–4/179). Levinas's discussion is complicated and non-linear. The title of the
book itself, *Totalité et Infini*, is of course vital for understanding his
argument, for, as he explains in his Preface, it is the 'infinite' that
enables us to escape the closure of totality. And one of the sources
of the infinite is precisely the Other, whose face reveals transcendence to us. Levinas's ideas are not easy to pin down, in part
because his whole philosophy opposes any such definition, and in

part simply because his terminology has such a range of non-standard meanings. The face is a case in point, referring not so much to the physical aspect of the Other as to his presence to me in alterity and mastery which frees me from my hateful selfhood and self-possession:

> For me to be able to free myself from possession itself [...] I must encounter the indiscreet face of the Other that calls me into question. The Other – the absolutely other – paralyzes possession, which it contests through its epiphany in the face. (TI, 145/171)

Relations with the Other save me from self-sufficiency and open me up to ethics and transcendence (TI, 167/193). The Other is not merely different from me in a specific and relative way, he is 'infinitely transcendent, infinitely foreign' (TI, 168/191). And my relationship with him cures me of what Levinas calls my 'allergy' (TI, 172/197), in other words my hostility to otherness. In this way, the Other does not limit my freedom but rather justifies it by enabling it to become responsible (TI, 171/196). By putting my self in question, the Other paradoxically frees me and allows me to become ethical: 'To be for the Other – is to be good' (TI, 239/261). He makes me ashamed of the arbitrary nature of my freedom: 'The Other [...] has the face of the poor, of the stranger [...] and, at the same time, of the Master' (TI, 229/251).

Like the face, desire for the Other is not primarily or solely physical. Unlike need, desire can never be satisfied: 'the strange desire of the Other that no voluptuousness comes to crown, nor to close, nor to put to sleep' (TI, 154/179). Desire is unquenchable, 'inassouvissable' (TI, 134/150), not because it is infinite but rather because it is always precisely for the alterity it can never know: 'in Desire, there is no sinking one's teeth into being, no satiety, but an uncharted future before me' (TI, 89/117). Levinas discusses erotic love in similar terms; it is not a matter of possession, indeed possession would entail the death of 'voluptuousness' ['*volupté*'], whereas 'voluptuousness does not come to satisfy, it is this desire itself' (TI, 237/260). The lover's caress, like the face and desire, is not merely physical, and the pleasure it gives transfigures the subject by revealing to him his passivity and lack of mastery:

Voluptuousness transfigures the subject itself, which henceforth owes its identity not to its initiative of power, but to the passivity of the love received. It is passion and trouble, constant *initiation* into a mystery, rather than *initiative*. (TI, 248/270)

Erotic love frees me from the encumbrance of my self. This liberation has several dimensions. In the first place it drives me towards the Other and away from my enclosure within myself; secondly, it reveals to me my passivity and lack of mastery and this is itself a liberation; and thirdly it is ultimately my means of transcending death. This final dimension needs further explanation.

Paternity and discontinuity

As we saw already in *Le Temps et l'Autre*, death and time are intimately interrelated. Subjectivity is not so much 'towards death' ['*pour la mort*'] as 'against death' (TI, 199/224), and temporality is paradoxically the mortal subject's way of escaping death, not of course in perpetuity but by deferral: 'to the inevitable violence of death it [temporal being] opposes its time, which is the time of adjournment itself' (TI, 199/224). Mortality frees us from the chains of causality, from the 'limitation of fate' (TI, 260/284) by its interruption of the natural, causal order of things. And yet this is not simply the end of our lives, nor does it render our lives pointless; 'the life between birth and death is neither folly nor absurdity, nor flight, nor cowardice' (TI, 27/56). My relations with the Other free me from myself and from death in a further sense in so far as they produce a child who is both 'other and my-self', (TI, 244/267):

> The self [*le moi*] is, in the child, an other. (TI, 244/267)
>
> My child is a stranger [. . .] but a self that is a stranger to itself [C'*est moi étranger à soi*]. (TI, 245/267)
>
> In fecundity, the self [*le moi*] is other and young. (TI, 246/278)
>
> My self [*le moi*] divests itself of its tragic egoity. (TI, 251/273)
>
> I do not have my child, I am my child. (TI, 254/277)

Paternity, which Levinas claims need not be biological, introduces discontinuity into the self without annihilating it entirely. Paternity conquers death, but without the stasis that immortality would entail:

> In paternity, where the Self [*le moi*], across the definitiveness of an inevitable death, prolongs itself in the Other, time triumphs over old age and fate by virtue of its discontinuity. [. . .] This triumph of the time of fecundity over the becoming of the mortal and ageing being, is a pardoning. (TI, 258–9/282)

> Fecundity opens up an infinite and discontinuous time. It liberates the subject from its facticity. (TI, 277/301)

> The discontinuity of generations – which is to say death and fecundity – releases Desire from the prison of its own subjectivity and puts an end to the monotony of identity. (TI, 281/304)

Paternity, then, triumphs over death. But death itself, as we have seen, is a liberation from causality. The imminence of death is double-edged, simultaneously a threat and a deferral. And death is not, ultimately, what we should fear most. After all, we will not be around to see it; as Levinas comments drily 'the last part of the journey will be made without me' (TI, 211/235). Here Levinas may seem momentarily close to Sartre. But where he differs radically from Sartre, though he is close to Marcel, is in his comments on the suffering that precedes death, for illness and suffering put us cruelly to the test as subjects: 'In suffering, the will is defeated by sickness' (TI, 215/238). We are passive in the face of suffering, and our will and freedom are thereby weakened and destroyed: 'It is not the nothingness of death that has to be surmounted, but the passivity to which the will is exposed insofar as it is mortal' (TI, 220/243).

But since Levinas considers liberty and will as inferior to our passivity before the other, perhaps even suffering and illness should also be seen in terms of liberation from destiny and causality. At the end of *Totalité et Infini* we may wonder whether Levinas has yet followed his insights and intuitions about subjectivity and mortality to their ultimate conclusions. For this we will have to await *Autrement qu'être* of 1974.

Otherwise than being: passivity and subjection

One of the most striking differences between Levinas's two major works concerns my relations to the Other. We have seen in *Totalité et Infini* that the Other is my master, my means of access to ethics, to alterity, to fecundity, and to the overcoming of death. In all these ways, the Other is essential to my escape from and transcendence of the limited causal order of nature. But it would be hard to find passages which envisage the Other as actually constituting me. On the contrary, we read that otherness depends on me for its existence: 'L'altérité n'est possible qu'à partir de *moi*' (10). In *Autrement qu'être*, by contrast, the Other is not only my Master, he is also my creator in the fullest sense of the term. *Autrement qu'être* arguably goes as far as is possible without abandoning the subject entirely, towards a dissolution of subjectivity in passivity and fragmentation. It is significant that the first chapter starts with an epigraph from Jean Wahl concerning the importance and significance of passivity, and it is certainly the notion that underpins all the major arguments of the work. Rather than something ambiguous whose negativity paradoxically frees me from stasis, passivity is presented as positive, creative, and liberating. It is the passivity and vulnerability of the subject in the face of the Other and of death that open him up to an experience of transcendence and infinity. Like mortality, erotic love creates a wound which saves the subject from lethal self-sufficiency and solitude. Levinas discusses subjectivity in terms of subjection and of broken identity:

> This rupture of identity [. . .] is the subjectivity of the subject or its subjection to everything, its susceptibility, its vulnerability, which is to say its sensibility. Subjectivity – the place and non-place of this rupture – comes to pass as a passivity more passive than all passivity. [. . .] Vulnerability, exposure to outrage, to wounding, passivity more passive than all patience, passivity of the accusative form, the trauma of accusation suffered by a hostage to the point of persecution, calling into question the identity of the hostage, who substitutes himself for others: Self, a defection or defeat of the Ego's identity. And this, pushed to the limit, is sensibility. That is to say, sensibility as the subjectivity of the subject. (AQE, 17–18/14–15)

The terminology of violence is striking: subjection, vulnerability, insult, wound, trauma, accusation, persecution, hostage, defeat, but it is clear that this depiction of subjectivity is precisely what allows it to go beyond being, into a realm which is not subject to the limits of ontology and identity. And the subject thus defined, or thus evoked, is not an ethereal, spiritual being; on the contrary he is irremediably physical, subject to pain, sickness, and ageing, not so much impeded by his embodiment as identified with it:

> Adversity assembled into corporeality, susceptible to so-called physical pain, exposed to outrage and wounding, to sickness and ageing, but adversity: there since the fatigue of the body's first efforts. (71/55)

Of course the embodied subject is not merely open to wounding, he is also simultaneously open to *jouissance* and to the caress: indeed, 'sensibility can be a vulnerability, an exposedness to the other [. . .] only because it is *jouissance*' (93/74). It is the very same vulnerability to age and to suffering that enables the subject to welcome the Other he encounters in erotic love, and at one point Levinas even identifies the alterity at the heart of the subject with the soul: 'the Soul is the other in me' (86/69). Having discussed paternity as transcending time and death in *Totalité et Infini*, Levinas now identifies maternity as the paradigm of the other within the self, 'maternity, gestation of the other in the same' (AQE, 95/75), though once again he does not seem to limit this to physical childbearing for he says it goes beyond the natural. But it is clear that the subject is, from the outset, always already incarnate:

> The so-called incarnate subject does not result from a materializa-
> tion [. . .] that would have been realized by a consciousness. [. . .]
> It is because subjectivity is sensibility – exposure to others, vulner-
> ability and responsibility in the proximity of others [. . .] – that the
> subject is of flesh and blood, a man that has hunger and eats.
> (97/77)

And this flesh-and-blood subjectivity, this inescapable alienation of the self by the other, 'the incarnate ego, the ego of flesh and blood' (100/79) is precisely what could only seem incomprehensible or miraculous to a Cartesian conception of human dualism

(99/79, 181/133). Thus, my skin which experiences the caress is not just a surface protecting an organism, it is rather described as the gap between the visible and the invisible (AQE, 113/89); similarly the wrinkled skin on my face which bears witness to my self and to my past: 'wrinkled skin, a trace of itself' (115/90) is described as a 'forme ambigüe', an epiphany rather than a physical phenomenon. Once again, the face is ambiguously situated between physical physiognomy and a transcendence that reveals a form of alterity. It is 'a trace of itself' which does not so much signify what is hidden (a 'hidden God' 119/94) as invite us to approach it.[18]

The bodily subject then is transformed by all that it undergoes: age, illness, pleasure, pain. These are not undergone by the body alone, indeed there is no 'body alone', which is why Levinas refers to 'so-called physical pain [*la douleur* dite *physique*]', they are intrinsic aspects of 'the corporeality of the subject' (AQE, 70/54). I age as subject, not just as body: Levinas's references to 'a subjectivity of ageing' (69/54) and to 'subjectivity in ageing' (67/52) may show that he is uncertain of exactly how to speak of such a degree of intimate integration but the problems are linguistic not conceptual. Subjectivity could hardly be further from an identification with the reflexivity of consciousness (156/125).

Levinas tries repeatedly to find the formulations that will do justice to his conception of bodily selfhood without lapsing into yet another hypostasis, though he recognizes that this is probably inevitable. But what matters is the understanding that the self is dependent from the outset on the other, and cannot be justified from within itself. From birth onwards the subject is prey to the other, subject to 'the erosion of ageing, in the permanence of a loss of the self' (136/107) until death, which always comes too soon, 'always violent and premature' (135/106). Although Levinas does not seem to use the phrase, he could, like Merleau-Ponty and Sartre, subscribe to the notion that I am my body, and that there is no ultimate distinction between body and soul:

> The body is neither an obstacle opposed to the soul, nor a tomb that imprisons it, but that by which the Self is susceptibility itself. The extreme passivity of 'incarnation' – to be exposed to sickness, suffering, death, is to be exposed to compassion, and, as a Self, to a gift that costs. (139/195)

The subject's radical passivity is part of his very constitution, his compassion and responsibility for others can never be escaped since without them there would be no subject to speak of:

> Responsibility for another is not an accident befalling a Subject, but precedes Essence in the Subject. [...] Ipseity, in the passivity without *arche* characteristic of identity, is a hostage. [...] The passivity undergone in proximity by the force of an alterity in me [...] is not, however, the alienation of an identity betrayed. [...] I am assigned. *Through* the other and for the other, but without alienation: I am inspired. This inspiration is the psyche. The psyche can signify this alterity in the same without alienation, in the guise of incarnation, as being-in-one's-skin, as having-the-other-in-one's-skin. (145–6/114–15)

In the fullest sense of the word, the self is a subject, Sub-jectum, subject to others, responsible for others (147/116). Levinas refers to this radical passivity as 'the Passion of the Self' (149/117) and argues that this primary condition of the self as dependent on others is what explains human pity, compassion, and forgiveness.[19] Subjection to the other is also described in very physical terms as 'substitution operating in the entrails of the self, tearing its interiority, throwing its identity out of phase' (152/196). And since it is part of my self-constitution, my responsibility for the Other is unlimited, extending as far as my death, 'a deathly passivity' (159/124). But we must remember that this subjection is precisely what liberates me from my chains: 'Substitution frees the subject from ennui, from the enchainment to itself, where the Ego suffocates the Self' (160/124).

Like any religious thinker, Levinas does not seem to believe that this is a high price to pay, and nor is it reversible: I must die for the Other, but I can never ask the Other to die for me, since this would involve commending human sacrifice (162/126). But it is dying for the Other rather than myself that gives my life meaning: on its own, death might render all my care for myself pointless and even tragi-comic, but in so far as I give my life to and for others, it can be seen as infinitely valuable without any need to rely on a notion of personal immortality (166/129). For it is my radical responsibility for others that ultimately makes me human and gives me a soul:

> Through this alteration the soul animates the subject. It is the very
> pneuma of the psyche. [...] An undoing of the substantial nucleus
> of the Ego that is formed in the Same, a fission of the 'mysterious'
> nucleus of the 'interiority' of the subject by this assignation to
> respond. (AQE, 180/140)

And although Levinas is wary of too facile a reversal of failure
into success, loss into gain, he does none the less describe the
eventual position of the persecuted subject, hostage to the Other,
in terms of glory. Not of course, glory on his own account, but
rather the glory of the Infinite, or the Divine. The subject has been
freed of his noxious imperialism and opened to the glory of God:
'The ego stripped by the trauma of persecution of its scornful and
imperialist subjectivity' (AQE, 186/146) can bear witness to the
Infinite. And Levinas quotes Claudel: 'God writes straight with
crooked lines' (187/147).

We may not wish to follow Levinas in his religious conclusion,
and indeed Ricœur reproaches him with it as a theological and
non-philosophical parti-pris,[20] but we must admit none the less
that Levinas has had the courage of his religious convictions.
Death may not be the gateway to the immortality of the individual soul, but it is what frees us from stasis, introduces creative
discontinuity into the natural order through the birth of children,
and makes life meaningful if it has been led for others. Levinas
does not have to take a position on the question of life after death:
human passivity and passion ensure that the self will continue in
and through others, others we encounter as well as others we
engender.

Autrement qu'être is probably Levinas's most fully developed
account of the interweaving of subjectivity, mortality, alterity, and
passion. Texts of the mid 1970s, collected in book form in 1992
as *La Mort et le Temps*[21] contribute somewhat less than their title
might suggest to our understanding of Levinas's views on death
since they are transcriptions of lectures given at the Sorbonne in
1975–6 and in them he is primarily concerned to discuss the views
of others. None the less, certain major themes emerge very clearly
within the relative simplicity of the lecture format. Levinas defines
his own thought in relation, and often in opposition, to the philosophy of Heidegger, Hegel, Bergson, Bloch, and Kant among
others. He returns repeatedly to the idea that an understanding

of death, such as it is, comes to me through the Other: the Other whose mortality reveals to me the truth and reality of death; the Other whose face witnesses to his soul while he is alive; the Other for whose death I am irremediably responsible. Indeed, my own identity as subject which, as we have just seen, comes to me from the Other to whom I am hostage, is necessarily fissured by his death: 'Being affected [*l'affection*] by death is affectivity, passivity, a being affected by the beyond-measure [*la dé-mesure*], an affection of the present by the nonpresent, more intimate than any intimacy, to the point of fission' (DMT, 24/15). It is the incomprehensibility, meaninglessness, and ultimately madness of death that save me from the stasis of self-identity.

Levinas is vigorously opposed to Heidegger's dismissal of the importance for me of the death of the Other: on the contrary, the Other's death is all that really matters to me since my responsibility for him is what makes me unique and irreplaceable (38/29). My guilt for the death of the Other is ultimately what lies at the heart of my own death: his death is the first death and entails my own (DMT, 49/43). Indeed, every death is the first death. In other words, I am responsible for the Other in so far as he is mortal and mortality lies at the heart of my self. And Levinas draws his lectures to a close in a poetic evocation of the inextricable relationship between love and death, quoting Diotima from Plato's *Symposium* who identifies love with the desire for immortality, but for the beloved rather than the self:

> Thus we come back to the love 'as strong as death' [Jankélévitch]. It is not a matter of a force that could repel the death inscribed in my being. However, it is not my nonbeing that causes anxiety, but that of the loved one or of the other, more beloved than my being. What we call, by a somewhat corrupted term, love, is *par excellence* the fact that the death of the other affects me more than my own. The love of the other is the emotion of the other's death. It is my receiving the other – and not the anxiety of death awaiting me – that is the reference to death.
>
> We encounter death in the face of the other. (121/105)

But Levinas's very last word turns again to the Divine: 'the relationship with the infinite is the responsibility of a mortal being for a mortal being', for, as Abraham understood, 'I am, myself, ashes and dust' (133/117).

We are of course free to question Levinas's ultimate turn to religion, as Ricœur does. It is clearly a move that is vital to Levinas himself, but it is striking how late he always seems to leave it, as though he wants to carry his philosophical reflections through to their ultimate conclusions before considering how these relate to religious questions. So the religious *per se* may seem an irrelevance or a distraction, but at least it cannot be accused of having distorted and dominated Levinas's philosophical enquiry. If his reflections are consonant with a religious position, or seem to him to point to the Divine, others are left free to draw different conclusions, agnostic or atheist.

Indeed, it is noticeable how the four philosophers whose work we have examined in this chapter determinedly leave religion proper aside in their quest for the truth about love, death, and the subject. None the less, they seem to come closer than many other thinkers to what feels like a proper understanding of the interrelationship of mortality and subjectivity. Belief in God and eternal life is not necessary for an appreciation of the way in which love conquers death by denying it, and individual immortality depends on the love and thoughts of others (Marcel); the notion of ipseity depends on the idea that the other constitutes part of my identity so that loss of the other involves the loss of myself (Ricœur); mortality gives meaning to life by creating the fragile and vulnerable heart of joy, love, and passion (Jankélévitch); death frees me from stasis and self-identity and allows me to be open to radical alterity (Levinas). In all cases, passion entails both Eros and suffering; love and death are intrinsically intertwined.

4

Psychoanalytic Thought: Eros and Thanatos, Psyche and Soma

Jacques Lacan, Didier Anzieu, Julia Kristeva

Love and soul are indissociable. (Kristeva) [1]

The sufferings of neurosis and psychosis provide us schooling in the passions of the soul. (Lacan) [2]

Freud would have recognized many of the preoccupations of the philosophers of the previous chapter, though his interpretation of them would have been rather different. The relationship between love and death lies, of course, at the heart of psychoanalytic investigation, as we see in the famous opposition between the death instincts or drive (Thanatos) and the life instincts or libido (Eros). Indeed, in *Civilization and its discontents*, Freud describes the evolution of civilization itself as 'the struggle between Eros and Death, between the instinct of life and the instinct of destruction, as it works itself out in the human species' (*Civilization*, vol. 12, 314). Freud's conception of this relationship was complex, evolving, and at times apparently contradictory. He rejects entirely any suggestion that destructiveness is an integral part of the sexual instinct, but does maintain that there is a destructive element associated with all love, possibly excluding a mother's love for her son.[3] His explanation for this ambivalence is in terms of the dual status of our relationship to those we love, which involves simultaneously identity and difference: 'These loved ones are on the one hand an inner possession, components of our own ego; but on the other hand they are partly strangers, even enemies' ('Thoughts for the times on war and death' vol. 12, 87).[4] It is this dichotomy that lies at the heart of our mixed feelings at the death of someone we love. On the one hand, we may collapse completely when a loved one dies: 'Our hopes, our desires and our pleasures lie in the grave with him, we will not be consoled, we will not fill the loved one's place' (78). On the other hand, our unconscious death-wish arising from an element of unspoken hostility creates a conflict in us and may lead to neurosis (88). Mourning is thus a complex process in which the libido that was invested in the loved one must be gradually recovered before it can be reinvested elsewhere. This process is painful, prolonged and often resisted. Although our everyday familiarity with mourning allows us to take the process for granted as natural, Freud claims to find it puzzling from a psychoanalytic point of view: 'Why it is that this detachment of libido from its objects should be such a painful process is a mystery to us and we have not hitherto been able to frame any hypothesis to account for it' ('On Transience', vol. 14, 289).

Similarly, and perhaps more puzzling to the layman, we are not even whole-heartedly life-seeking for our own account. Psychologically and biologically we seek life and reproduction, but we also seek to recover a prior state without tension, which Freud calls the Nirvana principle[5] and which forms part of the death instincts ('Beyond the pleasure principle', vol. 11, 329). There is thus an opposition between our unceasing drive for life and our need for equilibrium, whether this be in the release and reduction of tension or in a constant level of tension (329). Freud was led to posit the existence of the death instincts from his observation of the compulsion to repeat as well as of ambivalence and aggression. Initially, this 'strange assumption' (319) seemed to him incompatible with the well-known struggle for life and self-preservation of organisms, but ultimately natural science appeared to confirm rather than refute the dichotomy.

'Our expectation', Freud writes, 'that biology would flatly contradict the recognition of death instincts has not been fulfilled. We have unwittingly steered our course into the harbour of Schopenhauer's philosophy. For him death is the "true result and to that extent the purpose of life", while the sexual instinct is the "embodiment of the will to live"' (322). But Freud's conception of the relationship between the pleasure-seeking libido and the death instincts is not entirely clear: having insisted throughout 'Beyond the pleasure principle' that the two are quite distinct, indeed opposed, he concludes by saying that the pleasure principle is in the service of the death instincts in so far as it guards against excessive increases of stimulation (338). Freud did not consider that he had satisfactorily resolved the issue and indeed claimed that he was not himself fully convinced of the truth of his own hypotheses (332).[6] His conclusion to 'The Ego and the Id', written three years later, in which he follows up his speculations from 'Beyond the pleasure principle' is similarly uncertain.

Freud recognizes the way in which 'the claims of Eros, of the sexual instincts' counteract the 'continuous descent towards death' (387), but argues that 'the pleasure principle serves the id as a compass in its struggle against the libido' and its disturbances, and helps it fend off fresh tensions by satisfying them as swiftly as possible, before they become too powerful. 'This', he claims, 'accounts for the likeness of the condition which follows complete sexual satisfaction to dying', and explains why some animals die in the act of reproduction, 'because, after Eros has been eliminated through the process of satisfaction, the death instinct has a free hand for accomplishing its purposes' (388). None the less, Freud once again refuses to give the last word to the death instincts:

> Eros and the death instinct struggle within [the id] . . . It would be possible to picture the id as under the domination of the mute but powerful death instincts, which desire to be at peace and (prompted by the pleasure principle) to put Eros, the mischief-maker, to rest; but perhaps that might be to undervalue the part played by Eros. (401)

The role of the other in the constitution of the self is also a recurrent topic of speculation in Freud's theorization. In Freud's view, 'a unity comparable to the ego cannot exist in the individual from the start; the ego has to be developed' ('On narcissism' vol. 11, 69) and this development takes place in part through attachment to others which interrupts the sterility of narcissism: 'Love for oneself knows only one barrier – love for others, love for objects' ('Group psychology', vol. 12, 78). And Freud describes sexual passion as the most advanced form of such love: 'The highest phase of development of which object-libido is capable is seen in the state of being in love, when the subject seems to give up his own personality in favour of an object cathexis' ('On narcissism', 68).

Or as he writes elsewhere: 'When somebody is completely in love . . . altruism converges with libidinal object-cathexis' (*Introductory lectures on psychoanalysis*, vol. 1, 467). We might well speculate whether Freud has not begun to propose an answer here to his own question about the pain involved in mourning, when the libido is forcibly detached from its object. The imbrication of subjectivity and alterity must provide at least a partial explanation of the 'mysterious' distress caused to the survivor by the radical separation of self and other in death.

Of course, Freud's reference to the 'highest phase of development' is descriptive rather than moral, he would not necessarily ascribe fully to Levinas's belief that the source of all ethics lies in the face of the Other, though he does maintain that the death of the loved one inaugurates ethics: 'Thou shalt not kill', applied initially to those we love, then to strangers, and 'finally even to enemies' ('Thoughts on war and death', vol. 12, 84). Questions of love take up a large part of his meditations on mental health and happiness, and he frequently reflects on the role of the development of an ability to love in our progress towards maturity:

> Here we may even venture to touch on the question of what makes it necessary at all for our mental life to pass beyond the limits of narcissism and to attach the libido to objects. The answer which would follow from our line of thought would once more be that this necessity arises when the cathexis of the ego with libido exceeds a certain amount. A strong egoism is a protection against falling ill, but in the last resort we must begin to love in order not to fall ill, and we are bound to fall ill if, in consequence of frustration, we are unable to love. ('On narcissism', 78)

Levinas would probably not recognize the value of 'a strong egoism', but he would surely subscribe to Freud's view that an inability to love would be highly damaging.

Jacques Lacan

Lacan too, for all his insistence on a 'return to Freud' would reject the notion of a 'strong ego'. But he would understand the thinking of both Freud and Levinas in respect of the damage caused by a failure to love, despite his notorious comments about love, Woman (*La femme*), and sexual relations. In this chapter we will explore the work of three major French psychoanalysts of the second half of the twentieth century and their understanding of mortality and subjectivity, love and death.

Love and desire

One of Lacan's most important contributions towards a clarification of these questions depends on his elaboration, around 1960, of a distinction between pleasure and *jouissance* which we shall explore shortly. The distinction parallels, to some extent, the opposition between love and desire, familiar to us already from other philosophers such as Sartre, though Lacan's understanding of it is rather different. Love involves the sublimation of desire (as is clearly manifest in Courtly love);[7] furthermore, it implies the death of desire in so far as it seeks a union which would necessarily annul the difference and alterity sought by desire. As Lacan writes in *Séminaire VII*, sublimation has to be paid for and the price we pay is the loss of *jouissance* ('a pound of flesh', SVII, 371/322). Love, Lacan maintains, is the illusory substitute offered by civilization in return for the relinquishing of unbridled desire, it is also, as we shall see, a compensation for the absence of any real sexual relations between men and women, formulated repeatedly in Lacan's notorious 'there is no sexual relation' [*il n'y a pas de rapport sexuel*], (SXX, 17/12).

But love is doomed to disappoint us, for it can never measure up to the demands of unconditionality we make of it. It makes promises of union and permanence that it can never keep, and is ultimately a *tromperie*, a deception (SXI, 121/147). Love is originally narcissistic; it arises from our relations to our self, and these are necessarily imaginary in so far as they depend on the ego, which is, as it is for Sartre, an imaginary construct, a coherent unity we create from our fragmented and intermittent subjectivity. Indeed, Lacan reverses Proust's insights into the 'intermittences du cœur' when he writes that the subject:

> transfers the permanence of his desire to an ego that is nevertheless obviously intermittent, and, inversely, protects himself from his desire by attributing to it these very intermittences. (E, 815/691)

It is not desire that is intermittent but rather the subject: 'The subject is never more than fleeting [*ponctuel*] and vanishing, for it is a subject only by a signifier and for another signifier' (SXX, 130/142). Indeed, desire is never truly mine, it is always 'the desire of the Other', in the dual sense of subjective and objective genitives: desire for the Other and the Other's desire. For desire arises from the unconscious and is, in Lacan's terms, unaware of what it seeks, which it conceals by misunderstanding and denial ('dénégation') (E, 815/691). Desire is insatiable, and is for the radically Other, whereas Love, though also insatiable, is never for the truly other but is always a form of self-love (SXX, 12/5–6). Desire can never be satisfied not for contingent reasons but because it is for something impossible, an alterity which is forever unknowable. Lacan has many ways of describing the origin of desire: it is what remains of our demand for unconditional love after need has been satisfied (E, 691/580); it arises from an original separation or split in the subject (SXX, 114/126).

In Lacan's early writings (1938), this original separation is described in biological terms and connected to the 'weaning complex', for in his view the immaturity of the human infant at birth means that its separation from its mother is premature and prevents it from ever experiencing itself as whole and complete except in imagination. Weaning is thus not merely a separation from the comfort and nourishment of the maternal breast, but also a re-enactment of the initial separation of birth. But even at this early stage, Lacan does not consider the complex to be a primarily biological feature, it is on the contrary psychological, though it has a biological underpinning ('Les Complexes familiaux', AE, 30–6).

Pleasure and *jouissance*

Impossible desire and illusory love pursue, then, quite different aims and are radically incompatible.[8] This is bad news for romantics among us, but will be no surprise after our readings of Sartre[9] and Jankélévitch. Jankélévitch, as we saw, opposed the unending yearning of desire to the trivial contentment of happiness. Lacan makes a similar move: desire cannot be satisfied, and this constitutes both its pain and its greatness; pleasure alleviates desire temporarily and can thus provide a limited 'bonheur'. This is how Lacan comes to oppose pleasure and *jouissance*: the former is what Eros and the other 'pulsions' all seek, but it is in fact a mere trap and diversion. Pleasure, even that of orgasm, usually termed *jouissance* in French (hence many of the apparent paradoxes), puts an end to desire but satisfies without slaking. Sexual *jouissance*, Lacan claims, does not truly relate to the Other who is reached only through fantasy (SXX, 14/8). Post-coital *tristia* is thus not just regret at the cessation of pleasure, it bears witness to a more fundamental disappointment which recognizes that orgasmic satisfaction in no way puts an end to human yearning. Physical desire (or need) may be temporarily muted, but true desire for the Other which arises from the unconscious remains as acute as ever.

This explains in a way much clearer than Freud ever dreamt of, why the pleasure principle is not really the life force we would expect, but seems to have a darker side and be linked obscurely to the death drive. Pleasure keeps us away from the depths of our desire ('the pleasure principle, which can only have one meaning – not too much *jouissance*', SXVIII, 108), and this helps life to run more smoothly without too much pain, but also masks from us the way in which desire is linked at heart to death; the subject may lose conscious control at the point of orgasm ('l'évanouissement du sujet', E, 774/653), but true *jouissance* would entail death.

This goes some way towards explaining the many ambivalences surrounding the notion of *jouissance*, such as the way in which it is both proscribed and prescribed: on the one hand forbidden because of its links to death, but on the other an insistent command from the superego: 'the superego is the imperative of jouissance – *Enjoy!* [Jouis!]' (SXX, 10/3). This command may initially seem surprising, but in fact it is an integral part of the double-sided nature of pleasure and *jouissance*.

The superego orders *jouissance* precisely because of its ambiguity: phallic *jouissance* is exactly that – *jouissance* of the phallus rather than of the body of the woman, in this sense it is a limit and a form of castration (13/7, 74/79). This makes of *jouissance* a kind of double-bind which means that the subject is fated to be always in the wrong. And because sexual *jouissance* is phallic and non-reciprocal, it can never be taken as a sign of love, however intense it may be: 'Jouissance of the Other [*La jouissance de l'Autre*] [. . .], of the body of the Other which symbolizes the Other, is not the sign of love' (SXX, 11/4). Paradoxically, Lacan claims, castration, which would put an end to phallic *jouissance*, would be the only path to real love and sexual relations:

> There is no chance for a man to have jouissance of a woman's body, otherwise stated, for him to make love, without castration [*à moins de castration*], which is to say, without something that says no to the phallic function. That is the result of the analytic experience. That doesn't stop him from desiring woman in every way, even when that condition does not obtain. He not only desires her, but does all kinds of things to her that bear an astonishing resemblance to love. (SXX, 67/71–2)[10]

We note that Lacan here refers explicitly to men: he has in fact another, very different, notion of *jouissance* which is feminine, non-phallic, non-castrated, and supplementary, to which we will return in due course, and which is not solely the domain of women (SXX, 26/23, 68/72, 75/81).[11]

Subjectivity, language and death

A similarly ambivalent structure is attributed by Lacan to language: it is language which makes us subjects rather than mere animals, and which, by the same token, makes us aware of our own mortality (81/88). 'Man becomes human when he enters the Symbolic Order' (SI, 178/155). The relationship between language, subjectivity, and death can be understood in many ways: because of its complexity and importance we will look at several of Lacan's discussions of the link. One of the simplest is through the notion of absence: all language is necessarily a marker of absence, the signifier stands in for the absent signified, so, for example, in the case of Freud's observation of his grandchild's game of Fort-da, the signifier is a means of mastering (maternal) absence by a process of control and self-mastery.

Indeed, in Lacan's terms, the symbol kills the thing it represents: 'Thus the symbol first manifests itself as the murder of the Thing, and this death constitutes the subject through the eternal perpetuation of its desire' (E, 318–9/261–2). This gives us another way of understanding what Lacan means by his famous claim that the unconscious is structured like a language: both mask as well as reveal human mortality and lack. In the case of the phallus further complications arise, as Lacan maintains variously that the phallus is 'the reason for the desire of the Other', 'the desire of the mother [*le désir de la mère*]' (E, 693/582) and 'la jouissance sexuelle' (SXVIII, 34), and also that it is a signifier without a signified (SXX, 75/81),[12] so that phallic *jouissance* is not only useless ('serves no purpose' [*'qui ne sert à rien'*], SXX, 10/3), but also meaningless: 'the jouissance of an idiot' (75/81).

Conversely, *jouissance* may come from an unlikely source, that is, talking about love: 'speaking of love is itself a jouissance' (SXX, 77/83). This would seem to be the answer to the puzzle Lacan posed early on in the Seminar, for having opposed love and desire and argued that love is the illusory compensation for the non-existence of sexual relations, he went on to claim that he would demonstrate how love and sexual *jouissance* were in fact linked (48/50). The process is perhaps more logical than it might at first seem: as we know already from the *Ecrits*, the subject is intimately related to the signifier, and Lacan in fact maintains that the signifier represents the subject to another signifier: 'the subject is nothing other than what slides in a chain of signifiers [. . .]. That effect – the subject – is the intermediary effect between what characterizes a signifier and another signifier' (SXX, 48/50). And whereas *jouissance* does not seek the subject but rather the Other, love, on the contrary, seeks precisely the subject, and the 'sign' of the subject, and this 'sign' is what can trigger off desire:

> In love, what is aimed at is the subject, the subject as such, insofar as it is presumed in an articulated sentence. [. . .] A subject, as such, doesn't have much to do with jouissance. But, by contrast, the sign of the subject is capable of arousing desire. Therein lies the mainspring of love. The course I will try to continue to steer [. . .] will show you where love and jouissance meet up. (SXX, 48/50)

Love then cannot produce *jouissance*, but talking about love may: 'Where it speaks, it enjoys and knows nothing' ['*Là où ça parle, ça jouit, et ça ne sait rien*'] (SXX, 96/105). 'The unconscious is not the fact that being thinks [. . .] the unconscious is the fact that being, by speaking, enjoys and [. . .] wants to know nothing more of it' (SXX, 95/104–5). And of course, since desire is born from the originary division of the subject, and since that division is due in part to language, then the cause of desire is (the fall into) language and can therefore be partially assuaged by language (114/126). So the *jouissance* of the Other may not be a sign of love (125/137), but speaking of love may bring *jouissance*: 'Such is the substitute that – by the path of existence, not of the sexual relationship, but of the unconscious, which differs therefrom – constitutes the destiny as well as the drama of love' (SXX, 132/145)

In *Séminaire XI* Lacan poses the same problem:

> The whole question is to discover how this love object can come to fulfil a role analogous to the object of desire – upon what equivocations rests the love object's possibility of becoming an object of desire. (SXI, 169/186)

Given the opposition between the narcissism of love and the alterity of desire, how can the one lead to the other? Once again, the answer is through the imaginary, the 'phantasy' ['*fantasme*'] (SXI, 168/185) and 'pulsions partielles' which all arise from the fact that 'le sujet naît divisé' (SXI, 181/199) and seeks to complete itself. Lack lies at the heart of desire, both in so far as the subject depends on the 'signifiant' which is the domain of the Other, and also in so far as sexuality and reproduction are related ultimately to the death of the individual who is not immortal (138/150 and 229/254). Lacan offers a psychoanalytic version of Plato's myth of Aristophanes:

> To this mythical representation of the mystery of love, analytic experience substitutes the search by the subject, not for the sexual complement, but for the forever lost part of itself that is constituted through the fact that it is only a sexed living being, and that it is no longer immortal. (SXI, 187/219)

Access to the opposite sex is thus only ever through partial 'pulsions' through which the subject seeks an object which will complete it (E, 849/720).

In the *Ecrits* Lacan explains this once again through the relationship between the subject and language: 'The moment at which desire is humanized is also that at which the child is born into language (E, 319/262). Entry into the Symbolic Order is conditional on the initial renunciation of *jouissance* in the castration complex; because the signifier creates and splits the subject, it thereby introduces into it an awareness of death and lack. The speaking subject reveals that the libido is linked to death (its meaning is 'mortifière') and that every pulsion is part of the death drive (848/719) and divides the subject and desire (853/724). Lacan does not subscribe to the notion, suggested by Freud, that the death drive can be reduced to the Nirvana principle, the natural principle of entropy. The 'pulsion de mort' is, on the contrary, far more directly destructive (SVII, 251/340).

Similarly, *jouissance* is also destructive, it arises from and thrives on transgression, and is described by Freud himself in *Civilisation and its Discontents* as an evil: 'jouissance is evil [. . .] because it involves suffering for my neighbor' (SVII, 217/184). What *jouissance* ultimately seeks is to satisfy the 'pulsion de mort', that is to say the insatiable, fruitless quest for the primordial lost object of desire. This is why desire has to be stopped and moderated, as is carried out by civilization and its discontents; or, in Lacan's more philosophical terms, by the brakes imposed on us by ethics and aesthetics, 'the good' ['*le bien*]' and 'the beautiful' ['*le beau*']; or, in cruder terms, false promises of future happiness on the one hand, and pain on the other (SVII, 280/239).

Goodness offers attractive but ultimately illusory substitutes for the satisfaction of free-ranging desire; beauty – as Sartre showed at the end of *L'Imaginaire* – disarms, suspends, and forbids desire (SVII, 279/238–9). *Jouissance* is sacrificed to sublimation in art, language, and culture, and this sacrifice may in fact be a necessary evil (SVII, 371/322). Indeed, given the radical aggressivity of prelinguistic desire and its moderation and mediation by language, sublimation, and the Symbolic Order are, in Lacan's view, what save us from mutual destruction:

At first, before language, desire exists solely in the single plane of the imaginary relation of the specular image, projected, alienated, in the other. The tension it provokes is then deprived of an outcome. That is to say that it has no other outcome – Hegel teaches us this – than the destruction of the other. The subject's desire can only be confirmed in this relation. [. . .] But, thank God, the subject inhabits the world of the symbol, that is to say a world of others who speak. That is why its desire is susceptible to the mediation of recognition. Without which every human function would exhaust itself in the unspecified wish for the destruction of the other as such. (SI, 193/170–1)

These discussions are complex and difficult, but the role of language and the Symbolic Order in protecting us from the death and destructiveness of unbridled desire and *jouissance* is clearly vital. Although Lacan speaks at times as though the pleasures of art, language, love, and ethics were but a poor substitute for the deeper joys of transgressive desire, a careful reading reveals that he too is ultimately on the side of civilization.[13] We should perhaps note in passing, that despite his repeated and provocative insistence that the goal of psychoanalysis is truth rather than healing, his willingness to employ the tools facilitated by transference (which he describes as a form of love that has been artificially produced: E, 348/288) shows clearly his conviction that illusion and imagination have an important role to play in self-understanding, even if they can never provide the whole truth.

Mortality and the death drive

What is not yet fully clear is to what extent the death drive which we have been discussing is linked to death in the sense of physical mortality. Freud's own 'biologism' is well known, and indeed he considered that science would one day clarify many of the obscurities of psycho-analytic theory, in particular with respect to the death drive: the 'bewildering and obscure processes' are, he maintains,

merely due to our being obliged to operate with the scientific terms, that is to say with the figurative language, peculiar to psychology...The deficiencies in our description would probably vanish if we were already in a position to replace the psychological terms by physiological or chemical ones (*Civilization*, 333–4).

Lacan of course recognized that Freud was a product of his age in the sense that he envisaged biology as a model of scientific rigour, but argues that Freud was not reductive and that he reworked and renewed any concepts he took from biology. Moreover, Lacan insists that, vital as the death drive is in Freud's theory, it is not ultimately a biological notion (E, 124/101, 317/261, 342/287). What is more, Lacan himself sometimes uses concepts borrowed from biology, such as that of 'imago' and 'dehiscence' (E, 96/78, 181/148, 188/153), which he reworks within a symbolic framework. And he occasionally illustrates his work with examples from animal behaviour, as in his references to pigeons and locusts in his account of the mirror stage (E, 95/77), and to crustaceans in his account of mimicry (SXI, 91/99). Indeed, the early Lacan is quite prepared to recognize a biological foundation to psychological phenomena: 'In opposing complexes to instincts, we do not deny complexes any biological foundation. [...] While instinct has organic *support* [...], the complex has only organic *relation* [rapport], when it supplements a vital insufficiency through the regulation of a social function' (AE, 34–5).

But there are still significant differences between Freud and Lacan in this respect, perhaps most marked in their understanding of sexuality and castration, and in particular the distinction between Freud's concept of the penis and Lacan's of the phallus, though Lacan's own reading of Freud plays down this difference in so far as he maintains that Freud regards the imaginary function of the phallus as equivalent in both sexes, and comments that this equivalence is incomprehensible to those who maintain a strictly biological or naturalist interpretation of Freud (E, 543/455). Indeed, in Lacan's dense and difficult essay on 'La signification du phallus', he attributes to Freud a depth of intuition into what he himself believes to be true with respect to the phallus and relations between the sexes, in a way that moves the biological dimension away from sexual difference and reinstates it in language, as he uses images of swelling, turgidity, and 'flux vital' to describe his own discourse. By this kind of argumentation Lacan blurs the difference between Freud and himself, and between the biological and the symbolic, in a rhetoric that is very difficult to resist or even to clarify, and which has been called an eroticization of the language of theory.[14]

Similarly, with respect to the death drive, it is clear that throughout the 1950s Lacan still insists on the biological underpinning of the human relationship to death, explaining that although it is our 'symbiosis with the symbolic' that enables us to imagine our own mortality, this symbiosis would not be possible without the preceding 'béance' or gap that is opened up in the imaginary during the 'stade du miroir' because of the (biological) prematurity of human birth (E, 97/78). Lacan situates the death drive first in the imaginary order (AE, 35) and later in the symbolic, going so far as to maintain that 'the death instinct is only the mask of the symbolic order' (SII, 375/26). The symbolic is persistently linked with death by Lacan, not only in his argument which we have already examined that symbol represents the 'murder of the thing' and thereby makes desire eternal, but also in his claim that the tomb is the first human symbol and that it marks the significance of the individual, setting him apart from the interchangeability of the animal realm (E, 319/262).

Perhaps unsurprisingly, Lacan takes suicide as the supreme representation of the relationship between desire and death, in so far as it refuses to accept the impossibility of desire and by this very 'dénégation' finds a paradoxical form of triumph over the mechanisms of its own alienation: 'It is not, in fact, a perversion of instinct, but rather a desperate affirmation of life, which is the purest form in which we recognize the death instinct' (E, 320/263). Suicide represents a refusal of the compromises of civilization, a refusal to accept the illusions of love in place of the impossible satisfaction of desire in true *jouissance*: 'The subject says 'No!' to this elusive game of intersubjectivity in which desire gains recognition for a moment only to lose itself in a will that is the will of the other' (E, 320/263).

So if we seek what pre-existed the subject's entry into the Symbolic Order, what was truly prior to his birth into the symbolic, we find it, Lacan argues, in death, which is precisely what gives existence meaning. And here Lacan does seem to be referring not merely to symbolic death but also to real, physical death, for he says that this 'sens mortel' reveals a centre that is external to language and not merely metaphoric. And he insists once again on his fidelity to Freud in these meditations, refusing to privilege Freud's biological references above his cultural allusions: 'Allow me to laugh if these remarks are accused of turning the meaning of Freud's work away from the biological foundations he would have wished for it, toward the cultural references with which it is rife' (E, 321/264).

Death then is both inside and outside language; we are forever marked by an irremediable sense of loss, absence, and death. Language implies and enshrines absence in so far as the signifier can never do more than represent the signified, but it also compensates for it, precisely standing in for what is absent, as the word 'Mother' stands in for and masks the absence of the maternal object of desire that it both evokes and summons. Language of course does not create death, any more than it banishes the mother from the baby's side, but it signifies it, and by this signification changes forever human awareness of our own mortality.

So physical death is necessarily part of Lacan's psychoanalytic theory: indeed, without it there would be nothing to symbolize and possibly no symbolization, for as we have seen death is the primordial symbol. But he does not theorize about death itself, rather about our awareness of death, and our symbolic relationship to it. Should this surprise us in a psychoanalyst whose concern with the soma is professionally limited to its interaction with the psyche? Probably not, but one critic at least considers that Lacan does not have enough to say about the Real which underlies both our Imaginary and Symbolic relations to death:

> Death is endemic to the signifying chain, and the structure of the human subject is always one of catastrophe: logic says so, and polysemantic writing says so too [...]. Let us grant for a moment that death is the ubiquitous condition of human speech, and that the only opportunity we have for saying *no* to mortality lies, fragilely, in speech itself and in the action that it may provoke. We still have a lopsided and implausible account. For we die inside the signifying chain, but outside it too. We die many times before our deaths, but we die at our deaths too and watch others dying at theirs. We die as organisms and as citizens. Death is too complex a biological and social fact to be located pre-emptively in any one place. And although Lacan deploys a sophisticated topological

imagery in order to make the point that death is both intrinsic and extrinsic to the words that speak us, he is often prepared to grant those words, and whatever lies inside them, outrageous privileges. [...] Suffering and death need to be given more weight – silently, and in the Real.[15]

Feminine *jouissance*

Lacan's refusal of biological determinism may lead him, at least in the opinion of some critics, to underplay the physical realities of sex and death in favour of a symbolic account of their significance. None the less, biological and bodily features are recognized as important for their impact on the human psyche, and a possibly unexpected consequence of Lacan's resolute opposition to reductivism is that he can discuss sex and gender in a way that is potentially recuperable by, and productive for, feminist theorists. His account of feminine *jouissance* probably represents the best example of his transcendence of the biological towards the symbolic.

Jouissance, as we have seen, is held in check by the pleasure principle, since its full realization would mean the end of desire and the death of the subject (*'la jouissance mortelle'*, SXVIII, 108). Moreover, sexual *jouissance*, or orgasm, is but a poor substitute which is, paradoxically, a way of keeping true *jouissance* at bay, and is not even a sign of love (SXX, 27/25). There is no 'rapport sexuel' (AE, 413),[16] because no reciprocity is possible: we know each other merely as imaginary constructs so can never provide what the Other might truly desire. Nor does love offer a solution, for that too is based on illusion.

But despite this series of apparently pessimistic 'truths' about human relations, Lacan still at times surprises us by his unexpected comments. In 'Subversion du sujet et dialectique du désir', for example, he claims both that 'I can, at most, prove to the Other that it exists [...] by loving it', even though he deems this 'too precarious a solution'; and says of *jouissance* that its absence would make the whole universe pointless (E, 819/694), even though he immediately adds that it is usually forbidden. And although this interdiction is enshrined in the Law, the Law merely reinforces a pre-existing barrier which operates, as we have seen, through the pleasure principle. So what is prohibited is, in fact, already impossible (E, 821/696).

So what hope is there for *jouissance*, for love, or for sexual relations? When the term is not qualified, *jouissance* is paradigmatically phallic: that is to say that it is necessarily non-reciprocal, imaginary, and a form of castration (SXX, 14/9). But in *Séminaire XX*, in 1972–3, Lacan offers an alternative, 'la jouissance féminine', which is non-phallic, non-totalizing, and not necessarily restricted to women: '*Were there another one*, but there is no other than phallic jouissance – except the one concerning which woman doesn't breathe a word, perhaps because she doesn't know it, the one that makes her not-whole' (SXX, 57/60).

Feminine *jouissance* cannot be known because it cannot be spoken: since it is the fall into language and the Symbolic Order that castrates desire and impedes *jouissance*, an other *jouissance* would of necessity be silent ('we repress the said jouissance because it is not fitting for it to be spoken [. . .]. It is precisely because the said jouissance speaks that the sexual relation is not', SXX, 57/63).

Speech, *jouissance*, and sexual relations are mutually incompatible. What then, if anything, can be said of *jouissance féminine*? It 'makes her not-all', woman is not 'toute', not whole, she does not *have* a (so-called) phallus, though according to some she *is* the phallus (E, 825/699). For this reason her *jouissance* may not be phallic, and therefore not be subject to castration. We have already seen Lacan argue that unless the phallic function is negated by castration, a man cannot relate directly to a woman in sexual relations: his *jouissance* is limited to the phallus rather than the woman's body (SXX, 67/72).

Indeed, Lacan refers to the polymorphous perversion of the male,[17] by which he means that the aim of his desire is deviated from its true object, the body of the woman (SXX, 68/73). And since the phallus is not the penis, women too may experience phallic *jouissance*, just as Lacan has indicated that men may go beyond it. But because '*La* Femme', as a universal, does not exist (SXVIII, 108), she is not complete ('toute'), not a totality, and thereby not limited by her essence (AE, 537/*Télévision* Eng. 37). For this reason she has the capacity for another kind of *jouissance* which Lacan calls supplementary. So in a familiar form of 'qui perd gagne', women's lack and incompleteness and partial exclusion from the Symbolic Order is seen as a potential entry to non-phallic, non-castrated *jouissance*:

> A woman can but be excluded by the nature of things, which is the nature of words, and it must be said that if there is something that women themselves complain about enough for the time being, this is it [*c'est bien de ça*] – put simply, they don't know what they are saying. That's the whole difference [*toute la différence*] between them and me. The fact remains that if she is excluded by the nature of things, it is precisely in the following respect: being not-whole [*pas toute*], she has a supplementary jouissance compared to what the phallic function designates by jouissance. (SXX, 68/73)

Behind Lacan's teasing allusions to feminist demands, we can see a serious argument. Women may enjoy a kind of *jouissance* that goes beyond the phallus ('au-delà du phallus', SXX, 69/74): 'There is a jouissance that is hers [*à elle*], that belongs to that "she" [*elle*] that doesn't exist and doesn't signify anything. There is a jouissance that is hers about which she herself perhaps knows nothing, if not that she experiences it – that much she knows. She knows it, of course, when it comes [*ça arrive*]. It doesn't happen to all women [*Ça ne leur arrive pas à toutes*]' (SXX, 69/74). So all women may not experience it, and nothing can be said directly about it precisely because it is excluded from the Symbolic Order, but Lacan clearly has considerable time for the notion of feminine *jouissance*. Indeed, he reverses the common psychoanalytic reductivism which explains (away) the ecstasy of the female mystics of the Middle Ages as nothing more than non-sublimated orgasm:

> I believe in the jouissance of woman insofar as it is extra [*en plus*]. [. . .] What was attempted at the end of the last century, in Freud's time [. . .], was the bringing of mysticism back to matters of fucking [*affaires de foutre*]. If you look closely, that's not it at all. Isn't this jouissance that one experiences and yet knows nothing about what puts us on the path of ex-istence? And why not interpret one face of the Other, the God face, as supported by feminine jouissance? (SXX, 71/77) [. . .] It is insofar as her jouissance is radically Other that woman has more of a relationship to God. (SXX, 77/83)

And if some religious readers are offended by Lacan's association of the divine with feminine *jouissance*, this can only be because they have not understood how seriously, indeed philosophically, Lacan takes *jouissance*. Men too can have access to this kind of *jouissance*, but the price to pay will be the same as that paid by women: exclusion from the universal, and incompleteness (74). Freud may have claimed that libido was exclusively masculine, but in Lacan's view this was to exclude precisely what Freud himself claimed not to know: 'Was will das Weib? What does woman want?' (SXX, 75/80). What women do not want, and need not envy, is phallic *jouissance* which never relates to the truly other (l'Autre), but only to the 'fantasme'. Women, on the contrary, have the chance of relating to the Other: 'Being in the sexual relationship, in relation to what can be said of the unconscious, radically Other, woman is that which has a relationship to this Other' (SXX, 75/81).

L'âmour

Encore also gives a glimpse of a potentially less pessimistic view of love. No longer described solely in terms of narcissism (see AE, 195)[18] and *tromperie* (trickery, deception), its ability to substitute for the absence of *jouissance* and of sexual relations is converted into a kind of success through failure. Love fails most seriously when it slides into mere tenderness (neurosis) or mere eroticism (perversion), which happen when it convinces itself that it knows what the other needs or desires. Conversely, the acceptance of one's ignorance of the other, and of the lack of any real reciprocity, opens the way for love: 'Love demands love. It never stops demanding it. It demands it *encore*. *Encore* is the proper name of the gap [*faille*] in the Other from which the demand for love stems' (SXX, 11/4). Of course, this demand for love is necessarily expressed, which is why love and speaking of love are described as equivalent (SXX, 77/83). Love accepts to forego bodily *jouissance*, it is connected with the soul (*l'âme*), if the soul exists, and is what traditionally enables us to put up with what would otherwise be intolerable (SXX, 78/84). And just as women are most likely to experience non-phallic *jouissance*, so too it is women who are most likely to love (*aimer d'âmour*).

Lacan's account of love at the end of *Encore* is deeply bewildering, as it turns around a series of negations which replace one another in what seems to be an unstoppable whirligig, and which he terms with apparent insouciance 'the displacement of negation' (SXX, 132/144). It is ultimately this 'déplacement' which constitutes what we might call the heart of love, Lacan's term for it is love's drama: 'Such is the substitute that – by the path of existence, not of the sexual relationship, but of the unconscious, which differs therefrom – constitutes the destiny as well as the drama of love' (SXX, 132/145). In the end, the only conclusion possible is that Lacan's conception of love is ambiguous, perhaps even aporetic. He does not resolve the contradictions he has set up, but rather uses them to reveal the inherent conflicts of human (non) relations.

Love may be born from the failure of *jouissance*, it may be an illusion, but it is also all we have, and in a form of *qui perd gagne* (loser wins) it may allow us to delight, however paradoxically, in the very impossibility of *jouissance* and in the impossible *jouissance* of the other. In the final paragraphs of *Encore* we see love defined as an approach to the other that is only tenable through failure ('which is upheld only in failing [*qui ne se soutient que de se rater*]', SXX, 133/145–6). But this failure is precisely what saves us, since success in love ('la vraie amour'),[19] which presumably would imply truly knowing the other, could only end in hatred. It is the failure of love which ultimately preserves us from mutual oppression, just as the failure of *jouissance* saves us from mutual destruction, and just as the failure of the feminine insertion into the Symbolic Order saves (some) women from merely phallic *jouissance*.

Seminar XX is difficult, provocative, and frustrating. But it also provides the most positive indication we have seen so far that something beyond the dissatisfactions of desire and the disappointments of love might be possible. Lacan's punning meditations on the body and soul in which love is referred to as *l'âmour* because it relinquishes the body and contents itself with the soul, 'it souloves' ['*il âme*'], may distract us from the seriousness of his intentions. Feminine *jouissance* is not certain, it is not necessarily restricted to women, and it is not the lot of all women to experience it; it cannot be spoken of but this does not mean that it has no reality. There is much on offer here for women (and others), psychoanalysts, and philosophers to meditate on.

A footnote on Irigaray

Luce Irigaray's ambivalent relations with Lacan are well known: having attended Lacan's seminars at Vincennes where she also taught courses, she fell out of favour after the publication of *Speculum. De l'autre femme* in 1974, and lost her position in the institution. Like *Speculum*, much of her subsequent work consists in meditation on and critique of the Freudian and Lacanian positions. Indeed, she is often seen primarily as contesting Lacan's views on, for example, feminine sexuality, though an alternative and arguably more judicious reading considers her work as refining and extending Lacan's analyses rather than simply refuting them. In 'Cosi fan tutti' for example (from *Ce sexe qui n'en est pas un*, 1977), in which she responds precisely to *Encore*, she picks up Lacan's claim that women do not understand and cannot speak of their own feminine *jouissance* and sets it up in opposition to his other claim that 'parler d'amour est en soi une jouissance'. But of course, as we have seen, Lacan himself is well aware of the apparent contradiction, and it underlies much of the paradoxical discourse in which he revels.

Similarly, Lacan does not need Irigaray to tell him that just because sexual relations cannot be spoken of, this does not mean that they do not *exist*, in the usual sense of 'exist'. As a post-Heideggerian, Lacan is using 'exist'/'*il y a*' in a precise and quasi-philosophical sense, and is well aware of the provocative effect his laconic claim will have. This pattern of correcting Lacan with tools he has himself provided continues throughout Irigaray's essay, from the interpretation of Lacan's notorious '*La Femme n'existe pas*', to that of his claim that in psychoanalytic discourse woman exists primarily as mother. Irigaray concludes by arguing that Lacan has seen much of the truth about feminine sexuality but has failed to recognize that this is, like his own discourse, historically determined:

> Psychoanalytic theory thus utters the truth about the status of female sexuality, and about the sexual relation. But it stops there.

Refusing to interpret the historical determinants of its discourse [...] and notably what is implied by the hitherto exclusively masculine sexualization of the application of its laws, it remains caught up in phallocentrism, which it claims to make into a universal and eternal value. (*Ce sexe*, p. 99/102)

I would suggest that Irigaray has failed to appreciate the full implications of what Lacan has to say about feminine *jouissance*, and that if he does remain trapped in a phallocentric position (which is certainly a complex question) it is arguably not for the relatively simple reasons she outlines.

Didier Anzieu

Didier Anzieu, like Luce Irigaray, undertook analysis with Lacan who, it emerged later, had also psychoanalysed Anzieu's mother, Marguerite – the Aimée of case-history. This family romance is one of Lacan's controversial *causes-célèbres*, and consequently Anzieu, like many others, came to reject much of his former analyst's teaching. In terms of theoretical positions, rather than professional deontology, Anzieu has two major differences of opinion with Lacan – one concerning the *moi*, the other concerning the unconscious. For Lacan, like Sartre, as we have seen, the *moi* or self (in Sartre's terminology the ego), is an imaginary construct and a potential source of sclerosis for the subject, whereas for Anzieu it is a vital element in the construction of personal identity. And whereas for Lacan, the unconscious is famously structured like a language, for Anzieu the unconscious is the body.[20] These differences have, of course, significant implications for the way Anzieu views subjectivity, passion, and mortality.

The skin-ego: embodied subjectivity

One of Anzieu's main claims to originality lies in his elaboration of the *moi-peau*, or skin-ego, a notion that lies at the heart of his theorization of the way in which the self is constituted at the earliest stages of life. It can be seen to derive from Freud's description in 'The Ego and the Id' of 1923, of the ego as bodily: 'The ego is first and foremost a bodily ego; it is not merely a surface entity, but is itself the projection of a surface.' This remark is accompanied by an explanatory footnote, approved by Freud, which further explains the notion of surface: 'The ego is ultimately derived from bodily sensations, chiefly from those springing from the surface of the body. It may thus be regarded as a mental projection of the surface of the body' (SE, vol 19, p.26).[21] It is not necessarily easy at first to understand the relationship between ego and bodily surface and Anzieu devotes several texts to its explanation.

Put simply, his argument is that the ego, a psychic phenomenon, arises initially from the infant's experience of its body, and more particularly of its skin which constitutes not only a container for all that lies within the body, but also a limit to the body, and a means of contact with the outside world (*Moi-Peau*, 61–2/40)[22] The skin is liminal, marking simultaneously the boundary of the self and its access to the world. The skin both incarnates and circumscribes our individuality. When a mother holds her baby, it is their skin that indicates the boundary between them as well as constituting their point of contact.

But Anzieu's *moi-peau* is much more than simply a way of describing the initial construction of our bodily identity, it provides the basis for all psychic structures (*Une Peau*, 71). All the mechanisms of thought arise from agreeable biological functions which are represented symbolically, metaphorically or metonymically (*Psychanalyse des limites*, 24). It is the pleasure of proprioception that underpins the development of the thinking self: 'the Skin Ego founds the very possibility of thought' (*Moi-Peau*, 62/41). 'For no psychic reality other than the skin-ego does pleasure so manifestly ground the possibility of thought (*Créer/ Détruire*, 205).

And in *Le Penser: du Moi-peau au Moi-pensant* of 1994, he lays out, in a detailed series of propositions, exactly how he envisages the inseparable union of mind and body. Anzieu's understanding of the self is resolutely anti-dualist: psyche and soma are not separable, even theoretically; subjectivity is not just embodied, it is embodiment. He starts *Le Moi-Peau* with what might sound like a declaration of deterministic materialism: 'The dependence of thinking and of the will on the cortex is now scientifically established, as is the dependence of emotional life on the thalamus' (MP, 25/3), but goes on immediately to express regret that a consequence of such psychopharmacological research has been to reduce the 'living body' to the nervous system, and concomitantly to relegate psychology to the status of poor relation of cerebral neurophysiology.

For Anzieu, like René Kaes, the psyche depends on both the biological and the social body, which are themselves mutually inter-dependent (MP, 26/4). And what is more, of course, psychoanalysis is concerned not just with the psyche of psychology, but also with the conscious, preconscious, and unconscious fantasies that construct a bridge between psyche and soma, world and other psyches. But just as we may feel we have understood the *moi-peau* as a bodily construct underpinning the psyche, we learn that it is 'a reality of the order of phantasy' (MP, 26/4). What is more, the *moi-peau* is not only fantasmatic but fragile, and some patients encountered by Anzieu are uncertain precisely of their boundaries: where are the boundaries between the psychic and the bodily self, between the real and the ideal self, between self and others? Such uncertainty and weakness in what he calls the psychic skin makes for huge vulnerability to narcissistic wounds and personal alienation (MP, 29/7).

One aspect of the *moi-peau* that is initially puzzling is the significance it necessarily accords to the surface. If the self is the projection of bodily surface, this runs counter to our intuition that the self lies somehow deep inside us. Like Sartre, who argues that the ego is outside in the world, transcendent not immanent, Anzieu too inverts the natural intuition – expressed in the metaphor of the shell and the kernel[23] – that what is most important is always hidden within,[24] and uses the morphology of the brain itself to show how, apparently paradoxically, the centre (here the cortex) may be located on the periphery.[25] Indeed, Anzieu elaborates a whole series of paradoxes about the skin which jolt us out of many of our comfortable assumptions about how selfhood is constructed: skin is permeable and impermeable, deep and superficial, true and misleading, regenerative and dying, solid and fragile, uniting and separating. In short, the skin exemplifies what Pascal would have called our *grandeur* and our *misère*, our superiority as a species as well as our profound vulnerability (MP, 39/17).

From self to subject

It is this vulnerability, of course, that explains why Anzieu and Lacan disagree so fundamentally about the status of the *moi*. Anzieu maintains that Lacan seeks to demolish the *moi*, envisaged as an obstacle to 'the assumption of the I',[26] whereas he himself tries rather to restore the *moi* of his unhappy, wounded patients and not merely to help them realize their potentially (self-) destructive desires. But the issue is not necessarily so clear-cut: Lacan's hostility to ego-psychology is well known, but although he notoriously denies any therapeutic goal for analysis which he sees as aiming for truth rather than happiness, truth ultimately offers a means of liberation for the analysand, which is also why Lacan values transference as the highest form of love. Moreover, Anzieu's attempt to heal the *moi* of his patients is not technically a form of ego-psychology, except in the loose and general sense of focusing on the ego.[27] Indeed, the *moi*, or *moi-peau*, is for Anzieu just an early stage on the path to full subjectivity. The new-born infant has no *moi-peau*, it must construct one, and then leave it behind as its experience broadens and deepens:

> Only by breaking with the primacy of tactile experience and by constituting itself in a space of *intersensorielle* inscription, in *sensorium commune*, can the ego (*moi*) subsequently pursue its structuration. (*Créer-Détruire*, p. 229)

In *L'Epiderme nomade et la peau psychique* of 1990 Anzieu sets out what he describes as the four stages in the organization of the human psyche. First comes the constitution of what he calls the *Soi*, the fragmentary, disorganized elements of infantile experience; next is the constitution of the *Moi*, which involves, as we have seen, developing a container for the previously disparate elements and recognizing psychic boundaries; third is the constitution of the *Je*, which involves a degree of reflexivity; and finally, the subject itself is constituted on the basis of the *Je*.[28] So, for Anzieu as for Lacan, the *je* and the subject are valued as higher levels of human psychical organization, and the *moi* (whether the *moi-peau* or the *moi* of the mirror stage)[29] is left behind and transcended. To those of us outside the quarrels of the psychoanalytic community, the similarities might seem just as striking as the differences, even though the emphasis is clearly placed on different moments of psychic development.[30]

Lacan certainly describes the self-identification of the mirror stage as a fiction which 'symbolizes the mental permanence of the *I* at the same time as prefiguring its alienating destiny' (E, 95/76), and argues that the mirror stage transforms the 'fragmented image of the body' into 'the assumed armour of an alienating identity' (E, 97/78), but we cannot fail to note that his essay also attributes to (even) Sartre an essentializing of the *moi* which only a wilfully perverse reading could maintain. And if the inertia of the *I* and the capture of the subject within his situation (E, 99/80) provide Lacan with a definition of madness, it is also made explicit that love (embodied in psychoanalytic transference) can recognize this knot of (imaginary) servitude and cut through it or untie it.

So if we read Lacan's text carefully, we will notice that the alienation of the mirror stage is an inevitable moment of development at which 'mediation through the desire of the other' contributes to the infant's subject-formation, even as it opens him to the suffering of potential neurosis and psychosis in 'the school of the passions of the soul' (E, 99/80). Lacan may lament this moment, while recognizing its inescapability, whereas Anzieu celebrates it as a necessary phase without which the future subject could not come into existence: neither analyst envisages the *moi* (or self or ego) as more than a stage on the long path to free subjectivity. And it is Lacan who points out that the analyst can be no more than a facilitator in this respect, unable to accompany the patient on his journey: 'it is not in our sole power as practitioners to bring the patient to the point where the true journey begins' (E, 100/81).

The *moi* of the mirror stage is, then, a necessary moment of identification and alienation which precedes the development of subjectivity that will shortly be enabled by language. And the *moi-peau* is far from being the stagnant ego rejected by Lacan as an alienating *alter ego* (E, 374/312); unlike the Ego psychologists, Anzieu never confuses the *moi* with the subject (E, 178/145), but envisages it rather as a stage on the way to subjectivity, and as a necessary illusion, like several other forms of imaginary identity.[31]

Love and death

Just as Anzieu and Lacan disagree over the status of the *moi* while being, on closer inspection, in less radical opposition to each other than at first appears; so they disagree over questions of love and death, but again a close reading reveals that there is a (possibly wilful) misunderstanding underlying their opposition. Anzieu claims that Lacan not only undermines the *moi* but also 'discredits love' ['*déconsidère l'amour*'] (*Une Peau*, p. 68), which he links to death. In his view, much of what Lacan has to say about love applies only to borderline patients who are dominated by the 'pulsion de mort'.

However, we have already explored the complexity of Lacan's conception of love, and its evolution in *Encore*, and need not repeat this now, except to remark that it does not seem accurate to restrict the applicability of Lacan's view of love to a sub-set of patients, nor to simplify his position to one in which love is down-graded. On the contrary, love may involve illusion, but it is argu-ably all we have, and it is rather *jouissance* that is ultimately linked to death. If we turn to Anzieu's own understanding of love, we will see that it is equally possible to argue that it is he, not Lacan, who has downgraded its importance.

In his interviews with G. Tarrab, Anzieu is asked why psycho-analysts consider love as a form of regression. His reply is in terms of different levels of attachment and 'psychic levels' ['*niveaux psychiques*'] (*Une Peau*, p. 122). Love, he explains, is both a state and a process. For neurotic subjects it will involve complementary fantasies; for narcissists, symmetrical ideals; for dependent subjects, reciprocal needs; and for psychotics, a form of antagonism. Anzieu's psychoanalytic pragmatism about love contrasts strongly with Lacan's arguably near-mystical romanti-cism. Anzieu is quite clear about the potential benefits and draw-backs of love: it can be used well or badly, involve generosity or suffocation, and may embody the ambivalence of what he calls poisoned presents. At its best, however, love helps form the healthy subject:

> Love demonstrates intelligence when it contributes to the con-struction of a supple yet firm envelope that delimits and unifies the child, the friend, the companion – a bark [*écorce*, also 'shell']

for their trunk, oxygen for their leaves, a living skin for their thoughts. (*Une Peau*, p. 181).

Similarly, Anzieu's passing remarks about love may seem to paint a picture which comes closer to ordinary human experience than what often feels like the reductiveness of psychoanalytic accounts, be they those of Freud, Lacan or Anzieu himself. Of the sexual caress, for example, he writes: 'love presents a paradox, simultaneously bringing about both the deepest psychical contact and the most complete form of skin contact with one and the same person' (MP, 32/19). None the less, closeness to common experience is clearly no guarantee of truth, and in the Preface to the new (French) edition of *Le Moi-Peau* in 1995, Evelyne Séchard criticizes Anzieu precisely for privileging attachment over libido, and thereby downgrading and desexualizing love (MP, 12).

It does seem that Anzieu's unremitting focus on the body as what has been most relentlessly repressed in twentieth-century theory, far more than sex, which was rehabilitated by Freud (MP, 43), has – paradoxically perhaps – led him away from passion and left him with (mere?) affection and pleasure. This is not, of course, to say that Anzieu does not discuss sexuality, it would probably be difficult for a psychoanalyst not to do so, and all his texts and many of his case studies give considerable weight to the sexual, but it certainly does not seem to hold pride of place in his theory or practice, and the dark, deep connection between Eros and Thanatos is largely absent from his writings.

If we turn now to death, however, an interesting picture emerges. When Anzieu discusses pain, trauma, and death, the link with love seems to surface again, though his discussions of love rarely allude to death. In his essay on Bacon, for example, he uses Freud's analysis of his reaction to Michelangelo's 'Moses' to explain his own emotive response to Bacon's work:

> The shock of an encounter with the work, comparable to being lovestruck or to the terror of a near-death experience. The work of art or of thought, at the intersection of the two axes of human experience: love and death. (*Francis Bacon*, 13)

And in this essay, Anzieu employs a more lyrical and passionate tone when he speaks of how Bacon's triptych represents the potentially devastating effects of a lack of response to love, when 'a void installs itself in place of the heart' (21):

> The series of these paintings develops the allegory of man aban-
> doned by his gods and fellow creatures, wounded in flesh and soul,
> and who loses his sweat, his blood, his substance. (21)

> Upright [. . .] a woman [. . .], breasts swollen and sagging, without
> doubt and abundantly a wetnurse. But the head, sealed in a plastic
> bubble, with neither affectionate mimicry nor regard for the runt,
> who, filled with a milk that does not sate, proclaims its hunger for
> love in a desert. (23)

But it is not merely that Anzieu (like Merleau-Ponty) needs the stimulus of a powerful work of art to enable him to write powerfully himself, there is also a theoretical underpinning to his emphasis on trauma, and he agrees with Bion that our early experience of pain marks us far more strongly than that of pleasure:

> The psychotic kernel – discovered by Bion – that, to a greater or
> lesser degree, is active in everyone tends to reproduce the first
> experiences not of pleasure but of pain, tends to panic in the face
> of their return and to have recourse to the most archaic, the most
> expedient means to eliminate their horror. (63)

Similarly, just as sensation makes us feel alive, the withdrawal of sensation has an even more dramatic effect in giving us a foretaste of death (71), and it is precisely this that forces us to *think*. Thought, then, as it is conceived here, is not so much an attempt to recreate in imagination primitive satisfactions, as to mourn their loss:

> Thinking is not seeking to recover primitive satisfaction. To think
> is to reflect on the absence of the breast and foremost to represent
> it to oneself. [. . .] Thinking in images repeats the painful hallucina-
> tion of the inevitable traumatisms of childhood. (82)

Anzieu's sensitivity to suffering is evident throughout his work. Elsewhere in the essay on Bacon he discusses the way in which our grasp on reality is undermined by bodily weakness: 'it remains at the mercy of fatigue, of depression, of illness' (81–2). And illness and fatigue certainly find a place in Anzieu's thinking about the body that they do not have in Lacan, for example, and which Sartre struggles unsuccessfully to accord them. Of course, as an analyst whose aims are explicitly therapeutic, and whose conception of psychosomatic integration is so central to his work, bodily suffering inevitably looms very large in his understanding of the human and is recognized as impacting powerfully on subjectivity, thought, and desire:

> As every one of us knows from experience, intense and lasting pain disorganizes the psychical apparatus, threatens the psyche's integration with the body, affects our capacity to desire and the activity of thinking. Pain is not the opposite or the reverse of pleasure: their relation is asymmetrical. (MP, 227/200)

Indeed Anzieu comments in a footnote on how little attention has been paid to pain in psychoanalytic literature. Anzieu's own case histories all concern bodily disturbances, and in particular of course, disruptions and traumas to the *moi-peau*, be these matters of physical lesions, as is the case with patients suffering from burns, or more psychic lesions, as in cases of failures of mother-love and nurturing, where infants have been left to survive rather than helped to thrive. In all cases, psychoanalytic healing necessarily involves both psyche and soma.

It would be easy for Anzieu to claim originality here, when we consider how little attention Lacan, for example, seems to have paid to the bodily suffering of his patients, but he is impressive in his refusal to be seduced by such temptations. So when G. Tarrab, for example, suggests in an interview that previous psychoanalysts have tended to ignore the body, Anzieu points out that this is quite simply untrue, and that ever since Freud's first studies it has been clear that 'the body is the bedrock of the psyche' (*Une peau*, 71). It is his conception of the skin ego that is original, and also his awareness of, and extended theorization of, bodily pain. Similarly, he is more acutely aware of the effects of human ageing than philosophers who have a less concrete and pragmatic conception of subjectivity, and he describes the way in which middle age brings us to a position in which we are forced to face the certainty of eventual death and can either start to come to terms with it or else retreat into a form of paranoia and denial; the choice is between 'beginning to mourn one's own impending death instead of feeling persecuted by it' (*Psychanalyser*, 114–15, 165).

If we are able to embark on the process of (self-) mourning we may consequently become more courageous, loving, and understanding as our ability to sublimate is strengthened. However, Anzieu's discussions of death, and particularly of the *pulsion de mort* which he frequently associates with logical paradoxes and double-binds,[32] rather than with more self-evidently violent or aggressive drives, often tend to retain a positive note potentially at odds with the realities of human mortality, bodily or psychic. Indeed, he describes thought as essentially a deferral of immediate response (which he explains with reference to the Derridean notion of *différance*)[33] to the major questions of death and sexuality:

> The two challenges presented by Nature to the human mind are the existence of sexuality and that of death. Perhaps the mind even created thought, if not to respond completely to these challenges, then at least to contain their anxiety, to recognise reveries and fantasies, and deal with the intra- and inter-psychic conflicts elicited in humans by their impotence, their finitude, their dereliction, their narcissistic wounds, their failures, their boredom, their vanity, their circumstance, their excess and their nothingness: the marks of original sin, according to Pascal, that psychoanalysis calls the castration complex. (*Le Penser*, 5)

Anzieu clearly recognizes the suffering and traumas that beset mortal subjects, and his work offers much to the sick, weary, and ageing; whether his theoretical – as opposed to therapeutic – contribution will be significant in the long term is not yet clear.

Julia Kristeva

Of all the theorists and philosophers discussed in this book, Julia Kristeva is possibly the most evidently concerned with the interrelationship of two of its most central preoccupations: passion and subjectivity. Like Anzieu and Irigaray, Kristeva too situates herself in relation to Freud and Lacan, but she gives an arguably more accurate and sympathetic account of their views as well as developing a distinctive theory of her own.

Love and subjectivity

From the 1970s onwards Kristeva's work can be read as an extended meditation on the nature of love, primarily romantic passion and maternal love, but also the love enacted in psychoanalytic transference. What is most interesting for our purposes is the link Kristeva establishes between love and subjectivity. *Histoires d'amour* (1983) consists in a series of essays devoted to different conceptions of love, from Plato and Plotinus through a variety of religious philosophers to nineteenth and twentieth-century writers and psychoanalysts. It is not always easy therefore to disentangle Kristeva's own ideas from those of the writers she is discussing. But her first essay, 'Eloge de l'amour', seems to sketch out a view of love that underpins all the consequent analyses. While explicitly recognizing the variety of components in love, and their contradictory and even antagonistic natures, she never sets up an opposition between love and desire as we have seen, for example, in Sartre and Lacan.

Love, as described by Kristeva, is far closer to romantic passion as we usually understand it, and is reduced neither to the masochistic self-objectification it risks becoming in Sartre, nor to the idealizing delusion of the Lacanian substitute for *jouissance*. And whereas Sartre and Lacan can only contemplate the necessary *failure* of love, since its success would involve an alienation either of the other (Lacan) or of the self (Sartre), Kristeva, like Freud,[34] seems prepared to envisage love as a successful mode of human relations in which the subject is born through openness to the other, 'l'ouverture à l'autre' (HA, 25/14). Indeed, the link between love and subjectivity is a cornerstone of Kristeva's conception of the subject: 'I am, in love, at the zenith of subjectivity' (HA, 14/5). 'If it lives, your psyche is in love. If it isn't in love, it is dead' (25/15). But this is not to say that Kristeva views love as a purely benevolent state. On the contrary: 'this exaltation beyond eroticism is as much exorbitant happiness as it is pure suffering' (9/1), 'however enlivening it is, love never inhabits us without burning us' (12/4). It is a powerful source of pain, both psychic and physical (13/4), it overwhelms our body and its symptoms are extraordinarily similar to the symptoms of fear (palpitations, dry throat etc., 15/6). Indeed Kristeva describes it as an unstable point between death and rebirth: 'a fragile crest where death and regeneration vie for dominance' (13/4). She considers that the pain of love ('blindness', 'physical ailments', 17/8) is precisely the aspect that philosophers – from Plato to Hegel – have tended to elide in their identification of love with a search for the Supreme Good or the Absolute Spirit.

Why then is love, as Kristeva describes it, such a painful state? There are several ways of answering this question. In the first place, what Kristeva means by love includes, as I have indicated, elements that many other thinkers would attribute rather to desire. Lacan, for example, concludes Seminar XVIII with a radical opposition between love and *jouissance* in which love is set up precisely as an obstacle to *jouissance*; quoting Ecclesiastes, he writes: '*Enjoy with the woman you love*' ['Jouis avec la femme que tu aimes'] and comments: 'It is the height of paradox, because it precisely from loving that the obstacle comes' (XVIII, 178).

Conversely, Kristeva's more inclusive definition of love necessarily incorporates both the joys and sufferings traditionally associated with desire as well as those traditionally associated with love. And the joys are precisely the reverse of the pains: fusion with the loved one, for example, may be experienced as a potential loss of self, feared just as much as it is desired: 'fear of crossing and desire to cross the boundaries of the self' (17/6). Love can be seen as a supremely positive state: 'in the rapture of love, the limits of one's own identity vanish', but this very loss of self in the other also represents a potential threat to identity, a 'state of instability in which the individual ceases to be individual and allows itself to become lost in the other, for the other' (13/2–4). This kind of love, desiring love, *l'amour-passion*, is not calm and harmonious but rather 'delirium, disengagement, rupture' (13/4–5). Another way of answering the question of why love is so painful comes from Freudian psychoanalytic discourse: in so far as (passionate) love includes desire, it involves both narcissism and idealization, that is to say both self-glorification and self-destruction, self-unification and the breakdown of the self.

Love is essential for life, but in its most passionate form it represents what Kristeva describes as a 'chaotic hyperconnectivity', which is still to be preferred to the 'death-dealing stabilization of love's absence' (25/15). Love is renewal and renaissance for the human subject, but such renewal disconcerts, troubles, and disrupts. 'The state of love' is 'a disconcerting dynamic' at the same time as being 'the supreme guarantee of renewal' (27/16). 'Love is a putting to death that makes me be' (50/35). What is more, despite her 'Eloge de l'amour', Kristeva apparently agrees with Lacan that love involves a form of self-deception or *tromperie*, though one she believes is vital to human existence. In preferring the imaginary to the real, love enables self-development and *jouissance* (17/7).

'Freud et l'amour: le malaise dans la cure' (cleverly translated as 'Freud and Love: Treatment and its Discontents'), elaborates further the use Kristeva makes of Freud in her theorizations of love. While taking from Freud the conception of love as ultimately narcissistic, she has a more positive view of its benefits and its structure, which she sees as not so much a matter of madness and blind criminality, as of (self-) construction and (self-) protection (HA, 36/25). Love may be a form of narcissism, but it none the less has an external object (47/33); amatory identification may only provide a screen for the emptiness within, but this screen precisely offers a defence against the pain of separation; like Narcissus, the narcissist (that is, of course, all of us lovers) seeks someone to love, even if ultimately that someone bears an uncanny resemblance to himself; narcissism strengthens the ego and the subject and helps exorcize our primal loss.[35] Using Melanie Klein's terminology, Kristeva describes love as a way of incorporating the other through identification; in this way, the object of love is a metaphor for the subject (that is, it represents the subject), rather than involving the metonymic structure of desire (43–4/29–30).

Even this brief account of Kristeva's analysis reveals love at the heart of the psyche, indeed, it is love that enables the constitution of the subject. The structure of narcissism establishes a form of reflexivity that passes through the other in order to construct an identity for the subject after the grief of maternal loss. It could indeed be said that love is always love for the mother, but via a third party. When we are not loved, we fall ill; this is because the failure of amatory, idealizing identification drives the psyche to identify with a somatic symptom or illness (52/37). Of course, love cannot fully heal the wounds of maternal loss, nor do more than provide an always fragile bridge over the abyss, but it can help us conceal and control the pain of primary separation and resist the 'pulsion de mort' and its accompanying aggressivity (59/43). Love may not ever entirely fulfil our yearning, and it may be ultimately based on illusion, but, for Kristeva as for Lacan, it may still be all we have.

Love stories

The intrinsic ambivalence of love, and its intimate relationship to human subjectivity has of course made it a privileged source of material and reflection for writers and philosophers, and Kristeva's *Histoires d'amour* explores a wide range of the various theories – or stories – of love. Her theoretical analyses, as we have seen, are developed primarily in response to previous psychoanalytic models, but the stress she places on love is certainly original. She considers conceptions of love from classical philosophers such as Plato and Plotinus, through the Old and New Testaments, medieval theologians such as Thomas Aquinas and Saint Bernard, the courtly troubadours, literary figures from Don Juan to Romeo and Juliet, as well as psychoanalytic theories of transference and of maternal love. What is unique in Kristeva's account is the significance she gives to her subject: love is not merely an aspect of the theories she explores, it lies at their heart and constitutes their most vital element. Her discussion of Plato's *Symposium* and his *Phaedrus* makes clear for the non-Lacanian reader exactly what Lacan means by 'l'âmour': 'Psyche speaks and unfurls herself only in love' (HA, 77/59). Psyche is, of course, the soul (*âme*), and her lover was Eros, l'Amour. The Greek myth of Psyche and Eros makes possible a French pun (*âme/amour*) which cannot be translated into English, but its significance is clear: it expresses the intimate interdependence of love and the soul for human subjectivity, for the soul is the receptacle of 'amorous passion' and love is an element of the soul. (82–3/63). But Eros itself is extraordinarily complex, on the one hand sado-masochistic delirium and madness, on the other the aspiration towards the Good and the

Beautiful: as Kristeva crisply expresses it, pederast and philosopher (81/62). In both cases, Eros represents a yearning for what is lacking, be it a beautiful boy or a beautiful truth. Kristeva's focus is precisely on the transmutation of sexual desire into a more complex human love, both of which are contained, she maintains, within the Greek term Eros which covers a wide range of physical and psychological experiences including the tenderness of friendship (philia).

Both the *Symposium* and the *Phaedrus* make clear that love is itself a form of desire: 'Everyone sees that love is a desire' (82/63; *Phaedrus*, 237d). But in the *Phaedrus* it is love as the desire to possess which is dominant, whereas in the *Symposium* love is represented less as possession than as fusion, though even this idealized conception (to which 'Platonic' love is usually reduced) makes clear that love is for what we do not have (94/73). As Kristeva's chapter title suggests, Eros is both 'manic' and 'sublime', 'mortelle et procréatrice, ravageante et idéalisante' (98/76). Eros here is, like the Freudian libido, predominantly male and indeed, for Plato, homosexual, that is to say for another (idealized) self.

This form of erotic love is taken up and further elaborated by Plotinus in the Narcissus myth which embodies 'love centred on itself, though aspiring to the ideal Other' (HA, 78/59). The *Enneads* describe the way in which (self-) love constitutes the internal unity of the soul: Kristeva shows Narcissus in anguish as his love finds no (external) object, for he is both subject and object of his own desire (147/116). But the melancholy and indeed the death-wish of Narcissus do not depend solely on his perversion, they are rather endemic in erotic experience as its reverse side, manifest when the object of love is removed or absent.

Plotinus himself might seem to share in the suffering subjectivity of the Ovidian myth, in his notorious attempt at the end of his life to neglect and reject his dying body and become all soul in order to fuse with the divine (149/117), entailing a further refusal of alterity in union with the One (152/120). But Kristeva is sensitive to what separates Plotinus from Narcissus, which is precisely the Divine. Plotinus believes that his soul can overcome its solitude in loving union with the One; whereas Narcissus – closer to us moderns as Kristeva remarks – takes the opposite path from the mystic and finds in death neither salvation nor fusion but rather the alienation which constitutes his own image: 'If he is alone by himself, his otherness is not secured within a totality, it does not become interiority. It remains open, gaping, mortal, because deprived of a One' (153/121).

Narcissus makes frequent further appearances in Kristeva's texts. She explores in particular, of course, the Freudian rehabilitation of narcissism (155/122), but she also traces the fortunes of the myth through a variety of manifestations from the Middle Ages through to Mallarmé, Valéry, and Gide in the modern period, showing how it lends itself to two antithetical interpretations in terms of either ironic self-dispersal and emptiness on the one hand, or an auto-erotic sacralization on the other (170/136). But it is perhaps in Christianity that Narcissus plays his most significant and arguably least-expected role – in connection with the Incarnation. In a general, philosophical sense, incarnation (or, in contemporary terms, embodiment) is clearly a question at the heart of all enquiry about the human; it represents one way of looking at the relationship between mind and body, or body and soul. In Christian theology, it is usually reserved for the expression of the way in which God became man in the form of Christ, still fully God and yet fully human, divine ideal, and bodily form, born from God's love for himself.

But Kristeva traces the notion back to the Judaic texts of the Old Testament, and in particular the Song of Solomon, or the Canticle of Canticles, in which human and divine love become indistinguishable as *'ahav*. The biblical command to love God (Deuteronomy 6:5) and your neighbour (Leviticus 19:18), which Kristeva terms the Law of Love, has, she argues, tended to mask the more complex forms of love represented in the Canticle (108/85). The Canticle represents love not as a duty but as a powerful antidote to death: 'Love is strong as death, jealousy as relentless as Sheol' (118/93). It shows a love that is neither dutiful nor fusional but rather yearns for the absent beloved, who is separated from the lover and forbidden. It is a physical love that longs for the body of the loved one, for his kisses and caresses which, like wine, intoxicate without slaking (115/90). The lover is subject to the beloved, but embraces the subjection that opens her to otherness through amorous identification in both ecstasy ('la sortie hors de soi') and incarnation ('devenir-corps de l'idéal'). In its very pains – 'I am sick with love' – love creates an inner life, a psychic interiority which Kristeva describes as prefiguring romantic mysticism. The Canticle combines idealization and sensuality in a way which an allegorical reading cannot defuse: physical passion for the body may be identified with love of God, but its eroticism remains undeniable – permitted, Kristeva suggests, only because it is never consummated. The Law of Love embodied in the Song of Solomon becomes the love of the impossible, and thereby creates an extraordinary dialectical synthesis of (universal) sensuality and melancholy with the (specific) Judaic legislative imperative (124/98). Body and soul are inextricably linked in what Kristeva describes as a unique erotic abstraction and an idealized sensuality. She also sees the text as an early statement of feminism, affirming woman as lover and beloved, passionate, desiring, suffering, divided, sovereign: in short, exemplar of the modern subject (126/100).

Passion

Christianity takes the idea and ideal of love further, through Paul in the first place and most especially though John. Saint Paul defines God as love (II Corinthians 13:11), who sacrifices his Son for us, unworthy mortals, and who asks us to love not only our neighbour but also our enemy. Christ's passion and death are described as scandal and madness. God's love for us is not the yearning of Eros but the free gift of Agape, bestowed on us irrespective of our merits. God is prepared to have his Son die for us, precisely because of our sins, not our virtue. And his death itself is a pure act of love, not a sacrifice demanded by law or contract but rather a gift, the gift of death which permits us to transcend our own mortality in an idealizing identification with God-made-Man.

All this is, of course, part of traditional Christian theology, but Kristeva inscribes it within a psychoanalytic framework which fits so well that it seems to have been created specially for the purpose. Perhaps this is to say no more than that psychoanalysis grew up in a Christian, or post-Christian, era, but such a reductive explanation is less easy to proffer for Kristeva's analyses of Plotinus, the

Old Testament, or Plato. In any case, Christ's death on the cross is of course a passion in many different senses, it represents both the demolition and the apotheosis of the body, destroyed but resurrected, traumatized, and defiled only to be taken up to heaven in a resurrection of the body as well as the soul. In Saint John's Gospel, the idea that God is Love is taken a step further, for his love is said to pre-exist the creation of the world and thereby takes on truly cosmic dimensions. In this sense, God's love can only be for himself for he has no external object. John's Gospel is traditionally identified as a paean of love, but such a version of Christian love is certainly less painful and violent than that described in Paul's threnody where the body of Christ on the cross is the primary emblem of divine passion.

Similar analyses are given by Kristeva of the writings of Saint Bernard, whose works represent love initially as violent desire and lack, and who constitutes a hierarchy of stages of love moving upwards from the flesh, through reason to wisdom (HA, 196/156). So, bodily love is seen to lie at the heart of all love, however ultimately spiritual. And love is a form of self-love, 'loving oneself in God' ['*s'aimer en Dieu*'], a *jouissance* of the soul that has not renounced the body but rather glorified it. In Kristeva's terms, bodily love has been violently transformed into a jubilatory state of self-idealization passing through a successful identification with the Other (206–7/163–4). The soul has been ravished from the body, in a passion which also unites, so that we love our spirit carnally and our flesh spiritually, to use Bernard's terms (211/166). Narcissism is satisfied and also transcended.

As Kristeva comments, it is not yet thinking (the *cogito*) that constitutes the subject, but rather loving (215/169). Her comments on the writings of Saint Thomas are just as analytically illuminating, though she does come close to apologizing for interpreting the Thomistic conception of self-love as secondary narcissism (217/170). But in fact Kristeva avoids reductivism, in part, of course, because for her psychoanalysis does not need to be reductive. Aquinas's idea that love of others depends on an initial love of self, which indeed constitutes the self as a being capable of love, lends itself almost too well to analytic exploration. He gives an account of passion, which he sees as a form of desiring love, as a kind of gravitational pull towards its object in a quasi-physicalist description that Kristeva links to Lacanian 'drives' ['*pulsions*'], and refers to as 'the angelic treatment of alienation' (235/183).

Mother love

Kristeva's other major contribution to the theorization of passion and subjectivity lies in her discussions of mother love. In 'Freud et l'amour', Kristeva suggests that Freud's famous question: 'What does a woman want' is perhaps no more than an echo of a more fundamental question: 'What does a mother want', 'Que veut une mère?'(HA, 57/41). 'Stabat Mater', first published in 1977 under the title 'Héréthique de l'amour', an essay on the history of representations of the Virgin Mary, is devoted to Christian conceptions of motherhood and femininity. It has an unusual construction: a theoretical analysis, into which is inserted an irregular column of personal, poetic meditation on maternity and childbirth. Here Kristeva discusses what is usually excluded from literature and even more so from theory: the experience of giving birth in all its physical and emotional reality – pain, bodily and psychic, placenta, after-birth, bone marrow, mother's milk. And, even more poignantly, the psychological experience of separation from the child that has been part of the mother's own body for the past nine months. The contrast with Beauvoir's account of the alienation of pregnancy could not be more pointed. Kristeva describes a mother's love as stronger and more real than any romantic passion; referring to maternal sacrifice and devotion, she writes:

> A price that is borne all the more easily since, contrasted with the love that binds a mother to her son, all other 'human relationships' shatter like flagrant simulacra. (HA, 310/247)

Elsewhere, Kristeva has argued that the refusal of maternity by certain feminist groups cannot be generalized. Pregnancy involves a unique experience of personal identity, one of self-doubling and an illusion of completeness:

> Pregnancy is a dramatic ordeal: a splitting of the body, the separation and coexistence of self and other, of nature and consciousness,

of physiology and speech. This fundamental challenge to identity is accompanied by a fantasy of wholeness – of narcissistic self-containment. Pregnancy is a sort of institionalized, socialized and natural psychosis. (*Nouvelles maladies*, 324/219)

And similarly, in implicit contra-distinction to Lacan, she describes childbirth as epitomizing the pain of loss far more powerfully than any failure of sexual relations:

A mother is continuous separation, a division of the very flesh. And consequently, a division of language – and it has always been so.
  Then there is this other abyss that opens up between the body and what had been its inside: there is the abyss between the mother and the child. What relation is there between myself, or even more unassumingly between my body and this internal graft and fold, which, once the umbilical cord has been severed, is an inaccessible other? My body and . . . it. No relation. [. . .] To say that there are no sexual relationships amounts to a meagre assertion in the face of the dazzling light of the abyss between what was mine and is henceforth irremediably strange. Trying to think through that abyss: staggering vertigo. (HA, 317–18/254–5)

Kristeva's essay concludes with a discussion of a possible new ethics that would involve the contribution of woman and, more importantly for our purposes, a brief consideration of the relationship between the symbolic and the biological. Like Lacan, and unlike Anzieu, Kristeva assigns a primary role to language in all her analyses. We have just seen mothers described in terms of separation ('partage') and the division of both flesh and language. Now we see mother-love described as a refuge when language breaks down and biology shows through; mother-love precedes the symbolic, and represents the original safe haven from which we are all in exile:

But it is there too [in maternal love] that the speaking being finds refuge when its symbolic carapace cracks and a crest emerges where speech causes biology to show through: I am thinking of the time of illness, of sexual-intellectual-physical passion, of death . . . (HA, 327/263)

Mourning and melancholia

In *Soleil Noir: dépression et mélancolie* (1987), Kristeva develops further the notion that the symbol instantiates a denial of loss and absence, that is to say, originally, the psychic and biological loss of the mother. From a psychoanalytic point of view, depression arises from an inability to deal with the loss of the mother, a loss which we all share, as we have already seen in our discussion of Lacan, because of the prematurity (psychological as well as physical) of human birth: 'the premature being that we all are' (SN, 25/15). Kristeva refers to this as the 'unfulfilled mourning' (72/61) or the 'impossible mourning for the maternal object' (19/9).

Although Freud and Melanie Klein analyse depression in terms of ambivalence or aggressivity towards the lost object of love, Kristeva prefers an interpretation derived from the contemporary analysis of narcissism, that is as a sign not of hostility but of a wounded, incomplete self whose vulnerability is envisaged as congenital rather than as caused by an external object (21/12). What we are mourning is not so much a specific object as 'la Chose', the Thing, that is to say something indeterminate, ungraspable, 'the real rebels against signification, the pole of attraction and repulsion, the seat of the sexuality from which the object of desire will be detached' (22/13).[36] In this sense there is nothing that we can really blame for our feelings of loss and sadness. And Kristeva is clearly drawn to the views of Klein who envisages sadness precisely as a (perhaps paradoxical) way of countering the worst effects of the potential disintegration of self that primal loss risks producing. According to this view, sadness provides a means of affective cohesion and personal integrity in the face of symbolic breakdown, just as 'schizoid fragmentation' (30/21) is itself a defence against death, somatization, and suicide.

> The discourse of the depressed [...] is the 'normal' surface of a psychotic risk: the sadness that overwhelms us, the retardation that paralyzes us are also a rampart – sometimes the last one – against madness. (53/42)

> Such affective pain, resulting from denial, is a *sense without signification*, but it is used as a screen against death. (61/49)

So the series of defences against the 'pulsion de mort' is long and complex, but in all cases, the pain – be it of depression or schizophrenia – has a positive side in so far as it protects the human organism from self-destruction. Kristeva does not refer here to Freud's notion of the gain to be derived from illness, but a parallel could perhaps be drawn. Unlike schizophrenia, depression is not so much a defence against death as against Eros, which in turn makes the depressive vulnerable to the lure of Thanatos. And it is in this connection that Kristeva theorizes the question of feminine *jouissance*. Like Lacan she describes two kinds of *jouissance* as open to women: phallic *jouissance* which is competitive or identificatory, relates to the symbolic realm, and is experienced through the clitoris; and 'an *other jouissance*', which goes deeper into both psychic and bodily space, is fantasmatically imagined, and is (perhaps controversially) defined as vaginal. This latter form of feminine *jouissance* is what may save us from depression and death in so far as it constitutes a triumph over 'la mere mortifère' and a true openness to the other as a sexual partner who is life-giving in both the psychological and biological senses (*Nouvelles maladies*, 292–3/241–3).

Language

Drawing on Freud's claim that the unconscious does not recognize negation or death, Kristeva argues, together with André Green,[37] that this must mean that the Ego is split into two parts – the one, unconscious, that does not admit negation, though it is permeated through and through by it; the other, the realm of the imaginary and fantasmatic, which both bears witness to death and also counters it in its representations of it (SN, 36–7/26). Kristeva argues that the consequent cathartic effects of language, and in particular literature, need to be utilized by psychoanalysis as a tool which may not match analysis in its powers of elaboration but which offers possibilities of sublimation that should not be ignored:

> If psychoanalysis considers itself more efficacious [than literature] notably in its reinforcement of the ideatory possibilities of the subject, it should also enrich itself by paying greater attention to

these sublimatory solutions of our crises, not to be a neutralizing
anti-depressant, but a lucid counter-depressant. (35/24–5)

Furthermore, the symbol, itself a denial of loss, may be in its turn
denied. And Kristeva explains the difference, in psychoanalytic
terms, between *déni* and *dénégation* (*Verneinung* and *Verleugnung*)
as she understands it, but even without this technical explanation
her main point is clear. If the consoling and therapeutic effects of
language as a screen against loss and absence are rejected by the
depressive patient, the rejection represents an inability to let go
of the lost object, and can engender a form of hatred of it. (36/26).
This entails a consequent refusal of introjected objects and leads
to a deep-seated refusal of self-worth, an inability to enjoy the
pleasures of narcissistic identification, a rejection of all meaning
and significance, and an ultimate refuge in suffering and maso-
chism (61/50).

However, by what looks like a form of *qui perd gagne*, a
certain degree of melancholy or depression can be seen to
enhance creativity by increasing linguistic diversity, subtlety, and
refinement. To put matters simply, it seems as though a measure
of depression is a powerful and even constructive element in
human experience, whereas too much depression needs psychoanalysis and/or medication to help counter it. If we remain
focused on literary language, we may initially be tempted to
suggest that symbolization can master biology up to a point,
but that biology will win in the end. However, this would be
inaccurate, since psychoanalysis is of course itself a process of
symbolization, albeit one which depends on input from an
external source, the analyst.

Psychoanalysis and neuroscience

Soleil Noir, in its discussions of biology, illness, passion, and death,
bears clear witness to Kristeva's determination to refuse the
common dichotomy between psychoanalysis and neurology.
Indeed, although she has not (to my knowledge) participated in
collaborative enterprises with neuroscientists and biologists, of
the sort discussed in my Introduction and attempted by Ricœur,
for example, she is clearly familiar with them, and she seems in

fact to have gone a considerable distance in her attempts to counter the prevalent philosophical opposition between psychoanalysis and science (or psychiatry).

The big question here of course is how depression, melancholy, and sadness are related, and what relationship there is between these psychical phenomena and chemical conditions in the brain. Kristeva does not propose a firm definition of these terms but prefers to use them fairly interchangeably, within a broadly Freudian perspective. But she devotes part of her first two chapters to an account of the neuro-science of depression, in terms of brain function, serotonin, noradrenalin, and 'cholinergic hyperactivity' (SN, 47/35, 51/39).

Her footnotes show her to be apparently up-to-date in her reading of the literature of the time on the pharmacology of depression. Biology and symbolization may be radically separate domains but they are not mutually exclusive, and she describes melancholy as lying 'at the frontier of the biological and the symbolic' (19/65).

For Kristeva, neuroscience in no way interferes with psychoanalysis: on the contrary, knowledge of the way we respond to, process, represent, and express our states of mind (or our passions) cannot come into conflict with knowledge of the brain. However, this does not mean that we have made any real progress to date towards an understanding of the way in which mind and brain are correlated:

> And yet there is nothing today that enables the establishment of some kind of correspondence – aside from a leap – between the biological substratum and the level of *representations*, be they tonal or syntactic, emotional or cognitive, semiotic or symbolic. (SN, 51/39)

In *Les Nouvelles maladies de l'âme* (1993), Kristeva returns to the question of the relationship between neuroscience and psychoanalysis, arguing again that rather than science invalidating psychoanalysis, it can serve as a means of its renewal. The book's title is clearly provocative in its reference to the apparently outmoded notion of the soul, a provocation echoed by the subtitle of the present book. Kristeva starts her text with a rhetorical question: 'Do you have a soul? [. . .] Does the soul still exist?'

(NMA, 9/3), and proceeds to a brief and allusive account of the fortunes of the Greek *psyche* on its path to becoming the Latin *anima*.

Medical doctors of Antiquity, she explains, took over the metaphysical distinction between body and soul, and constructed a parallel set of illnesses, prefiguring modern psychiatry: the 'maladies somatiques' and the 'maladies de l'âme', which included the passions such as sadness, joy, and delirium. Although the parallelism led some thinkers to a monist view of the human being, it led the majority to dualist views that stressed rather the radical separation between psyche and soma. What is more, the localization of the psyche has always posed a problem: is it to be found in the heart, the humours, or the brain?

Kristeva initially situates Freud on the side of philosophical dualism, in so far as the psyche is not reducible to the body and is given priority over the body; but she goes on to show how psychoanalytic theory itself necessarily puts dualism in question through its theory of 'pulsions', its recognition of the way in which sexual desire determines human meaning, and its acknowledgement of multiple elements which transgress the boundaries of body and soul. In the original German, Freud uses *Seele* (soul) apparently interchangeably with *Geist* (mind), though the etymological link is obviously clearer in English than French, just as the link between *Anima* and *âme* is more apparent in French.[38]

Just as for Aristotle, the *anima* was life-giving, so for psychoanalysis, human life depends precisely on the life of the psyche, be it painful, intolerable or jubilant (13/5): 'With Freud, the *psyche* is reborn [...] the soul becomes multiple and polyphonic, the better to serve the 'transubstantiation' of the living body [...] From this valorization of the soul, Freud crafted an indistinctly moral and therapeutic course of action' (14/6).

And, contrary to initial expectations, biology and neurobiology have, Kristeva argues, in their latest advances, drawn on many of the features traditionally associated with the soul, such as the notions of subject, representation, image, and teleonomy. Rather than an 'age-old chimera' (14/6), the soul is, on the contrary, the very place where dualism may be overcome, in so far as it is inseparable from the body, in, for example, passion, or, in more psychoanalytic terms, 'pulsions':

The assault of the neurosciences is not destroying psychoanalysis, but invites us to rework the Freudian notion of the drive: the pivot between 'soma' and 'psyche', between biology and representation. (NMA, 53/30)

Cognitive science and neurobiology, rather than revealing the soul as definitively no more than a mere ghost in the machine, show it to be a necessary element in the latest experimental and theoretical advances. The terminology is of course different, but the arguments are clear. If there is cognitive determination, it does not seem to run in the direction we might have expected, and Kristeva quotes from recently published work by neuroscientists to demonstrate her thesis: 'Cognitive architecture is not limited by the nervous system; on the contrary, the nervous system is penetrated by the cognitive architecture that takes place there' (14/6).[39]

Of course we know, and I have already discussed this in my Introduction, that neuroscientists and philosophers differ radically in their interpretations of the data derived from cognitive and neurological experimentation. The point here is not even to attempt to take up a firm position in what is an extraordinarily technical debate, but rather to demonstrate that the jury is still ultimately out on the mind–body problem, and to explain the continuing appeal of the soul, with its – at first sight surprising – potential to bridge the gap. It was in a slightly different context that Michael Dummett argued that 'We can reestablish communication only by going back to the point of divergence [. . .]. It's no use now, shouting across the gulf',[40] and in their reversion to the notion of soul, philosophers such as Kristeva are attempting precisely such a return.

It would seem, then, that the three psychoanalysts explored in this chapter all have something markedly different to contribute to our understanding of subjectivity and mortality, passion and death. Lacan's account of desire, subjectivity, and mortality reveals their interrelationship in a radical and acute form but, according to some critics, lacks bodily foundation and fails to address death 'in the Real'. Anzieu puts the body in pride of place, and foregrounds the dependence of subjectivity on its bodily foundations, making substantially more room for illness and death than his fellow analysts, but arguably underplays the intensity of love and passion. In Anzieu's universe, pain may be vivid, death may be certain, but love seems a matter of attachment rather than libido, affection rather than passion. Kristeva writes wonderfully well about love as constituting the subject, and about mortality, but despite her powerful account of the experience of maternity and her excursions into neuroscience and biology, the real, physical body, whether ageing, sick or dying, does not always figure decisively in her analyses. We will now turn finally to deconstruction to discover whether the most apparently abstract of theories can produce an account of subjective embodiment which does full justice to passion and death.

5

The Deconstruction of Dualism: Death and the Subject

Jacques Derrida and Jean-Luc Nancy

The gods do not have a body and a soul
But solely a body, and are perfect.
It is the body that takes the place of their soul.
(Pessoa, quoted by Nancy)[1]

Love is a series of scars. 'No heart is as whole as a broken heart', said the celebrated Rabbi Nahman of Bratzlav. (Elie Wiesel, quoted by Nancy)[2]

I think about nothing but death. (Derrida)[3]

Jacques Derrida

Death and the sign

Death has been at the heart of Derrida's meditations on subjectivity, writing, and difference since his first philosophical work in the late 1950s. Indeed, a paper on Husserl delivered in Cerisy la Salle in 1959, entitled '"Genèse et structure" et la phénoménologie',[4] which was probably Derrida's first major incursion into academia, ends – perhaps unexpectedly – with a question about death. In reference to the possibility of the transcendental reduction, Derrida concludes by suggesting that the transcendental ego is called to reflect on the possibility of brute non-meaning in the event of its own death:

> The *transcendental I* that Husserl was tempted to call 'eternal'
> (which in his thought, in any case, means neither infinite nor anhis-
> torical, quite the contrary) is called upon to ask itself about every-
> thing, and in particular about the possibility of the unformed and
> naked factuality of non-sense, in the occurrence, for example, of its
> own death. (ED, 251/211)

And in his Introduction to Husserl's *Origin of Geometry* in 1962,
again in relation to the transcendental subject, Derrida shows how
the loss of meaning from past civilizations and illegible inscrip-
tions points to 'the transcendental sense of death' (OG, 85/88),
although Husserl's own argument rests rather on the claim that
meaning does not depend on any individual consciousness. For the
phenomenologist, the written text remains potentially intelligible
for a transcendental subject, even if not for a specific subject at
any particular moment. Indeed, in Husserl's view, once meaning
has appeared it can never be annihilated (OG, 92/95), though the
written sign itself can of course disappear. But Derrida maintains
that Husserl fails to face up to the implications of his own argument: he relegates the possibility of the loss or destruction of
meaning to that of a contingent accident and denies it any philosophical significance.

Truth, in Husserl's scheme, cannot be seen to depend on its
embodiment, even if it is that embodiment that guarantees its
durability and objectivity. Similarly, Husserl insists on the bewildering assertion that in the event of a total world catastrophe
wiping out all human life, transcendental consciousness would still
remain, since it is not dependent on any individual human consciousness. As would the truths of geometry that are independent
of all facticity. In Derrida's view, Husserl's position is ultimately
untenable and self-contradictory, and depends on a refusal to think
through the implications of his own conception of writing as the
incarnation of truth, rather than a mere, contingent, sensible
phenomenon.

A further ambiguity attaches to the other major reference
to death in this text, in relation to temporality: discussing the
phenomenological privileging of the present moment as an absolute origin, Derrida shows how this conception of time is undermined by Husserl's analysis of the imbrication of the present in
structures of retention and protention which ultimately reveal the

relationship of temporality to historicity, facticity, and death. Husserl, however, prefers to envisage the 'now' as a living present which stretches out indefinitely before us, and refuses to consider death as part of its meaning or its future, thereby relegating death to the status of an extraneous interruption to the temporal flow. It is true however that Husserl declared himself dissatisfied with his own reflections on temporality (OG, 150/137), so we might perhaps view their internal contradictions as evidence of unsolved problems rather than as wilful blindness. Derrida returns to the question of the phenomenological conception of the present again a few years later in 'Violence et métaphysique', an essay on Levinas, where he describes the present as 'violence' in so far as it occludes alterity:

> If the living present, the absolute form of the opening of time to the other in itself, is the absolute form of egological life, and if egoity is the absolute form of experience, then the present, the presence of the present and the present of presence, are originally and forever violence. The living present is originally marked by death. Presence as violence is the meaning of finitude, the meaning of meaning as history. (ED, 195/166)

The relationship between death and the sign, and between death and the present, in the phenomenological account is ineradicably marked by ambivalence and obfuscation. This will be thematized more explicitly, and become much clearer, in *La Voix et le phénomène* of 1967.

1967 was of course the year which launched Derrida onto the French philosophical scene with three major books: *La Voix et le phénomène*, *L'Ecriture et la différence*, and *De la Grammatologie*. The first of these continues his work on Husserl, in particular on the *Logical Investigations* (*Recherches logiques*, 1900–1). In it, Derrida explores in some detail Husserl's conception of language, presence, and meaning and analyses the ways in which Husserl's own arguments are at certain key points self-undermining. Once again, the relationship with death is significant: the very notion of presence implies my death in so far as it continues beyond, after, and without me:

> To think of presence as the universal form of transcendental life is to open myself to the knowledge that in my absence, beyond my

empirical existence, before my death and after my death, *the present is* [...]. The relationship with *my death* [...] thus lurks in this determination of being as presence, ideality, the absolute possibility of repetition. The possibility of the sign is this relationship with death. (VP, 60/54)

In other words, the sign implies my death (or the possibility of my disappearance) in so far as it must be able to continue to signify without reference to me, and it is for this reason effaced or undermined in metaphysical thought which does not wish to face its implications – and intimations – of mortality.

It is not however language and signification that bring me into contact with mortality, or in some way endanger me; the possibility of death is there from the outset and is inseparable from my being: '*I am* therefore originally means *I am mortal. I am immortal* is an impossible proposition' (60–1/54). The proposition is not meaningless, but it is both absurd and false. My mortality is already implicit in all my pronouncements: 'My death is structurally necessary to the pronouncing of the *I*' (108/96). Time and mortality enable subjectivity rather than limit it. As Levinas also argues, it is the vulnerability of the subject and its very subjection that marks its freedom. And this is one of the inevitable consequences that, in Derrida's view, Husserl persistently refuses (or fails) to draw from his own premises. 'Violence et métaphysique' also considers the question of the relationship between alterity, language and death; the very otherness of the other depends on finitude and mortality: 'The other cannot be what it is, infinitely other, except in finitude and mortality (mine and its)' (ED, 169/143). This poses problems, in Derrida's view, not only for Husserl but also for Levinas in so far as the infinite alterity of death and the infinite alterity of God (as positivity and presence) are radically incompatible, but these are part of another story.

It has already become clear that death is a perennial preoccupation in Derrida's work and lies at the heart of his thinking, whether this be on signification, temporality, alterity or subjectivity. Like absence, difference, writing, and imagination, death is one of the constantly effaced and suppressed poles which prevent presence, identity, speech, and perception – as well as life – from ever being pure and uncontaminated. Death is the truth of life, in all senses of the expression. The texts so far referred to have all been concerned with phenomenology, which was of course one of the major philosophical traditions with – and against – which Derrida defined his own way of thinking. We will now look at some other key texts where mortality plays a significant part in Derrida's work on subjectivity, on friendship, and on psychoanalysis, as well as at his obituaries for friends and colleagues, collected in *Chaque fois unique, la fin du monde*.

Death and psychoanalysis

Death is vital, of course, to discussions of psychoanalysis, in particular in relation to the death drive and the archive, and is first foregrounded in 'Freud et la scène de l'écriture' (1964) and later in texts such as 'Spéculer – sur Freud' in *La Carte postale* (1980), *Mal d'Archive* (1995), *Résistances* (1996) and *Etats d'âme de la psychanalyse*, (2000). In 'Freud et la scène de l'écriture', Derrida both sketches out the relationship of deconstruction to psychoanalysis and explores what Freud has to say about consciousness and memory in his 'Note on the Mystic Writing Pad' of 1925 (in the French translation we read 'magic').

Derrida is keen to explain how his conception of the historical suppression (G: 'Unterdrükung', Fr: 'répression') of writing since Plato is, despite appearances, not a psychoanalytic notion. Rather than understanding it by analogy with psychoanalytic repression (G: 'Verdrängung', Fr: 'refoulement'), it is itself the key to understanding how individual repression is possible (ED, 294/248). Derrida's main preoccupation, unlike Freud's, is not the individual psyche, it is the broader, philosophical question of the power of metaphysical thinking in Western history (broadly equatable with what he terms logocentrism). His essay sets out to show how the apparent opposition between the pleasure principle and the reality principle is, like all the major oppositions that interest him, in fact rather a relationship of interdependence and even complicity, and closely entwined with the relation between life and death:

> The difference between the pleasure principle and the reality principle, for example, is not uniquely, nor primarily, a distinction, an

exteriority, but rather the original possibility, within life, of the detour, of difference (*Aufschub*), and of the economy of death. (ED, 295/249)

Derrida is concerned to show how Freud's conception of the mnesic trace, left behind in the neuronal pathways of the brain after any psychic event, and particularly after a traumatic incident, is not a simple matter of an original inscription which may later be reactivated by similar events and indeed be all the easier to follow on successive occasions. On the contrary, and in a far more complex manner, Derrida argues, the apparently 'original' facilitation ('frayage') in the neural pathways, is itself already repeated, that is to say there is no *tabula rasa* in the brain but rather a system of pre-existing traces. Moreover, extreme pain, trauma or death cannot be easily processed by the psyche, and their effects may well be deferred for a later date. So the simple notion of inscription and revival is unable to cope with the complexities of psychic reality:

> Beyond a certain quantity, pain, the threatening origin of the psyche, must be deferred [*différée*], like death, for it can ruin psychical 'organization'.

> Isn't death already the principal of a life that can defend itself against death only through difference, repetition, reserve? (ED, 301, 300/254)

Life, Derrida shows, may well try to protect itself through repetition, the trace, and *différance*. But this does not mean that there is a pure, uncontaminated, original life that needs protection from later onslaughts: life is itself from the outset interwoven with death and deferral:

> Life must be thought of as a trace before Being may be determined as presence. This is the only condition on which we can say that life *is* death, that repetition and the beyond of the pleasure principal are originary and congenital to precisely that which they transgress. (ED, 302/255)

The paradoxical appearance of such statements depends, Derrida explains, on a vulgar concept of the present as a series of 'nows' which he has already deconstructed in his work on Husserl. Hence he can argue that 'the delay is originary' without absurdity (ED, 302/255). Derrida's paper concludes with an explicit statement of the relationship between the subject and writing or representation. The subject comprises a system of relations between layers, as in the magic writing pad itself where nothing is ever fully effaced; there is no simple, univocal subject:

> The 'subject' of writing does not exist if we mean by that some sovereign solitude of the author. The subject of writing is a *system* of relations between strata: the Mystic Pad, the psyche, society, the world. Within that scene, on that stage, the punctual simplicity of the classical subject is not to be found. (ED, 335/285)

Freud's own conclusions are less bold than Derrida's: he identifies mechanical representation with death, and ultimately opposes the magic writing pad to human memory, with which he has previously compared it. In this way Freud fails, in Derrida's view, to draw the conclusions from his own analyses which point to a much closer relationship between mechanical representation and memory, death and life. Rather than relegating the writing pad to being a mere material support without spontaneity, and thereby opposing it to the spontaneity of memory, Freud might have drawn the contrary conclusion: that the resemblance between memory and the writing pad points rather to the incomplete spontaneity of memory:

> Far from the machine being a pure absence of spontaneity, its *resemblance* to the psychical apparatus, its existence and its necessity bear witness to the finitude of the mnemic spontaneity that is thus supplemented. The machine – and, consequently, representation – is death and finitude *within* the psyche. (ED, 336/286)

The mode of inscription of the magic writing pad is not extraneous to memory, its resemblance is constitutive of memory, just as death does not interrupt life but rather founds it (337/287). So Freud, like Husserl, occludes death, and along with it the relationship to sex, despite his awareness of the unavoidable relationship between sex and writing, via the spilling of ink or semen, discussed in 'Inhibition, Symptom and Anxiety' of 1926 (SE XX; ED,

38/11). This will be foregrounded more clearly in Derrida's later explorations of Freud's texts.

'Spéculer – sur "Freud"' picks up discussion of the complexities of 'Beyond the Pleasure Principle' in 'La scène de l'écriture' and explores them in more detail. Derrida sets out to analyse further the puzzling contradictions of Freud's account of the fraught relationship between the pleasure principle and the reality principle, between life and death, disentangling the knots of the text to show how death is the 'end' of life, not primarily in the sense of conclusion but rather in the sense of aim: it is the point of life, it permeates life rather than simply causing life to cease (287/269); it is a law of life, not an accident (377/354). Pleasure and Reality are ideal limits, as destructive and 'mortelles' as one another (304–5/284–5).

Derrida points out that the *Lustprinzip* is translated as 'pleasure principle' but that *Lust* also means desire and *jouissance*. So, given the interdependence of the reality principle and the pleasure principle, when Freud insists that the sexual drives are hard to educate and to make conform to the reality principle, this in effect amounts to the claim that sexual desire cannot be bound even by pleasure or *jouissance*. This ultimately means that sex refuses its own conservation and exposes itself to death (306/286/7). None the less, despite the inextricable interweaving of pleasure and reality, sex and death, which Freud has progressively demonstrated, he remains determined to retain his original opposition between 'pulsions de vie' and 'pulsions de mort', and indeed declares himself a dualist on the issue, in implacable opposition to what he describes as Jung's monism. In this way, as Derrida demonstrates, Freud's conclusions are once again resolutely if unintentionally incompatible with the implications of his argument.

These meditations on the relationship between the pleasure principle, the reality principle, and the death drive are the major constants of Derrida's work on psychoanalysis, be it Freudian or Lacanian. Derrida frequently finds Freud unwilling to accept the implications of what he has himself uncovered, and describes him as struggling vainly in the toils of what appears to be an enactment of what he is describing, such as the compulsion to repeat. *Mal d'Archive* in particular returns to the question first raised in 'Freud et la scène de l'écriture', that of the archive and the relationship between memory and inscription. It is of course finitude and death that create the need for an archive: nothing persists forever, not life, nor love, nor memory, and the archive is charged with preserving what would otherwise be lost.[5]

However, this account is far too simple, and Derrida shows how the desire to construct an archive is related to power, to the compulsion to repeat, and thereby ultimately to the death drive, which means that there is an element of self-destruction inherent in the archive itself (24/10). This is one of the senses of 'mal' in *Mal d'Archive*: not just sickness but also longing – the longing of homesickness (*mal du pays*) – and, like all nostalgia, involving a yearning for an impossible return to an absolute beginning, prior to division and repetition (142/91). And Derrida holds Freudian psychoanalysis as itself partly responsible for fostering such a 'trouble d'archive', or disturbance in the archive, in so far as it encourages belief in a pre-lapsarian origin. Whereas, of course, according to Derrida's conception of writing, representation and temporality, the archive is only possible because it inscribes something that was always already fissured and iterable (153/100).This is the secret that psychoanalysis is burning simultaneously to reveal and to conceal.[6]

Résistances: de la psychanalyse (1996) continues Derrida's exploration of the aporias and internal contradictions of psychoanalysis. It contains three essays: an eponymous essay on Freud and resistance to analysis which Derrida locates as coming from within analysis itself; an essay on Lacan which develops the discussion of the archive and also relates conversations between Derrida and Lacan on the subject of death; and an essay on Foucault which continues the exploration of the pleasure principle. All are concerned to some degree with death and subjectivity, but do not add any radically new approach. *Etats d'âme de la psychanalyse* (2000) also focuses on death – on the death drive and on the death penalty. It constitutes an invited address by Derrida to the Estates General of Psychoanalysis, founded by René Major, in the Sorbonne on July 2000.

Derrida raises the major question of the relationship between psychoanalysis and ethics, law, and politics, with which it has not yet concerned itself (EAP, 21/245). Is there, he asks, anything *beyond* the death instinct? If this instinct lies at the heart of cruelty, is cruelty therefore ineradicable? And he suggests that psychoanalysis may currently be the only discourse able to deal with the question (12/240), but also that until now psychoanalysis has not shown itself willing to do so. New declarations of human rights, condemning genocide, crimes against humanity and 'cruel and unusual punishments' (55/262) such as the death penalty, have changed the shape of the relationship between the subject and the citizen, and between citizenship and democracy. If psychoanalysis, which is as 'mortal' as any aspect of civilization (27/247), does not take these mutations on board, it risks not only failing to make a much-needed contribution to political analysis, but also being left behind as the world moves on without it.

Freud himself was certainly concerned to consider human cruelty in times of war, not only in 'Thoughts for the times on war and death', of 1915, but also in his discussions with Einstein of 1931–2, published under the title 'Why War?', in which, as Derrida puts it, two specialists of *psyche* and *physis* collaborate in an attempt to understand what drives nations to attempt to destroy each other, in particular in a progressive, post-Enlightenment, civilization (35/252). If the death drive (and the 'drive of power and cruelty') is deeper-rooted and older than the principles of pleasure and reality, then arguably no politics will be able to eradicate it.

As Freud himself proposed, it is not possible to extirpate cruelty and aggression, but they may be counteracted indirectly in two ways: first, by the antagonistic force of love (Eros), and secondly by educating some men to combat their own aggressivity in the light of reason, and to lead others in the direction of civilization (75/272). For Freud, of course, the death instinct cannot be eradicated, not merely because it is deep rooted, but also because it lies at the heart of life itself, and is the dark side of the life force. This is why Freud strives constantly, against what seems to be all the evidence, to understand the death drive and its destructive powers in terms of the economy of life.

In fact, Derrida argues, there is no way that psychoanalysis can be expected to intervene in ethics and politics: its role is descriptive and explanatory, not prescriptive; any step beyond the death drive will be a step into the unknown and even the impossible, via what he says 'classical humanists' would call freedom and responsibility, and which necessarily involves a 'leap', a discontinuity, and a heteronomy (86/278). And perhaps, Derrida concludes, this might be part of a future task for psychoanalysis tomorrow: to join in the move from constative to performative, from 'is' to 'ought', in full knowledge of the leap that is involved; and perhaps then, still harder, to sign up to the difficult (or impossible) move towards an unconditional and impossible 'beyond of all cruelty' (87/278). In the last analysis, Derrida has used the invitation to address the newly founded Estates General to invite psychoanalysis to join deconstruction in its quest for an impossible ethics and justice.

Mortality and ethics

We will turn now to three texts where Derrida discusses death more directly, 'Donner la mort'.[7] *Apories,* and *Chaque fois unique, la fin du monde.* 'Donner la mort' his paper from the Royaumont conference of 1990, meditates on the writings of Jan Patočka in relation to the thought of Heidegger, Levinas, and Kierkegaard. It explores issues of responsibility, ethics, the secret, alterity, and death. In the context of our discussion, its most significant contribution is to the theorization of the relationship between mortality and individual singularity, or subjectivity, to use a term that Derrida prefers to avoid because of its humanist history. Derrida relates Patočka's belief that it is awareness of death that enables our freedom to Heidegger's 'being-for-death', but without assimilating them. For Patočka, looking death in the face is what produces, however paradoxically, the 'triumph of life' and, by the same token, responsibility and freedom. But Derrida is wary of the notion of triumph, which risks resembling the jubilatory phase of mourning, in which the survivor refuses to recognize his own mortality in that of the other. Derrida also compares Patočka's perspective with what Heidegger has to say about the specificity and uniqueness of individual mortality: the question of what it might mean to die for someone else is explored at length by Heidegger, and the impossibility of such an act is seen as the key to human singularity and responsibility. It is my mortality that makes me unique; in a sense the very limits of my finitude and facticity make me irreplaceable (DM, 45/45). My self is only possible because of my mortality.[8] And Derrida contrasts this Heideggerian conception of mortality with Levinas's insistence that it is precisely the mortality of the *other* that makes me responsible, and that is, indeed, logically prior to my own death.[9]

Patočka's view is subtly different from both of these, in part because of his Christianity: he conceives responsibility as a renunciation of self in the face of the other, and as an irreplaceable love for the other, which derives from death, or rather an awareness of death. It is my death and finitude which, although common to everyone, also make me irreplaceable, entirely singular, and this lies at the heart of my responsibility. 'In this sense', Derrida writes, 'only a mortal can be responsible'; 'Only a mortal can give', and he can give only to another mortal.[10] Derrida links these notions to his own conception of the paradoxical effect of language and writing. As he showed already in *Grammatology*, writing, with its essential iterability and its inevitable reduction of singularity in its obliteration of the proper name within a system, is precisely what constitutes the subject at the same time as effacing it.[11]

It is what at first appears as mere supplement that emerges as constitutive. In his discussion of Patočka, Derrida returns to his meditation on language as depriving me of my singularity – as soon as I speak I forego my uniqueness in the language of others.[12] My responsibility may be unique, but its expression can never be. This produces the inevitable aporia that responsibility must – ultimately – bypass speech in a form of silence and secret that contravenes all usual conceptions of the ethical. And for Patočka, responsibility also implies culpability: as a mortal, I am finite and responsible, and am thereby never equal to the infinite goodness of the gift:

> I am guilty inasmuch as I am responsible. What gives me my singularity, namely death and finitude, is what makes me unequal to the infinite goodness of the gift that is also the first appeal to responsibility. Guilt is inherent in responsibility because responsibility is always unequal to itself: one is never responsible enough. (DM, 55/51)

Much of Derrida's essay is concerned with Patočka's response to the story of Abraham's sacrifice of Isaac, and its differences from

Kierkegaard's account. For Kierkegaard, the necessary generalizability of the ethical reduces it and renders it inadequate to deal with the unique and absolute responsibility of the singular. Indeed, he describes the ethical as a temptation. Abraham's willingness to sacrifice his son Isaac involves a rejection of the ethical in favour of the absolute singularity of his relationship with God.

As Derrida points out in a footnote, Levinas strongly opposed the Kierkegaardian interpretation of the story, and suggested a radically different reading in which the ethical precisely instantiates the singular: it is the uniqueness of the subject which, in Levinas's account, makes Abraham pause in his sacrifice.[13] But this is another story.

Derrida leads us progressively to an understanding of the aporetic gulf between ethics and responsibility that can be summed up in the paradoxical notion of the irresponsibility of ethics.[14] He explores this at some length through an analysis of Kierkegaard's account of the story of Abraham, whose paradoxes woven around responsibility and irresponsibility, morality and immorality, are quite extraordinary.

But what is important for our purposes is not so much the analysis of the relation of ethics to duty, or even the way in which my response to the other necessarily involves the sacrifice of ethics. It is rather a matter of the way in which language (in its generality) deprives me of my singularity (DM, 61/60), just as ethics (in its generality) is unable to cope with the specificity and uniqueness of the other (68/67). Abraham accepts the death of his only son, the ultimate sacrifice, an absolute loss (96/95); and it is this relationship to death and suffering, without hope of reward or return, that marks the end of the old order, suspends the economy of exchange, and replaces justice by grace (105/113). Derrida is, in theory at least, still analysing the work of Patočka, but his own sympathies seem to be aroused by this version of Christianity, just as he was struck by Freud's allusion to love ('love thy neighbour as thyself', *Etats d'âme*, p. 74) as an (indirect) antidote to the cruelty of the death drive.

In his explorations of Husserl, Freud, Heidegger, Levinas, and Patočka, it is invariably the link between mortality (be it my own death or that of the other) and the self or subject in all its limitations and finitude that provides Derrida with his most poignant and thought-provoking analyses. What these analyses all have in common is their focus on death as intimately involved in subjectivity. It is our mortality that makes us free, responsible subjects, able to give, to decide, to make sacrifices, indeed to die for others. We are mortal because we live in time, not in eternity, and this constitutes also our singularity as subjects. Subject to time, subject to death.

Apories develops further the link between mortality and human subjectivity in an extended analysis of Heidegger. Derrida is concerned to explore the multiple senses of Heidegger's notion that death is the possibility of the impossible for *Dasein*, as well as to question the barriers Heidegger erects between authentic and inauthentic, human and animal, philosophical and biological forms of death. Derrida shows how aspects of death that Heidegger sees as specific to *Dasein* are in fact not unique, any more than the notion of the possibility of the impossible can be restricted to death, even though this may be its paradigmatic form. He spends a long time disentangling these questions, and concludes that if death is *Dasein*'s ultimate possibility, it is, paradoxically, precisely the possibility of non-existence, or, expressed in an aporia, the possibility of the impossible, the end of the world (for *Dasein*):

> The impossibility that is possible for *Dasein*, is indeed, that there not be or that there no longer be *Dasein*: that precisely what is possible become impossible, from then on no longer appearing as such: nothing less than the end of the world, with each death. (*Apories*, 131/75)

And this is, of course, the notion that is taken up in the title of the collection of Derrida's obituary texts in 2003, which we will examine shortly. In *Apories*, Derrida points out that – *pace* Heidegger – 'death' can stand in for a whole series of concepts which are only possible as impossible: love, friendship, the gift, the other, witnessing, and hospitality (137/79).[15] These are, of course, some of the many figures of the unconditional that have been subject to his deconstructive exploration, and perhaps we might say that it is death that lies at the heart of all of them, death and *différance*, which means that the gift, for example, can never be purely given, or that self and other cannot be ultimately and definitively separated. And in a sense, we seem to have come here full circle, for it was death that proved itself the unexpected and uninvited guest in the phenomenological enterprise, just as it is now *différance* that explains the inescapable permeability of 'opposites' (such as life and death, friend and enemy) that we might wish to hold apart. And Heidegger too, of course, is subject to this same impossibility of maintaining water-tight distinctions, in this context most importantly between human and animal, and between different conceptions of death and modes of dying. For if Heidegger maintains that only man as *Dasein* has a conception of death and a word for 'death', Derrida begs to differ, arguing – 'against, or without, Heidegger' – (A, 132/75) that animals too have a relationship to death, war, murder, and mourning, even if they do not have a language for it.[16]

Moreover, our human language does not guarantee the purity of our relationship to death, 'as such', or indeed to the 'other' as such: our own relationship to mortality and alterity is necessarily traversed by inauthenticity (to use Heidegger's terminology), and untruth (to use Derrida's). This is why, in the last analysis, the apparent disagreement between Levinas and Heidegger on the question of the primacy of my death versus the death of the other, necessarily loses its absolute pertinence. Since I am constituted from the outset by my relationship with the other, as s/he is by his/her relationship with me, the question of primacy can never be resolved.

And what is more, Heidegger's distinctions between modes of death (sterben: death; ableben: demise; verenden: perishing), some of which are restricted to *Dasein*, others of which are open to animals and to man as animal, are also based on unsustainable frontiers which Heidegger seeks to erect between animal and human, and between the human as animal and as *Dasein* (132/73). Indeed, Derrida maintains, as he did already thirty years earlier in 'Les Fins de l'homme', Heidegger cannot keep his philosophical thinking free of any of the elements which he would wish to see as extraneous to it, be these biological, anthropological, or theological. And Derrida draws up a brief list of parallels that can be drawn between Heidegger's thinking and that of Christian thinkers such as Augustine, Pascal, and Kierkegaard:

Despite all the distance taken from anthropo-theology, or indeed from Christian onto-theology, the analytic of death in *Being and Time* reinscribes or reimprints all the essential motifs of such onto-theology, through a repetition that still digs away at its originarity, right down to its ontological foundation, whether it concerns the fall, the *Ver-fallen*, into the inauthenticity of relaxation or leisure, or the *sollicitudo*, the *cura*, and the care (*Sorge*), or sin, originary guilt (*Schuldigsein*) and anxiety ... Neither the language nor the process of this analytic of death is possible without the Christian, or even the Judeo-Christian-Islamic, experience of death to which it testifies. Without this event and the irreducible history to which it testifies. (A, 138–9/80)

Heidegger's best efforts can never keep him free from 'contamination' by precisely those elements he is most keen to exclude.[17]

Impossible mourning

Apories is probably Derrida's most concerted attempt to grapple directly with the philosophical questions surrounding mortality. We will now look finally at some less theoretical and arguably more approachable texts. *Chaque fois unique, la fin du monde* is a collection of obituary speeches and letters written by Derrida between 1981 and 2003. The collection was originally published in English as *The Work of Mourning*, edited by Pascale-Anne Brault and Michel Naas, but, despite some misgivings, Derrida allowed a French version to appear in 2003. The work has a brief Avant-propos by Derrida, and a lengthy Introduction by the editors. Here we see in practice much of what Derrida has already discussed on a theoretical level, and in particular the uncertainties, aporias, and ambiguities associated with death and mourning. As Derrida writes in *Politiques de l'amitié*, all friendship is permeated and shadowed from the outset by the prospect of death: the law of friendship dictates that one friend will always die before the other. There is 'no friendship without this knowledge of finitude'; no friendship can escape time and mortality and this is what gives it its poignancy and intensity:

> *Philia* begins with the possibility of survival. Survival is the other name for a mourning whose possibility is never to be awaited ... The

anguished apprehension of mourning [. . .] plunges the friend into mourning before mourning. This apprehension weeps before the lamentation, it weeps for death before death [. . .]. Hence surviving is at once the essence, the origin and the possibility of, the condition of possibility of friendship; it is the grieved act of loving. (PA, 31/14)

In this way, for Derrida, mourning both precedes and follows death: we are always mourning. Indeed, 'originary mourning' is established at the origin of all relationships: 'Love or friendship would be nothing other than the passion, the endurance, and the patience of this work' (CFU, 182/146). And Derrida spends time repeatedly puzzling over the nature of mourning, taking issue with Freud in particular for his view of mourning as a way of coming to terms with loss and grief by means of an internalization of the loved one and a detachment of libido from him or her. In the first place, the status of mourning is already complex and problematic for Freud, since in his view there are healthy and unhealthy ways of effecting internalization, and the 'work of mourning' – referred to by Derrida as 'this confused and terrible expression *le travail du deuil*' (CFU, 242/200) – precisely involves a gradual cessation of grief.

Secondly, and closely related, Derrida is concerned to preserve what he calls 'fidelity' to the person who has died, which ideally would entail a loving internalization and remembrance of the friend, at the same time as respect for her alterity. Not surprisingly, these prove to be, at least theoretically, incompatible. And this incompatibility – 'the unbearable paradox of fidelity' (198/159) – permeates all aspects of mourning, so that in addressing our words directly to the dead, for example, we aspire to honour their memory but thereby risk taking them over as our own, and on some level denying the radical nature of their disappearance in a form of 'dénégation': 'two infidelities, an impossible choice' (70/45).

So grief is a minefield for Derrida, and so are obituary speeches, which must simultaneously reflect the singularity of the friend who has died, yet at the same time respect certain conventions. This makes speaking of the dead in a satisfactory manner impossible, yet it is clearly also necessary, and we have another example of an impossible yet unconditional demand: to speak well of the dead. And a further difficulty arises from the fact that the friend is not the only beloved person (ever) to have died: the element of repetition within what is a unique event may seem to undermine its singularity, but an alternative is clearly unthinkable.

This is beautifully expressed in the title of the collection: 'chaque fois unique, la fin du monde' – which captures the paradox of repetition ('chaque fois') and uniqueness, a paradox that is itself not restricted to death and mourning but which takes on a particular poignancy in that context. Derrida's meditations on mourning begin with the question of how to speak, and develop through linguistic concerns such as 'voice' and citation. Derrida continually asks: how can the I ever speak of the other – or indeed, not speak of the other – when the voice of the I is not distinct from the other's voice and yet is not the other's voice? In each of his various texts on mourning Derrida employs an intense and even uncanny form of intertextuality, where direct citation is interwoven within his own, intimate, elegiac writing.

As with so many Derridean preoccupations, language is undeniably troubled by mourning, but all his obituary texts share the same fundamental concerns with responsibility, fidelity, and the 'possibility of impossibility'. The challenge here is precisely to make the impossible a possibility in mourning; that is, to internalize what can never be internalized (for the dead may be 'within us' but they are 'not ours'); and also to establish a language for the unspeakable: how to mourn and how to speak in mourning, how to deal with the intolerable choice between what appear to be the two betrayals of silence and speech, 'Speaking is impossible, but so too would be remaining silent or absenting oneself or refusing to share one's sadness' (*Mémoires pour Paul de Man*, 15).[18]

This leads to the central paradox of mourning: that success appears to fail and failure to succeed (MPD, 54/35). This means that if we achieve in some way the successful (but impossible) internalization of the other, we in fact fail, because then the other is no longer other – we are no longer respecting the other's 'otherness' if we draw him or her into ourselves. And conversely, if we fail (which we are bound to), we succeed, because we have retained respect for the other as other. This is what makes 'true mourning' impossible for Derrida (MPD, 51/31): the possibility of internalizing what can never be internalized because of the infinite alterity of the other. Essentially, authentic responsibility to the other demands that s/he remain other, as Derrida states in 'Donner la mort': *'Tout autre est tout autre'*. But as he explains in *Mémoires pour Paul de Man*, this is not how mourning is usually conceived:

> Memory and interiorization: since Freud, this is how the 'normal' work of mourning is often described. It entails a movement in which an interiorizing idealization takes in or upon itself the body and voice of the other, the other's visage and person. (MPD, 54/34)

Derrida is painfully aware that any process of internalization is necessarily in tension with a concern for fidelity and responsibility, and he poses the question explicitly in his obituary of Roland Barthes: 'To keep alive, within oneself: is this the best sign of fidelity?' (CFU, 61/36). In *Mémoires*, Derrida maintains that it may be, but only if we are conscious that the friend is 'gone forever, irremediably absent, annulled [. . .] for it would be unfaithful to delude oneself into believing that the other living *in us* is living *in itself* (43/21) 'Phantoms: the concept of the other in the same [. . .] the completely other, dead, living in me' (CFU, 67/41–2). Thus, the impasse for Derrida's mourning is located in this problem of internalization, this challenge of making the impossible a possibility. However, in his efforts to maintain fidelity, to be *true to the original* (the other) in mourning, Derrida does perhaps approach a type of 'true mourning' which seems to offer a partial resolution to the problem, in the sense that in failing to unblock the aporia of how to mourn and how to speak in mourning, he manages at least to bear witness to the impossible choice between the two infidelities.

Derrida's 'impossible mourning' turns ultimately on the question of responsibility, both responsibility *for* the other (in the Levinasian ethical sense) and responsibility *to* the other (in the Derridean sense of fidelity). Of course, as we have just seen in *Apories*, impossibility is a Derridean preoccupation which extends far beyond mourning; it is clear throughout his writings that impossibility is a crucial aspect of his many accounts of responsibility, particularly in 'Donner la mort', where he explores the extremely complicated history of the responsible self. It is the struggle between silence and speaking, between the desire for presence and the acceptance of absence which dominates Derrida's reflections in *Chaque fois unique*.

Throughout his texts, Derrida is consumed by his search for the most appropriate way in which to mourn. He recognizes the double-bind which frames all his reflections on death and mourning, the conflict which persists between 'respecting the other's infinite remove' and the desire to speak of the other, to mourn for the other. However, his obituary texts make progressively clear that Derrida's own belief is that the greater betrayal would be silence.

In his search for a language of mourning, Derrida regularly looks to the words of the other, not to interpret their words, but rather to integrate them verbatim into his texts, for language is ultimately the means by which the living self assimilates the dead other in mourning. In *Adieu*, Derrida's funeral oration for Levinas delivered at the Pantin cemetary, he says, for example, 'allow me once again to let Emmanuel Levinas speak', and uses his friend's own writings to explore and respond to the implications of his death. Death is described by Levinas as a non-response met first in the face of the other, it is the other's death which is primary for me.[19] Death is not an empirical part of our facticity, Levinas maintains, that is to say, we do not understand the universality of death through a process of induction. Rather, the death of the other is an inherent part of my relationship with him; indeed, 'I am responsible for the other in so far as he is mortal'.[20] 'It is my mortality, my condemnation to death [...] that constitute that absurdity that makes possible the gratuitousness of my responsibility for the other'.[21] 'The death of the other affects me in my very self-identity.'[22]

In these phrases taken from *Adieu*, Derrida is not speaking unequivocally in his own voice, but rather, as he so often does, using Levinas's words to explore ideas he is evidently fascinated by but cannot fully sanction. With his application of what he refers to as 'the violence of the quotation', Derrida steers a path between the desire to speak and his concern with the inadequacy of words when mourning the other. He thereby creates a language of mourning which allows him to speak the unspeakable; and, most importantly, to do so while simultaneously fulfilling responsibility and maintaining fidelity to the other. Rather than bemoan the unintelligibility of death, Derrida's work on mourning begins to construct a way of dealing with it. He takes on the task of how to speak of mourning in a society which traditionally silences grief. Mourning is a genre governed by conventions of silence; it is fundamentally viewed as a 'private' experience, and to express mourning publicly, to break the silence and speak of this private experience is, according to some, itself a form of betrayal. To return once more – in an act of fidelity of our own to Derrida's words:

> One should not develop a taste for mourning, and yet mourn we must.

> We *must*, but we must not like it, mourning, that is, mourning itself, if such a thing exists: not to like or love through one's own tear but only through the other, and every tear is from the other, the friend, the living, as long as we ourselves are living, reminding us, in holding life, to hold onto it. (CFU, 141/110)

It is clear by now how intimately intertwined passion and death, love, friendship, and grief, are for Derrida. And he faces head-on the paradoxes, aporias, infidelities, and impossibilities that such an intertwining inevitably brings with it. His texts certainly feel as though they bring us close to the heart of the problem of death in so far as this can be equated with the problem of grief or with the philosophical question of the nature of human mortality, but whether they bring us close to an understanding of death as it is for the dying themselves is another matter. The body that appears in Derrida's texts of mourning is still primarily the body of the survivor, his tears, his sobs, his speaking voice. If we want to come closer to the body of the dying man himself, we must turn to the works of Jean-Luc Nancy.

Love of the body and sexual difference

But before leaving Derrida for Nancy we must spend a little longer on the body, not now in its mortality but in its erotic and amorous relations. As we have seen, Derrida writes frequently, indeed incessantly, about love and desire, passion and friendship. In *Politiques de l'amitié* he explores and questions a wide variety of traditional understandings of forms of love and friendship – Eros, agape, and philia, for example – just as he dismantles the identification of friendship with fraternity. His texts on love and desire – 'Envois' in *La Carte postale* is another important example – all refuse the limitations that the binary oppositions of cultural history and the policing of Eros[23] attempt to impose on our understanding of ourselves in relation to others. Sexual difference is another area where Derridean *différance* naturally comes into play, and indeed he claimed to consider it to lie at the heart of more formal, philosophical theorizations of difference.

Furthermore, his various 'Geschlecht' essays precisely explore the implications of Heidegger's exclusion of sexual difference from the domain of Dasein, which is limited to what Heidegger deems the proper realm of ontology.[24] It is true of course that radical feminist philosophers have made excellent use of *différance* to undermine established gender oppositions, and Judith Butler in particular has further unsettled the distinction between sex and gender, but Derrida's own role in this area of thought is arguably less clear, though *Glas* is a potentially important contribution to the debate.

But to mention *Glas* is implicitly to draw attention to the problem: the text is undeniably among Derrida's most difficult of access, and constitutes an allusive, dense, and teasing exploration, in parallel columns, of the writings of Hegel and Jean Genet. As so often, Derrida's discussions of sexual difference are indirect, mediated through his analyses of the texts of others, not only Heidegger, Hegel, and Genet, but also Levinas and Nietzsche in particular.

What role, then, does the body itself play in Derrida's texts, and in particular in those that concern love and sex? When he writes about Freud and Lacan, sexuality is inevitably an issue, and we have already looked, for example, at his discussion of the way in which the so-called Pleasure Principle ('Lustprinzip') is – in German – a matter of 'jouissance' and 'désir' ('Lust') as much as of pleasure (CP, 293/274). But this is arguably a textualized sexuality, a linguistic concern, if I may express myself in this way, it does not necessarily implicate the body in its physicality, any more than Derrida's professed 'desire' for presence involves physical desire. And again, even when Derrida links sex and death in *La Carte postale*, the very physicality of the image militates paradoxically against its being read in any more than a metaphorical fashion:

> I'd like to die. In the mountains, a lake, long before you. This is what I dream of, and this postal sorting nauseates me. Before my death, I would give orders. If you're not there, my body will be pulled out of the lake and burned, my ashes are sent to you. [...] And then you would enjoy mixing my ashes with what you eat (morning coffee, brioche, 5 o'clock tea, etc.) After a certain dose, you would start to go numb, to fall in love with yourself, I would watch you slowly advance toward death [...]. While waiting for you, I'm going to sleep, you are always there, my sweet love. (CP, 211/196)

Derrida's repeated fantasy of identification and reflection with the beloved – 'it suffices that you undress for me to see myself naked [...] and increasingly I metempsychose myself from you' (CP, 155/142) – works here through a kind of incorporation, but the dream of his lover devouring Derrida's cremated ashes mixed with coffee and brioche poetically and humorously resists a literal reading and can only be understood as an imaginative representation of a psychical identification.

Jean-Luc Nancy

In her 'Appendice' to Nancy's *58 indices sur le corps* (2004), Ginette Michaud makes a similar point. Contrasting Derrida and Nancy on the body, she remarks that even when Derrida discusses 'incorporation' (a term he prefers to 'incarnation' with its Christian overtones),[25] he seems to detach it from any biology and understand it solely in terms of a psychic process:

> It's as if Derrrida 'decorporated' incorporation, as if he decoupled it from any narrowly biological or organic conception of the body, only being able to accept it as a some kind of psychic process, a fantasmatic body (no less real or immaterial than the other kind),

by returning it to the domain of psychoanalysis and the internal
depths of some crypt, which is to say a form of radical expulsion
of the self, taking the self in itself out of the subject. (98)

Nancy, on the other hand, has a radically bodily understanding of
the notion:

> Nancy, by contrast, approaches the notion of incorporation from
> the other end, head-on [*à bras-le-corps*], dare I say it, to turn inside-
> out the notions of interiority and exteriority: not even the most
> organic of bodies incorporates itself or is incorporated, this is pre-
> cisely what it cannot make happen (except when dying), it is only
> outpourings [...] and ejections. (99)

Michaut remarks (somewhat over-allusively) that this very difference puts the two ways of understanding incorporation in
contact with each other. She does not explain precisely how,
but it would seem to be through the notion of expulsion or
ejection, which means that neither conception involves a simple
inside/outside relationship. The body as Derrida understands it
may be less physically immediate than it is for Nancy, but it is
no less fragmented. The body for Nancy may be more apparently organic and biological than it is for Derrida, but it is no
less elusive.

The soul and *jouissance*

There is a further aspect of Nancy's 58 *indices sur le corps* which
is important here, and that is the supernumerary 59th Index
which considers sexuality. Until this point in the text, the body
has not been evidently sexualized, but in the final index Nancy
seems to take sexuality as far as he can in two opposed directions,
the one physiological, the other provocatively spiritual. On the
one hand he refers explicitly to biological body parts: 'A body is
also a sex [...]: also breasts, a penis, a vulva, testicles, ovaries [...]
a type of chromosome.' And on the other he refers to sexual relations as a way in which the body goes beyond its own limitations:
'it enjoys [*jouit*], which is to say that the body is shaken outside
of itself. Each of its zones, enjoying for itself, outwardly radiates

the same. This is called a soul' (58IC, 66/160). This startling identification of soul and *jouissance* (orgasm) is part of Nancy's determined rejection of the mind–body dualism and something we will
return to shortly.

In her Appendix to the text, Michaut declares herself very
uneasy with much of what Nancy has to say in Index 59,
arguing that by relegating sexuality to a supernumerary entry he
at once emphasizes and downgrades it. Furthermore, she is wary
of both poles of his discussion, seeing him as simultaneously
running the risk of a kind of 'biologism', in which sexual identity is once again determined by anatomy rather than by something more deconstructive and post-feminist (113); and of falling
into essentialism: 'the body is sexed in essence. This essence is
determined as the essence of a relation to another essence. The
body is thus essentially determined as relation, or as in relation'
(66). Indeed, she goes so far as to envisage the two risks as
combined in an undesirable 'biological difference elevated to the
rank of essence' (113).

If we bear in mind, however, the lapidary format of the 'Indices',
as well as their studied self-contradiction (an essence which is
defined as a relationship seems quasi paradoxical) and think too
of Derrida's comments on Nancy's willingness to put to his own
purposes terminology which Derrida himself finds unuseable, the
references to anatomy and to essences can be understood as part
of Nancy's defiant project of deconstructive recuperation of
notions that have been appropriated by metaphysical, humanistic,
and Christian philosophies.[26]

None the less, I have my own reservations about Nancy's closing
remarks on sexuality, for irony (or its philosophical counterpart)
never completely destroys what is ironized, and Nancy's provocative relegation of sex to a post-script arguably reflects only too
accurately his approach to sexual embodiment. We will turn now
to a text in which sexuality is, ostensibly at least, the main subject
of discussion and see whether it is dealt with in a more convincing
manner.

In *L' 'il y a' du rapport sexuel* (2001), Nancy's response to
Lacan's (in)famous 'il n'y a pas de rapport sexuel' which we
discussed in the previous chapter, he takes as his starting position
a determinedly anti-dualistic identification of body and soul,
referring to *Eros* as 'the self-interpretation of the body' and

continuing 'which is to say, of the soul, if one prefers to give it this name' (IRS, 43). If we really accept the radical implications of this identification, it clearly cannot make sense to speak of thought or feeling as opposed to the body, love as opposed to sex: as Nancy writes in *Corpus*, when we touch the body of the other, we touch his heart, and vice versa; what touches us is always 'emotion' (C, 127/135): 'there is no sex without a minimum, even an infinitesimal (and wilfully denied) measure of love [. . .], just as there's no love without sex, even when imperceptible' (C, 36/37–9). This means that all relations are sexual, and that the very phrase 'sexual relations' is something of a tautology: 'The relation finds its fullest display and extension in the sexual' (IRS, 26).

Love and desire are two poles that cannot be separated: any attempt to do so necessarily participates, Nancy argues, in the Christian/Augustinian opposition between *cupiditas* and *caritas*, nature and grace, which he considers inferior to the older Platonic distinction between love of body and love of soul, in so far as the ancient philosopher allowed the possibility of movement between the two 'forms' (IRS, 48). Nancy of course recognizes that love and desire cannot simply be assimilated, but he insists – unlike Sartre and Lacan for example – that they are not mutually exclusive and are indeed mutually inter-dependent:

> In each gesture of desire, there must be some love, and *vice versa*. But that can, in each case, tend toward the fading away of the one or the other. Love and desire would thus be two poles of the relation. [. . .] Love gives that which it does not have (according to Lacan), and desire grasps at that which exceeds it. (49)

Even in their extreme forms, which Nancy names 'fidélité' and 'foudre' – loyalty and lightning-strike – love and desire are rivals rather than opposites, and though there is no transition between them they both participate in the same yearning for versions of infinity and eternity (it is perhaps interesting to note that the 'coup de foudre', here representative of desire, is referred to in English as '*love* at first sight', 50).

Similarly, the inextricability of self and other means that in sexual love bodies mingle not by penetration, which would bring death, but rather because they are already open to one another: 'Love is the touch of the open' (C, 28/29). Sexual intimacy does not entail a relationship between pre-existing entities, but involves a sharing of interiority in which the relationship itself constitutes the identities of its members, and in which there is nothing (no *thing* or entity) preceding or outside the relationship:

> Which interiority shares itself sexually? Precisely the interiority of no given identity, of no relation to self, which is also to say, of no relation in itself. (IRS, 31)

This means that there is, strictly speaking, no 'object of desire' because there is no strict subject/object division; just as the sexual relationship is not between pre-existing partners, so desire is not for a pre-existing object:

> Strictly speaking, there is no object of desire. What desire desires is not ob-jected against it [. . .] but is rather a part of its desiring movement. The thing of desire is no more ob-jectivisible than sub-jectivisible. (34)

Unsurprisingly, in the light of this, Nancy has a somewhat different view from Lacan of the (im)possibility of *jouissance* which he refers to as the corollary of Lacan's belief in the non-existence of the 'rapport sexuel'. Nancy rejects the opposition of desire and *jouissance*, or pleasure and *jouissance*. Just as he sees love and desire as inextricable, so he – like Kristeva – sees desire and pleasure (united in the German 'Lust') as intermingled rather than opposed; and if *jouissance* is impossible it is because it represents both an excess *and* a release of tension, an infinity of pleasure and desire, not because it represents a fantasy of impossible fusion (35). Nancy claims that if, as etymology suggests, desire is a 'désastre' (an inability to see the stars), it is indeed because it is insatiable – not because it cannot be satisfied, but because it does not participate in what he calls 'une logique . . . de la satiéte' (37). And he argues that the finitude of the 'rapport sexuel' and of 'jouissance' (which is what he believes Lacan means when he refers to their non-existence or their impossibility) is itself a 'punctuation' of 'l'infinité sexuelle' (39): an interruption, but also, I would suggest, a 'punctum', in Barthes's sense.[27]

It seems fair to say, however, in the light of our analysis of Lacan's arguments in the last chapter, that Nancy is taking a more optimistic line on very similar grounds: describing the glass, perhaps, as half-full rather than half-empty. And we should remember that Nancy's, albeit witty, summary of Lacan's position as 'Lorsque je baise, je suis baisé (*when I screw, I am screwed*)' (14), might have amused Lacan but was certainly not coined by him. Be that as it may, Nancy stresses that desire is not extinguished when it is calmed, and that pleasure does not bring it to an end, except temporarily (39). The deconstructive notion of 'différance' is brought into play here to explain how there is no fixed identity for the 'rapport sexuel', or for 'jouissance' or indeed for 'baiser (*to fuck*)':

There is no relation *qua* relation. Rather: fucking does not take place *as such*, but always otherwise [. . .]. Fucking takes place in accordance with its own impossibility. [. . .] But one fucks, and in fucking [. . .], *one burns and brands oneself with meaning* [. . .] *Jouissance* is nothing that one can attain [*atteindre*]: it is that which wounds itself [*s'atteint*] and consumes itself in attaining completion [*en s'atteignant*], burning the sense that is proper to it, which is to say, illuminating it by turning it to cinders. (52)

Nancy's description is more poetic than Lacan's, but it is not necessarily as different as he seems to believe. Indeed, I would suggest that it is ultimately an elaboration and explanation of Lacan's position rather than a refutation of it. Nancy's work on sex is undeniably stimulating and provocative, but it arguably lacks the deep originality that is, I would argue, so evident, and indeed so startling, in his thinking about human mortality.

A Portrait of Death

In *A plus d'un titre: Jacques Derrida* (2007), Nancy meditates on a portrait of Derrida by Valerio Adami, sketched in 2004. The drawing is described by the artist as an 'allegorical Portrait', and Nancy spends some time working on the question of allegory. But what is of more interest in this context is the relationship he discusses between the portrait and death. Of course, Nancy's monograph was written after Derrida's death, which obviously adds to the poignancy, but the link between portraiture and mortality transcends the physical demise of a particular individual.

As we see in *La Chambre claire* (1980), Roland Barthes describes time and death as creating the *punctum*, the uniquely personal meaning, at the heart of the most moving photographs of people, irrespective of whether they are still alive at the moment when the photograph is viewed. The person is preserved, as it were, in aspic, caught forever at a particular moment in time, and whoever the subject of the photo may be, baby or adult or old man, it is painfully clear to the viewer that the moment has passed, definitively, and can never return.

In the case of an artist's portrait, the same considerations apply, though arguably less acutely, in so far as the portrait is usually deemed to capture some version – however fragmentary and detotalized – of the 'essence' of its subject (even if the subject is a proponent of, for example, deconstruction or existentialism). But essences too clearly change in time (however paradoxical that may sound), so the issue of capturing on paper what is too fleeting to be captured in life differs only in extent between the photograph and the artist's sketch. Nancy's text begins with a reflection on death ('He who has disappeared, who will no longer ever appear. . .' p. 9), and he attributes the same preoccupation to Derrida, inserting quotations from *Mémoires d'Aveugle* into his own text:

> Already, when he was alive, he – Jacques Derrida – knew better than anyone that every image bears this 'death that comes through the eyes' and the 'originary ruin' that was the unique object of his haunting, of this thought, of wild desire plunged into 'narcissistic melancholy, a memory – in mourning – of love itself' that was his absolute desire and the inexhaustible pleasure waiting [*en souffrance*] in this desire [. . .]. But he, a portrait, what does he see in it? He sees death in it, the only resemblance [. . .], the image itself. [. . .] The only possible portrait of man. (10–17)[28]

Nancy is taking over Derrida's own procedure of weaving the words of his deceased friend into his 'obituary', in a sense thereby creating a double homage. The interplay between Nancy and Derrida is abyssal and may seem unending. Derrida himself noted in *Le Toucher: Jean-Luc Nancy* (2000), that ever since Nancy had known that Derrida was writing on the subject of touch he had delighted in referring to it on all possible occasions in his writings. So the intratextual exchange between the two philosophers is both self-conscious and reflexive.

Body and flesh

One of the most striking aspects of Nancy's thinking about the body concerns his terminology: in the first place his preference for 'corps' (body) rather than 'chair' (flesh), and also his repeated references to the soul ('âme'). In *Le Sens du monde* (1993), Nancy explains that the term 'chair' (as used, for example, in 'la passion de la chair') is overlaid with too much meaning and pathos:

> This is why the word 'body' ['*corps*'] should succeed the word 'flesh' ['*chair*'], which was always overabundant, nourished by flesh, and always egological. Herein lies the coming of the world of bodies, where suffering, dare I say it? is simply established, without any depth of passion. (226–7/149)

In *Le Toucher*, Derrida is harsher than Nancy about the use of the term 'chair' which he rejects decisively because of its phenomenological, and more especially Christian, overtones. Indeed, Derrida declares himself unhappy, for example, with Didier Franck's translation of Husserl's 'Leib' (the living body, 'le corps propre vivant') as 'chair' – especially given that Husserl specifically uses the word 'Fleisch' for flesh – though he does not claim to have a solution to the problem of translation (T, 204/349–50 n.13, 267/238). It is of course true that the German term 'Leib' renders many significant expressions where 'corps' or 'body' is usually used in both French and English such as 'Leib–Seele–Problem' (the mind–body problem, 'le problème corps-esprit') or indeed, and of particular relevance to Nancy, 'Leib–Christi', the body of Christ, 'le corps du Christ', in the Eucharist. Derrida suggests that the popularity of 'chair' derives in part from the extended use of it by Merleau-Ponty (as in 'la chair du monde'), but insists that it is in fact just a *part* of the body, and that its technical specificity (as it is used by the surgeon or the painter, for example) as well as its moralizing and Christian overtones ('le péché de la chair', 'the sin of the flesh') make it difficult to recuperate as a translation of 'Leib' (*Le Toucher*, p. 204/349–50 n.13). What is more, Husserl's use of 'Leib' and 'leibhaftig' tends to imply not only life but frequently also 'Esprit' (spirit or mind):

> By making flesh ubiquitous, one runs the risk of vitalizing, psychologizing, spiritualizing, interiorizing, or even reappropriating everything, there where one might still speak of a non-propriety or an alterity of the flesh. (*Le Toucher*, 267/238)[29]

'Corps', on the other hand, poses its own rather different problems. Michaud remarks that it has a quite different meaning from the English 'body' ('the Nancian body (*corps*) is as far as possible from the *body* and especially from *bodybuilding*' 'Appendice', p. 99), but, though the latter assertion is clearly correct, it does not seem to me to justify any overall distinction between 'corps' and 'body'. Nancy's own distaste for 'body building' (C, 69/75) is surely for the process which treats the body purely as an object to be worked on, rather than for the term 'body'? In any case, as *Corpus* (1992) makes poignantly apparent, both 'body' and 'corps' are clearly beset with problems for Nancy, arising in particular from the assumption of unity and significance that the terms usually express.

Almost all uses of the term 'corps' imply some form of meaning, whether it be religious, political, philosophical or literary and, in Nancy's view, these meanings are inescapably built into the term so that there is a sense in which 'corps' signifies meaning itself, be it 'sens' or 'signification' (C, 63/71). Indeed, Nancy describes this as a form of circular 'auto-symbolization', and sees it as the last thing to go in the decline and fall of Western metaphysics, like a kind of 'black hole' into which all meaning is eventually sucked (66/73). And since we are, he argues, 'organized' to create meaning, the current loss of meaning is necessarily painful, but it should not be referred to as a source of 'angoisse', for, unlike pain, anguish is itself a way of giving meaning to meaninglessness:

> Anxiety *is given as sense* [. . .]. But suffering is not given as sense. We suffer because we are organized for sense and the loss of it wounds us, cuts us. But suffering makes no more sense of this loss than it does of lost sense. It is only its edge, its burn, its pain. (C, 72/81)

And similarly, what Nancy describes as the 'wound' in the world, through which millions of bodies bleed to death in our techno-cratic massacres since the First World War, should not be described as a 'sacrifice', for the term gives too much meaning to the horror, be it natural or man-made. The wound is not a 'malheur', with its overtones of tragedy, nor yet a 'maladie', with its suggestion of knowable cause and possible healing, it is, purely and simply, a 'mal', an open wound through which the life-blood of human meaning drains away ('sense escapes from the wound, drop by drop', C, 71/81), even though we may still be unable to resist giving meaning to this very loss of meaning.

Body and soul

The body that Nancy wants to describe is then precisely *not* the religious body with which we are so familiar ('Hoc est enim corpus meum', pp. 7/5, 77/87), the body of the Incarnation in which the Word – or Spirit – is made flesh. It is rather a frag-mented, multiple body that has not been created by, or infused with, the spirit; it is 'a body given as multiplied, multi-sexed, multi-figured, multi-zoned, phallic and aphallic, cephalous and acephalous, organized, inorganic' (77/89). But if Nancy rejects a body that is infused with the spirit, this is not to say that he sets the body up in opposition to spirit or to mind.[30] Indeed, one of the problems with the term is that it is difficult to dissociate from its dualist history. As Derrida remarks in his discussion with Nancy in *Sens en tous sens* (2004), it is almost impossible to escape the metaphysical and humanist heritage that still attaches to so many philosophical terms such as 'creation', 'community', 'freedom', even after attempts have been made to deconstruct them, and 'corps' is no exception:

> Even the word 'body' [*'corps'*] is made of the same stuff [. . .]. Even if I temporarily accept it for strategic reasons, I will soon enough want nothing more to do with it. Body is the opposite of spirit and I know that you will still take me up on the old hat of binary oppositions, between what we'll call Platonico–Cartesian dualism and the 'flesh' of contemporary phenomenologists. Jean-Luc, too, does frankly much the same in *Corpus*. (*Sens en tous sens*, p. 168)

Nancy, however, is prepared to employ precisely the terms Derrida shies away from, and 'corps' in particular, in full knowledge of the uphill battle he will have to disentangle it from the 'esprit' that it inevitably implies and opposes:

> Why, then, a body? Because only a body can be cut down or raised up, because only a body can touch or not touch. A spirit can do nothing of the sort. A 'pure spirit' gives only a formal and empty index of a presence entirely closed in on itself. A body opens this presence [...]. It puts presence outside of itself, it distances it from itself. (*Noli me tangere*, 78/48)

But if Nancy is concerned to dissociate 'corps' and 'esprit', the same is not true of 'corps' and 'âme'. Indeed, his use of the notion of the term 'soul' appears at first (and arguably remains) both puzzling and provocative. Although body and soul are traditionally opposed as frequently as body and mind, Nancy's conception of the relationship between 'âme', 'corps', and 'esprit' is rather different. On one occasion, in a difficult and intriguing passage from *Tombe de sommeil* (2007), he puts body and mind together and opposes them to the soul:

> Never, however, never does the soul sleep. That absenting of self in self is unknown to it. Absence belongs to the body and to the mind; it is foreign to the soul. In sleep, the mind abandons itself to the body and disperses its location through it, dissolves its concentration into that soft, almost disjointed expanse. The body, for its part, abandons itself paradoxically to the very location of the mind [...] The man who sleeps is a mental body or a bodily mind [*un corps spirituel ou un esprit corporel*], one lost in the other, and in both cases, each from the standpoint of the other, a subject aspirated, extravasated, *ex-posed* or *ex-isting* in the strongest and moreover most problematic senses of these words [...] But the soul animates sleep as well as waking [...] Not indeed like a skipper in his ship, but spread throughout and mixed with the entire expanse of the body. (67–9/35–6).

Usually, however, the relationship between soul and body for Nancy is not one of opposition but something closer to the identity Pessoa attributes to the gods, in a poem Nancy quotes on several occasions in *Les Muses* (1994, 2001):

The gods do not have a body and a soul
But solely a body, and are perfect.
It is the body that takes the place of their soul. (64/35)

In *58 indices sur le corps*, whose 59th 'indice' we have already
discussed, Nancy gives a series of brief and contradictory notes
about the body, of which the first asserts 'The body is material. It
is dense' (58IC, 7/150) and the fifth, 'A body is immaterial'
(10/150). Many of these speak of the soul, and are equally paradoxical, number 8 for example reads: 'The soul is material, made
of entirely different matter' (13/151). Several give a lapidary
version of Aristotelian or Cartesian theories of the relationship
between body and soul:

> 6. The soul is the form of the organized body, says Aristotle. But
> the body, precisely, is what draws this form. It's the form of the
> form, the form of the soul.
>
> 7. The soul is extended everywhere along the body, says Descartes;
> it is entirely everywhere along the length of itself, all over itself,
> insinuated in itself. (12–3/151)

But there is nothing predictable about these 'definitions' as the
following example makes clear:

> 44 Soul, body, mind: the first is the form of the second, and the
> third is the force that produces the first. The second is thus the
> expressive form of the third. The body expresses the mind, meaning
> that it makes it spurt outside, squeezes its juices, draws its sweat,
> extracts its sparkle and throws it all into space. The body is a defla-
> gration. (50/157)

What starts apparently dryly and innocuously, becomes in the
space of a sentence an extraordinary poetic evocation of the power
of the body. But when we look closely at Nancy's writings on the
soul we see certain constants: the soul is the body's experience of
itself, 'What is the soul, if not the experience of the body?' (C,
127/134); the soul is the body as it knows itself, 'the body knows
itself as soul' (58IC, 74/139), 'the body is simply a soul' (24/152).
One of his most frequent references is to Freud's 'Psyche is
extended, knows nothing about it' (83/144), discussed in *Corpus*,

'the *soul* is the form of a body, and therefore a body itself (*psyche ex-tended*)' (C, 67/75), and echoed in the title of the brief 'Extension de l'âme' which follows the 58 *indices* and which itself echoes Descartes's own 'the soul is extended' (C, 71/150).

Here Nancy explores Descartes's famous letter to Princess Elisabeth of 28 June 1643 in which he discusses the union of body and soul, and argues that it can be interpreted very differently from the ontological dualism with which it is usually associated. The union is not a matter of accident, on the contrary it is what Nancy calls 'an ontology of the 'between'' (82/143):

> The soul marries the impulse of the body: if I walk, it is a walking soul; if I sleep, a sleeping soul; if I eat, an eating soul. If a blade or a shard cuts through my skin, my soul is cut to the exact depth, force and form of the wound. And if I die, the soul becomes death itself. (83/144)

The mortal body

Indeed, death is, as so often, the test-case of the kind of identity Nancy is concerned to tease out. Can our identification with our body cope with the implications of physical death? Nancy does not flinch from the consequences of such a radical identification:

> Our body is not only ours, but *us*, *ourselves*, even unto death, meaning its death and decomposition, in which we can be, and are, identically decomposed. (51/157)

Nancy is acutely aware of the difficulty of even starting to think properly and philosophically about the body. No way of speaking about it escapes the problems of expressing an identity which seems ultimately to defy our usual modes of conceptualization: whether I claim that I *have* a body or that I *am* my body I am doomed to incoherence:

> I can't introduce this instance – a 'self' able to say 'my body' or 'I am my body' – without keeping the body at a distance, distinct and disunited. And so I weaken the evident knowledge of the union. (75/140)

And of course, we come up against the limits of our thinking in our recoil from notions such as that of our own decomposition. Nancy himself, however, is prepared to face such issues head on, and his work in *Corpus* and *L'Intrus* in particular shows him troublingly and painfully forcing his reader to contemplate some of the radical consequences of really rejecting dualism and thinking of ourselves as truly bodily.

Nancy has clearly spent a long time meditating on the relationship between mortality and subjectivity and attempting to conceive of the body *as* mind, as soul, as subject. We have been focusing up till now primarily on the way in which this rejection of dualism prevents us from escaping the implications of our bodily selves into an ethereal realm, but as Nancy explains in an interview with Chantal Pontbriand in 2001, he does not consider the body as a primarily material object:

> The question of the 'body' must be defined or discerned with great precision and precaution. It is not a question of the 'sensible' versus the 'intelligible', or of 'matter' versus 'spirit' or 'soul': because as long as these oppositional pairs are employed we are trapped by them. If, implicitly, one speaks of the 'body' in a kind of rabidly anti-spiritualist or anti-intellectualist assertion, it risks falling short of the mark ... If you withdraw it from these oppositions, the 'body' actually designates two things which are intertwined: the first is coexistence, the second is being-outside-itself. Coexistence is existence insofar as it does not begin with a subject (who would then meet or recognize other subjects), but with the plurality of subjects, a plurality *which belongs to being subject* (as I like to say: the singular is plural). Plurality implies space, spacing, distance (distance and touch, the distance of touch). The materiality of bodies is not 'matter' in the physical-physiological sense of the term: it is not the material object, it is the spacing, the far and the near, the contact and the gap, the relation and the non-relation. This is what bodies are in the first place – and in this, once more, they are fundamentally not physical ... They are not physical but distant-near, reachable-unreachable, desirable-fearful, erotic, powerful, weak, fleeting, confrontational, etc. On the other hand, being-outside-itself means that a subject is only 'subject' in so far as it is exposed to and by the other of itself and in itself: the body is not the outside of an inside which remains autonomous, separated, ('soul' or 'spirit') and whose very relations with

the outside would therefore be hard to grasp; on the contrary, the body is the fact that the subject is in exteriority to itself, that its 'sameness' is played out precisely in this 'outside itself'. Through this double motif, which forms a single connection – being-several-outside-itself – the body corresponds to a world in which 'sense' can never be referred back to an interiority situated outside the world (in the heavens or the spirit: it comes to the same thing).[31]

For Nancy, ontology *is* the ontology of the body and he does not believe we have yet begun to think the ontological body. And he rejects the notion of 'my body' in favour of that of *corpus ego*, which, paradoxically, is without 'egoïté', and without egoism, because the body is never *me*, it is rather delivered up to others, known through others, just as I know others as bodies (C, 26/27). This is why death is necessarily taken with total seriousness: existence is not *for* death, death *is* the body: 'All its life, the body is a dead body, the body of a dead man, of this dead man who I am during my life' (C, 17/15). There is no being preceding or underlying the phenomenon: the decomposition of the body in death does not somehow house a pure inner self, on the contrary, that very decay *is* the subject, and is by the same token its freedom. It is always in relation to suffering and death that this strong identification between body and subject is most acute and most difficult to think. Nancy does not clothe his thinking about death in abstraction: he evokes with painful vividness the organs, wounds, blood, bruises, mutilations, and infections of the body. It is here that his reflection on bodily subjectivity seems to have its central focus as he writes:

> *Here*, at the point of suffering, there is only an open 'subject', cut, *anatomised*, deconstructed, disassembled, deconcentrated [. . .] in this anatomizing of organization, without which we would not be mortal. (C, 72–4/81–3)

Nancy quotes Elaine Scarry's phrase, 'the body in pain' to describe the dissolution, or 'decreation', of the world in the face of intense suffering.[32] If Psyche *is* the body, and *is* the subject, it is not the autonomous Subject of the subject/object dualism, but rather 'the subject of not being a subject, subject to not being subject, as one says "'subject to bouts of fever'"(C, 84/97). In this sense, the subject described by Nancy is passive not active, subject not only to fever but also to passion that moves and disturbs it, 'the body as emotion or commotion' (128/135). There is no Death or Resurrection for this body, this subject, but there is always *this* death (C, 85/97). Nancy is deeply preoccupied by illness: his seemingly endless list of bodily disintegrations and decompositions, 'clots, thromboses, aneurisms, anemias, haemorrhages, diarrhoeas, drugs, deleria, transfusions, scabs . . .', affects us by its density of enumeration not by its logic or sequence (C, 92/105). The body is, in Nancy's words, 'made in time' (C, 96/111). It is part of time and space, never existing elsewhere, only here and now. There is no other place for the subject outside the body that it is, the death that it awaits (C, 104/119).

Subjectivity and the heart of the other

In 1999, Nancy published an article – 'L'Intrus' – in a special issue of *Dédale* on the theme of *La Venue de l'étranger*, the coming of the stranger, or the foreigner. Nancy's intruder was the stranger within himself, literally within himself, for he had undergone a heart transplant about ten years earlier. In 'L'Intrus',[33] Nancy confronts the consequences of his philosophical identification of subject and body in an acute and radical form. What are the implications for subjectivity and identity of transplant surgery? *Corpus ego*, the singularity of the body *is* its subjectivity. The heart, in Nancy's words, *is* the body (C, 36/39). Traditionally, of course, the heart has been seen as the seat of selfhood: the seat, for example, of emotion, of moral orientation, and of pre-rational intuition.[34] Where does the heart of the other leave my subjectivity? Nancy's response is stunning in its simplicity and directness. In the first place, he assumes entirely the significance of his identification of body and subject even when extreme situations such as prosthetics are involved:

> I am illness and medicine, I am the cancerous cell and the grafted organ, I am immunosuppressants and their palliatives, I am the tips of the steel wire that brace my sternum and the site of injection permanently sewn under my clavicle. (*L'Intrus*, 449/C [Eng.], 170).

Nor does Nancy accept the usual, benign understanding of trans-plantation as a meeting between donor and receiver, which he refers to as 'politically correct' (440/162); he prefers to maintain the notion of the transplanted organ as an intruder, but precisely in order to be able to welcome it. This echoes Derrida's frequent meditations on hospitality, where the *hospes* is both guest and potential enemy, who must, none the less, be made welcome[35] Indeed, we might be tempted, in the light of Nancy's experiences, to extend this reflection to a consideration of the term 'hospital' itself. Nancy's paradoxical conception of the body as never mine, never a closed entity, a site of self-identity, mean that the trans-plant is at most another other, rather than a stranger within the autonomous self:

> The intruder is nothing other than myself and man himself. None other than the same, never done with being altered, simultaneously sharpened and exhausted, denuded yet overequipped, in the world as well as in himself, a disturbing thrust of the strange, the *conatus* of an excrescent infinity. (450/170)

For Nancy, who has argued that 'one cannot conceive a subject, a 'self', preceding a relation with others',[36] the transplanted heart is one more element in understanding an identity and subjectivity which is never self-sufficient and self-same:

> I really feel it, and it's much stronger than a sensation: never has the strangeness of my own identity, though for me it has always been so vivid, touched me so acutely. 'I' has clearly become the formal index of an unverifiable and impalpable change. Between myself and myself, there has always been some space-time, but at present there is the opening of an incision, and the irreconcilability of thwarted immunity. (447/168)

In *Le Toucher*, Derrida gives a profound response to Nancy's assumption of the radical implications of his bodily alienation. He reflects on the way in which Nancy's situation gives vivid and uncomfortable life back to metaphors of the heart: when we touch, for example, the heart of the matter, we do not usually expect to touch such a physical organ as Nancy confronts us with:

Never have I felt to this extent the enigmatic and troubling necessity of idioms, in expressions like 'messing with the heart' [*'toucher
au cœur'*] and 'touching the heart' [*'toucher le cœur'*], whether their
value is literal or figurative, or sometimes both, beyond all decid-
ability. (*Le Toucher*, 9/ix)

Derrida is of course in full agreement with Nancy over the question of non-self-identity, as has been clear since his work on
Husserl in the mid-1960s. There is no possibility of 'auto-affection': for Jean-Luc Nancy, as for us all, there can only ever be
hetero-affection and, indeed, the alternative would involve sterility, sclerosis and, as Sartre maintained, death. Nancy's 'intruder' is
a physical manifestation of our essential and unavoidable openness
to the other.

In his discussions of love and sexuality, illness, suffering, and
death, Nancy takes a radically anti-dualist position, refusing to
separate body and soul, heart and mind, self and other, and
driving the implications of mortality and of identification with
the body through to their most uncomfortable and disconcerting
conclusions. But whereas he is, I believe, refining rather than
breaking new ground in his reflections on love and sex, his meditations on mortality take him into areas where no other thinker
has so far dared to tread. Jean-Luc Nancy, more powerfully than
any other contemporary philosopher, has made the effort to
think the *bodily nature of the subject*, not merely in its philosophical implications as part of a radical rejection of dualism and of
hubristic humanism, but also as a concrete and inescapable
reality. Nancy forces us to think the mortality of the subject, his
thought is at times a kind of violence (to use Deleuze's expression), his enumerations of blood, pus, and pain make the body
as matter physically present, even in the face of the reader's
recoil and distaste.

The 'death of the subject' is never a mere metaphor for Nancy,
it is never a metaphor at all. The death of the subject is the
inevitable, *ontological* consequence of the subject as body, of the
bodily nature of the subject. In an interview with Derrida in
1989, Nancy questioned whether the term 'subject' was still
useable or if its heritage made it too misleading.[37] At that point
Derrida seemed to think the word could be reused and

reinscribed, perhaps by including animal subjectivities within its orbit. A few years later, Nancy too is willing to recover the term 'subject' from its classical, humanist overtones, this time by insisting on its bodily reality and mortality. Finitude and death are now what mark the subject, what enable the subject to exist, what free the subject from its subjection to sclerotic self-identity. Human, all too human, the subject is perhaps more precisely, mortal, all too mortal. (15026)

Epilogue

We unite with another, but it is to divide ourselves: that most intimate embrace is naught but a most intimate uprooting. In essence, the delight of sexual love, the genetic spasm, is a sensation of resurrection, of resuscitation in another, for only in others can we resuscitate and perpetuate ourselves. (Unamuno: *The Tragic Sense of Life*)

We have now explored a dozen different philosophical attempts to get to grips with some of the most fundamental issues in human experience and thought: the relationship between body and mind, heart and soul, and whether this be a matter of identity or difference; the relationship between love and sex, desire and passion; the relationship between self and other, and whether these are opposed or mutually imbricated and mutually constituting; and all this in light of the question from which I started – the relationship between subjectivity and mortality. To what extent I *am* my body, stark though that may sound in its simplest form, must surely determine to what extent my subjectivity is dependent on my mortality; to what extent I *am* my body, must surely determine how I conceive of love and desire. 'Love is a sexually transmitted disease'[1] is arguably more than a mere cynic's quip, it goes to the heart of what is most heart-rending in human co-existence and the passion of inter-subjectivity.

My initial, and strongly held, conviction was that to write a conclusion for this study would involve a betrayal of principle (or even worse, a *petitio principii*): how could I even start to conclude on a subject where I had been concerned precisely to show that phenomenologists, existentialists, religious philosophers, psycho-analysts, and deconstructive thinkers had all resisted the idea of closure; any attempt to draw together the threads of such a diverse and often difficult group of philosophers was bound to be both partial and problematic. But further reflection convinced me that these difficulties were ultimately what would make the enterprise of conclusion worthwhile, both necessary and impossible. What is more, philosophy is not of course the only way to approach the issues I have been exploring, and throughout my discussions I have drawn repeatedly on literature, especially in the epigraphs, for a complementary perspective. So what I want to attempt finally is two-fold: firstly to outline a brief conclusion in the form of an over-arching philosophical paradox; and secondly to make some methodological points about the way in which philosophy and literature (and indeed art) may be mutually enlightening on these mortal questions.

The possible/impossible aporia

– oh why
have to be human, and, shunning Destiny,
long for Destiny? . . .
Not because happiness really
exists, that precipitate profit of imminent loss.
(Rilke: *Ninth Elegy*)

One of the most constant and symptomatic elements in the philo-sophical discussions analysed in this study is their recourse to paradox and aporia. These paradoxes can perhaps be summed up within one over-riding maxim, that of *qui perd gagne* or loser wins – not, of course, in the merely trivial sense of some kind of fatal reversal or come-uppance, but rather in the profound sense of a salvation that comes through failure. The religious version of this paradox has been a constant (and 'scandalous') theme in Christian theology and soteriology. As the Beatitudes maintain, grief, and mourning are unavoidable prerequisites for redemption, and the 'folly' of Christ's passion and death on the cross is the highest form of wisdom, which goes beyond the limitations of merely human rationality and self-interest. It should not surprise us then if the religious philosophers I have discussed are thinkers of paradox and reversal, but what of the others? Existentialists too – and the 'qui perd gagne' paradox is most commonly associated with Sartre – are of course philosophers of paradox, most markedly where subjectivity is concerned. It is precisely our failure to achieve self-identity that allows us to be free: our non-self-coincidence, our *pour-soi* which is riven by self-division and is never *soi*, our 'diasporic' subjectivity provide the key to our ability to change, and to choose who we want to be.

In psychoanalysis also, paradox is a privileged structure of understanding: the death drive is essential to life; the pleasure principle protects us from an excess of *jouissance*. The psychoanalytic subject is again riven, whether born from the Freudian *Spaltung* (the splitting within the ego, or between Consciousness and the Unconscious) or from the Lacanian emergence out of the Imaginary into the Symbolic Order. Our inability to achieve completion defines us as human. Deconstruction too involves a strong version of 'paradoxical logic' in which *différance* ensures that the (self-)presence we may yearn for is forever impossible, and stasis is avoided in areas as diverse as signification, subjectivity, ethics, and politics. The *qui perd gagne* structure also operates deconstructively in areas such as mourning, where we have seen Derrida argue that 'successful' mourning fails to respect the alterity of the other, whereas 'a failed internalization . . . shows respect for the other as other', though of course Derrida will not accept this aporetic schema as doing any more than demonstrate precisely the impossibility of 'true mourning' (*Mémoires*, p. 50/30).

What are the implications of this paradoxical mode of thought for the relationship between subjectivity and mortality? This can perhaps best be expressed in the (post-Kantian) structure, popularized by, but not exclusive to, Derrida, which has come to be termed the 'possible–impossible aporia': X as a condition of both possibility and impossibility of Y. Derrida employs this structure to explore notions such as hospitality, the gift, forgiveness, and, as we have seen, mourning, where internalization could be described as its condition of both possibility and impossibility. I shall use this aporetic structure to express the relationship between subjectivity and mortality.

Mortality, I would suggest, is the condition of possibility and the condition of impossibility of subjectivity. This may initially sound Heideggerian, but it is not. Whereas for Heidegger, death was described as the ownmost possibility of Dasein, and indeed as the possibility of the absolute impossibility of Dasein, this is not the notion to which I am referring, though it is of course related to it. Heidegger is thinking in terms of being-towards-death as constitutive of Dasein's most fundamental being. It is a notion that we have seen Sartre in particular reject. For Sartre, death is *not* my possibility, it is rather an 'always possible nihilation of my possibles' (EN, 620/537, discussed above, p. 37).

What, then, does it mean to describe mortality as the condition of possibility and of impossibility of subjectivity? Subjectivity has been a constant issue for questioning not only by twentieth-century French philosophers, but also, of course, by many philosophers from Descartes and Kant onwards, though the term 'subject' is never used in this sense by the former, and is not used consistently by the latter. I have discussed this intriguing question in previous work on Sartre and Derrida[2] and will not repeat it here. But the specific relationship to mortality needs further thought. Human mortality and finitude are arguably what makes the subject in its traditional sense of self-sufficient, autonomous, spontaneous foundation of knowledge, understanding, feeling, and imagination an impossible ideal, and one nowadays generally considered philosophically outmoded and illusory. If the 'death of Man', celebrated at one point by Foucault among others, is no longer centre stage in contemporary French philosophy, this is not because of some kind of resurrection: it is rather because the considerable philosophical work that went into dismantling the humanist conception of the subject has been both assimilated and refined. The jubilation with which the subject's so-called 'death' was celebrated may have been crude and suspiciously over-emphatic, but it is best seen as an essential 'reversal phase' in any reinterpretation of subjectivity. In Derrida's own tentative terms:

> For these three discourses (Lacan, Althusser, Foucault), for some of the thinking they privilege (Freud, Marx, Nietzsche), the subject is perhaps reinterpreted, resituated, reinscribed, it is certainly not liquidated.[3]

Mortality and finitude bring us face-to-face with our fragility as subjects, and the loss of faith and its accompanying hope for life beyond death means that we cannot continue to wager on eternal life as saving our souls while our bodies die and decay. Mortality is the condition of impossibility of subjectivity, at least in any version of it which involves sovereign mastery or transcendence of the body. The very notion that I might 'shuffle off this mortal coil' has come to seem incoherent. Who am 'I' to shuffle off the very bodily existence that constitutes me? But this is not because the soul does not exist: on the contrary, it is because it does. Kristeva and Nancy envisage the soul as the place where mind–body dualism may possibly be overcome; for Lacan 'aimer d'âmour' is what enables us to put up with what is otherwise intolerable.[4] Derrida sees the soul more metaphorically as speaking to us of life and death, and as eliciting our dreams of immortality.[5] In Foucault's reversal of Plato, for modern man 'the soul is the prison of the body',[6] that is to say, what constrains bodily life and makes it subject to power and discipline. For Foucault, as for Nancy, I am subject *to* constraint, oppression, or sickness, not master of them (*subjectus* rather than *subjectum* or *hypokeimenon*).[7]

But it is also my mortality and finitude that constitute my subjectivity in the sense that the term is used by the philosophers studied here. Mortality is the very condition of possibility of subjectivity in the modern sense. It is precisely because I am *not* self-sufficient or self-identical or immortal that my subjectivity comes into being in its self-division and diaspora (to use Sartre's term) or *différance* (to use Derrida's). Sartre may not accept Heidegger's conception of Dasein as being-towards-death, but he describes the forward-looking, anticipatory nature of the *pour-soi* as structurally constitutive of our subjectivity or ipseity (EN, 622/538).

Derrida, even more clearly than Sartre, links selfhood to death, arguing in one of his essays on Paul de Man that 'we are never ourselves', and that the reflexive specularity which creates the self is never closed, and is brought into being by the possibility of mourning, so that our lack of self-identity coexists with our openness to the presence of the other (friend) within me, not only after his actual death, but during his life: 'There is no friendship without this knowledge of finitude' (MPD, 49/29). Nancy too describes our mortality as precisely what creates our subjectivity, leaving us wounded, open to the (heart of the) other within me (see *L'Intrus*). And Jankélévitch's reflections on transience similarly attribute the possibility of joy – which makes us truly human subjects – to the death that awaits us.

Subjectivity and mortality are then linked in an aporetic structure in which subjectivity is simultaneously created and abolished by mortality: made possible at the same time as made impossible. That mortality brings all subjects to an end, at least for themselves, of course needs no demonstration, though many of the philosophers we have discussed envisage some kind of continuity for our *être-pour-autrui* in the hearts and minds of others. That mortality undermines, makes insecure and fragile, the grounded, autonomous subject is what links death in the true sense (in what Lacan would call the Real, the domain of inassimilable trauma)[8] to the metaphorical (and much abused) notion of the 'death of the subject'. In this work I have focused primarily on the other side of the coin: on mortality as key to the kind of incomplete, un-self-centred, deferred subject which is thereby immune to the traps of hysteresis and fixity. The unattainability of sovereign mastery conditions and creates our subjectivity precisely as it renders it impossible. This possible–impossible aporetic structure is not restricted to the existential Heideggerian thematic of *Dasein*: it rather takes the question of the relationship between subjectivity and mortality further, beyond the pathos of finitude to the more strictly philosophical level of what Sartre calls 'le circuit d'ipséité'. That this schema does not exclude poetry and passion has, I hope, become evident for readers of this study.

La Melancolie de l'art

C'est pourquoi la beauté n'est jamais exempte de mélancolie: elle est comme en deuil de philosophie. (Sarah Kofman)

But reflection on death is not, of course, the monopoly of philosophy, any more than poetry and passion are the monopoly of art and literature. In *Demeure, Athènes*, Derrida offers us a series of meditations on Greek landscapes, people, statues, and photographs taken by Jean-Francois Bonhomme. Like Barthes, he is drawn to reflect on the paradoxical nature of the photograph, capturing a moment which is always already past and can never be retrieved. Whatever its subject and purpose, he argues, no photograph can avoid signifying death, and the images of ancient Greek statuary and contemporary village life provide an especially acute reminder of mortality in their juxtaposition of recent and distant past – are the street vendors of a few years ago any closer to us or more alive than the ruins of Ancient Athens? '[Each photograph] in any case recalls death fulfilled, the promise or threat of death, sepulchral monuments and memory in the form of the ruin' (*Demeure*, p. 11). Like Sarah Kofman, Derrida is vividly aware that the power of art comes in part from its multiple failures: its failure to represent, its failure to express, its failure to transcend, and its failure to retain and possess time passing. 'Beauty is thus never exempt from melancholy: it fails to mourn philosophy, weeps for the fragmentation of meaning, the loss of reference.'[9] The closer art comes to 'life', the more poignant its inevitable difference becomes, and there is something in the instantaneity of the photograph which points up the paradox particularly acutely.

Such is the message, of course, of all art, not just photography, indeed of all cultural products, intellectual and spiritual as well as aesthetic. Why otherwise are we so moved when texts of the ancient philosophers or poets come uncannily close to our own preoccupations? It is not so much, I would suggest, that we are surprised by the proximity of their relation to us – indeed, our universalizing humanism (however disavowed) has probably led us to expect it – but rather that our identification with them forces us to see our future in their past, and that future contains our inevitable mortality. As Shelley lamented in his sonnet 'Ozymandias', the eventual fate of our passions, like that of our works, and indeed our subjectivity, can only ever be wreckage, decay, and obliteration:

I met a traveller from an antique land
Who said: Two vast and trunkless legs of stone
Stand in the desert. Near them, on the sand,
Half sunk, a shattered visage lies, whose frown
And wrinkled lip, and sneer of cold command

Tell that its sculptor well those passions read
Which yet survive, stamped on these lifeless things,
The hand that mocked them and the heart that fed.
And on the pedestal these words appear:
'My name is Ozymandias, king of kings:
Look on my works, ye Mighty, and despair!'
Nothing beside remains. Round the decay
Of that colossal wreck, boundless and bare
The lone and level sands stretch far away.

Confronted with the ravages of time, our lips, hands, heart, and ultimately our selves, must give way to 'the lone and level sands'. Like the series of tombs described by Derrida, the monument itself expresses mourning, not simply in its purpose but also in its very structure: 'It mourns through its discrete structure (interruption, separation, repetition, living-on [*survivance*]), it mourns for *itself* beyond the trappings of death that provide its theme' (*Demeure*, 10).

What Derrida means by mourning inhering in structure rather than theme may perhaps be illuminated by some remarks of Jacques Rancière in reference to Classical Greek art. Rancière reminds us that Winckelmann, in his *History of Ancient Art* of 1764, described the headless and memberless Belvedere Torso as the utmost perfection of ancient sculpture, and the masterpiece of Greek art. Rancière explores the paradox that the model of supreme beauty should be embodied in a statue of a 'crippled divinity which has no face to express any feeling, no arms or legs to command or achieve any action',[10] and interprets the statue as paradigmatic of the collapse of representation. Winckelmann's beloved statue exceeds both expression and its sculptor's intentions: in a sense, the mutilation is emblematic of its perfection, for its form is beautiful, like the waves of the sea, because of, and not merely despite, its failure to represent.

Why, though, turn to Shelley, or to Greek sculpture and architecture, to explore the question of transience and desolation? Why, earlier in this work, quote Donne, Rilke, and Pessoa? Are Aristotle, Descartes, Sartre, and Derrida not enough? Clearly one possible answer is implied by the question: the deep and complex nature of the relationship between mortality and subjectivity, passion and death, body and soul, has been repeatedly analysed by philosophers, but conceptual analysis is not of course the only way of tackling the issue. An approach through art and imagination may provide a complementary perspective. It is true that philosophers sometimes draw on the literary resources of language to discuss these questions of life and death. Kristeva may come close to satisfying us in her 'Histoires d'amour', or Jankélévitch in his avowedly poetic and evocative paradoxes about love and death; indeed Nancy may bring some readers to the brink of tears with his lyrical philosophizing about heart and soul. But this only makes the point more powerfully: it is the philosophically dangerous refusal of conceptual clarity by literary language, and its embracing of ambiguity, connotation, and narrative, that allows it to weave its path through the imbricated Moebius strip of our mortal passions. Indeed, as Sartre argued in his much misunderstood *Qu'est-ce que la littérature?*, it is the very failure of poetry to communicate that is the source of its ability to suggest the incommunicable:

> If it is true that speech is a betrayal and that communication is impossible, then each word of itself conceals its individuality and becomes an instrument of our defeat and harbourer of the incommunicable. It is not that there is *something else* to communicate; but prose communication having failed, it is the very meaning of the word that becomes the pure incommunicable. (Sit II, 86/334)

However, it is, perhaps unsurprisingly, Sartre too who gives us the other side of the argument, the argument in favour of clarity and philosophical endeavour. If the literary writer succeeds, by a form of poetic *qui perd gagne*, in evoking the incommunicable, this is still far from being the end of the matter. Indeed, it is at most half the picture. Failure may be ineradicable, and may even be put to good purpose (as in the case of the proposed 'bon usage' of Jean Genet),[11] but mutual understanding must be our aim, even if we know only too well that it will always be partial: contaminated by originary *différance* in Derrida's terms, betrayed and impossible in Sartre's. This is all grist to the poet's literary mill:

> Moroever, it is not a matter of arbitrarily introducing defeat and ruin into the course of the world, but rather of having eyes only for them. Human enterprise has two aspects: it is both success and failure. (Sit II, 86/333)

But, in the last analysis, we must seek (impossible) success, not content ourselves with (inevitable) failure. And the notion of something that lies beyond communication, 'too deep for words', is viewed by Sartre as particularly vulnerable to hijacking by extremists: 'I mistrust the incommunicable: it is the source of all violence' (Sit. II, 305/229). This is, of course, why literature can supplement philosophy but not supplant it.

The philosophers whose work we have been exploring eschew dualism, just as they eschew myths of incommunicability, simplifications of subjectivity, and mystification about mortality. They all aim to overcome the natural human tendency (which could be termed that of 'folk psychology') to imagine the body and soul as separate, and to envisage the body as the primary site of death. But philosophical and literary history is littered with, and of course enriched by, others whose focus for death is unashamedly the body separate from the soul. In 'Sailing to Byzantium' Yeats presents us with a beautiful and radical expression of this dualistic view:

That is no country for old men. The young
In one another's arms, birds in the trees
– Those dying generations – at their song,
The salmon-falls, the mackerel-crowded seas,
Fish, flesh, or fowl, commend all summer long
Whatever is begotten, born, and dies.
Caught in that sensual music all neglect
Monuments of unageing intellect.

An aged man is but a paltry thing,
A tattered coat upon a stick, unless
Soul clap its hands and sing, and louder sing
For every tatter in its mortal dress,
Nor is there singing school but studying
Monuments of its own magnificence;
And therefore I have sailed the seas and come
To the holy city of Byzantium.

O sages standing in God's holy fire
As in the gold mosaic of a wall,
Come from the holy fire, perne in a gyre,

And be the singing masters of my soul.
Consume my heart away; sick with desire
And fastened to a dying animal
It knows not what it is; and gather me
Into the artifice of eternity.

Once out of nature I shall never take
My bodily form from any natural thing,
But such a form as Grecian goldsmiths make
Of hammered gold and gold enamelling
To keep a drowsy Emperor awake;
Or set upon a golden bough to sing
To lords and ladies of Byzantium
Of what is past, or passing, or to come.

In Yeats's words, man is, along with the rest of the natural world,
a prey to the ravages of time, unless 'soul clap its hands and sing,
and louder sing, for every tatter in its mortal dress'. It is the recognition of our own mortality that makes of us more than that
mortality. But Yeats's evocation of the immortal part of man, his
soul, is in terms not of the supernatural but rather of artifice. Our
progression towards physical death can never be fully redeemed
by our spiritual immortality. The human condition, 'sick with
desire, and fastened to a dying animal', is poignant and inescapable. Even the holy fire that allows us access to eternity will, by
the same token, necessarily exclude us from the powerfully evoked
sensual music of 'the young in one another's arms', 'the salmon
falls, the mackerel-crowded seas'.

But if Yeats, despite his dualist and religious outlook, is unable
to reconcile himself to the intimations of mortality and loss of
natural sensuality in ageing, other thinkers, poets and philosophers
alike, prove themselves better able to deal with, and even celebrate, the mortality and chronic loss at the heart of the human
condition. I have chosen to end this book with the most literary
of texts: two poems, by Shelley and Yeats. This is for the pleasure
and 'delectable pain'[12] of the reader – their evocations of the desolation wrought by time and of the inescapability of desire fit only
too well with my focus on passion and death, mortality, and subjectivity. They bring us face-to-face with the tensions and dilemmas and aporias of the mortal subject, and we delight in the

bitter-sweet experience of those ambiguities. But it is their very ambiguity and undecidability that we relish. As I have tried to show, twentieth-century French philosophy is also acutely aware that mortality and subjectivity are inseparable; that identity is fragile and even fictional, and that its imbrication with alterity is what keeps us from peaceful self-coincidence at the same time as constituting us as subjects.

This is what I have attempted to sum up by describing mortality as the condition of both possibility and impossibility of subjectivity. This is the paradoxical lesson of existentialism, religious philosophy, psychoanalysis, and deconstruction. And it is the serious, philosophical work of these philosophers that has enabled us to define this aporia with something approaching confidence. The questions explored here do not have easy answers; indeed some of them arguably have no answers at all. Perhaps answers would destroy the questioner, along with the questions. It is our very inability to be satisfied by either philosophy or literature that saves us from fixity, allows us to mourn the self-identity and presence that we cannot help but yearn for, and drives us to construct human subjectivity in the image we would wish for it: mortal, finite, passionate, and always incomplete.

Notes

1 Introduction: Love and Death

1. See Chapter 5 on Deconstruction.
2. Abjection, as Kristeva theorizes it, lies outside and beyond meaning, threatens our identity and boundaries, and is epitomized by the corpse. See Chapter 4 on Psychoanalysis.
3. Freud, 'On Transience' [1914], *Standard Edition*, 14, pp. 303–7.
4. Roland Bathes, *La Chambre claire: note sur la photographie* (Paris: Gallimard, 1980), trans. Richard Howard, *Camera Lucida: Reflections on Photography* (New York: Hill and Wang, 1982).
5. Rainer Maria Rilke, *Duino Elegies* [1922], trans. Edward Snow, North Point Press, New York, 2000, p. 51.
6. Rupert Brooke expresses this particularly well in his poem, 'Love':

   LOVE is a breach in the walls, a broken gate,
   . . . Love sells the proud heart's citadel to Fate.

7. See Jean Frère, 'L'âme et le corps selon Platon', *Le Corps et l'esprit*, ed. R. Quilliot, ellipses, Paris, 2003, p. 39.
8. 'De Anima', 'On the Soul', in *The Complete Works of Aristotle*, ed. J. Barnes, Princeton University Press, Princeton and Chichester, 1984. References are all to this edition of Aristotle, pp. 641–92.
9. *Articles on Aristotle*, vol. 4, 'Psychology and Aesthetics', ed. J. Barnes, M. Schofield, and R. Sorabji, Duckworth, London, 1979, p. 4. A footnote points out that '*philopsucheo*, "to love one's *psuche*", means in fact to fear death'.
10. These aspects of the soul are not shared with non-human animals but are peculiar to human beings and possibly also the gods. My thanks to Ralph Wedgewood for clarifying this issue for me.

11. Frère, 'L'âme et le corps', p. 46.

12. *Articles on Aristotle*, pp. 22 and 24–5.

13. 'On Sleep', 455a. For a stimulating discussion of this question, see Daniel Heller-Roazen, *The Inner Touch: Archeology of a Sensation*, MIT Press, Zone Books, 2007.

14. See also 'De Anima', Book III, 425b.

15. *Articles on Aristotle*, pp. 27 and 30.

16. These questions of equivalence or otherwise have been discussed by many specialists of Aristotle's work, for example by Charles Kahn: 'Sensation and Consciousness in Aristotle's Psychology', Jonathan Barnes: 'Aristotle's Concept of Mind' and Richard Sorabji: 'Body and Soul in Aristotle', all collected in *Articles on Aristotle*, vol. 4.

17. Descartes, *Les Passions de l'âme*, in *Œuvres et lettres*, ed. A. Bridoux, nrf, Bibliothèque de la Pléiade, Gallimard, 1953, art. 30–2, pp. 710–1. See Kahn in *Articles on Aristotle*, p. 26.

18. Art. 5–6, p. 697.

19. René Descartes, *Meditations on First Philosophy* (1641/1647), trans. John Cottingham, Cambridge University Press, 1997, Second Meditation, p. 17.

20. Ibid. Sixth Meditation, p. 54. As Cottingham indicates, the French version is more extended and includes the words in parenthesis (Pléiade, p. 324). Descartes's original Latin reads: 'certum est me a corpore meo revera esse distinctum, & absque illo posse existere'.

21. The French reads 'as a pilot in his ship' (Pléiade, p. 326).

22. Ibid. p. 56. We must of course remember that the mind–body connection discussed in Meditation 6 is offered as a solution to the a priori separation between them established in Meditations 1 and 2 which is 'certain' in a way that Meditation 6 does not claim to be.

23. Taken from the French, which contains the apposition (Pléiade, p. 331). Cottingham reads simply 'This argument would be enough to show me that the mind is completely different from the body . . .', p. 59. The apposition recurs later in the same Meditation, again in the French not the English.

24. For example in his letter to Mersenne in July 1641, translated by Anthony Kenny in *Descartes: Philosophical Letters*, Clarendon Press, Oxford, 1970, p.106 (Pléiade, 1124).

25. Ibid. Letter to Gibieuf, 19 January, 1642, pp. 125–6. (Pléiade, p.1142).

26. This notion of the 'esprits animaux' provides a good opportunity for me to draw apologetic attention to the leap I have made in

moving from Aristotle to Descartes without any discussion of medieval philosophy. An exploration of the ideas of Ficino in particular would have been interesting, with his conception of the layers of the soul, and the way in which he uses 'spirits' to refer to what we would now call the nervous system, as mediating between body and mind. In Plato too, of course, the 'Middle Soul', sometimes called 'Spirit', is responsible for initiative, activity etc.

27. E.g. Roland Quilliot, 'Introduction: pour ou contre le dualisme?', p. 9.
28. A. Kenny, letter to Hyperaspites, August 1641, p. 112. (Pléiade 1130–1).
29. A. Kenny, letter to Elizabeth, July 1644, p. 153. (Pléiade dates this letter July, 1647, p. 1280).
30. A. Kenny, letter to Elizabeth, 6 October 1645, p. 177 (Pléiade 1213–14).
31. A. Kenny, letter to Regius, May 1641, p. 102 (not in Pléiade selection).
32. A. Kenny, letter to Elizabeth, 28 June, 1643, pp. 141 and 143 (Pléiade 1158, 1160) and letter to Arnauld, 29 July 1648, p. 236 (Pléiade 1161).
33. A. Kenny, letter to Chanut (for Queen Christine of Sweden), 1 February 1647, p. 210. (Pléiade 1258). See also *Les Passions de l'Ame*, art. 107, p. 745.
34. Ibid.
35. Ibid.
36. Ibid. See also *Les Passions de l'âme*, arts. 79–82, pp. 732–3.
37. Ibid. p. 212. (Pléiade, 1261).
38. Ibid. See also Descartes's discussion of the way in which passion cannot be aroused by will but only by imagination in *Les Passions de l'âme*, art. 45–6, pp. 717–18.
39. See *Les Passions de l'âme*, art. 92, where Descartes discusses the kind of intellectual sadness which is not a passion, p. 739.
40. A. Kenny, letter to Elizabeth, 28 June 1643, p. 141 (Pléiade, 1158).
41. Benedict Spinoza, *The Ethics*, (1677), trans. S. Shirley, ed. S. Feldman, Hackett, Indianapolis/Cambridge, 1992, pp. 104–5 (Part III, Proposition 2).
42. Ibid. p. 95 (Part 11, Proposition 48).
43. Ibid., pp. 142–3.
44. B. Spinoza, 'Short Treatise on God, Man and his Well-being' [1662], in *The Essential Spinoza: Ethics and Related Writings*, ed. Michael Morgan, Hackett, Indianapolis, 2006. See also discussions of love in the *Ethics*, for example pp. 218–19. For two interesting discussions of this question, see Genevieve Lloyd, 'What a union!', in *The Phi-*

losophers' Magazine, 29, 1st quarter 2005, pp. 45–48; and Chantal Jacquet, *Le Corps*, PUF, 2001, pp. 163–184.

45. Nicolas Malebranche, *Dialogues on Metaphysics and Religion* [1688], trans. N. Tolley and D. Scott, Cambridge University Press, 1997.
46. G. W. Leibniz, *A New System of the nature and communication of substances, as well as of the union existing between the Soul and Body*, (1695), collected in *Philosophical Writings*, Everyman, Dent, London, 1995, pp. 131. Leibniz in fact takes this example from his friend, Christian Huygens, a Dutch mathematician and scientist.
47. Ibid. pp. 122–3.
48. G. W. Leibniz, *Discourse on Metaphysics*, collected in *Philosophical Writings*, p. 42.
49. *A New System of the nature and communication of Substances*, p. 124.
50. 'Second Meditation', Cambridge University Press. p. 16. (Pleiade, p. 274).
51. See, for example, his 'Méditations sur l'humilité et la pénitence' [1677], in *Conversations chrétiennes*, Folio Essais, Gallimard, Paris, 1994.
52. David Hume, *Inquiry concerning the Human Understanding*, (1748, 1777), Clarendon Press, Oxford, 1997, p. 67.
53. Immanuel Kant, *Critique of Pure Reason*, trans. Norman Kemp Smith (1781), Macmillan, London and Basingstoke, 1980, p. 360. (4th Paralogism).
54. Pierre-Jean-Georges Cabanis, *Rapports du physique et du moral de l'homme*, [1802] vol. I, L'Harmattan, 2005, p.151.
55. Julien Offroy de la Mettrie, 'La Volupté' [1746], in *Œuvres philosophiques*, tome II, Fayard, 1987, p. 130.
56. La Mettrie, Ibid. p. 112.
57. La Mettrie, 'L'Art de Jouir' [1753], in *Œuvres philosophiques*, p. 300.
58. Ludwig Wittgenstein, *Philosophical Investigations*, trans. G. E. M. Anscombe, Blackwell, Oxford, 1953, Part II, p. 178.
59. Gilbert Ryle, *The Concept of Mind*, (1949), Penguin Books, London 1990.
60. W. V. Quine, from *Men of Ideas: Some Creators of Contemporary Philosophy*, interviews with Brian Magee, BBC Press, 1978 and Oxford University Press, 1982.
61. See J-P Changeux, *L'Homme neuronal*, Fayard, Paris, 1983.
62. See for example, Paul Churchland, *Matter and Consciousness: A Contemporary Introduction to the Philosophy of Mind*, MIT Press, Cambridge MA, 1984 and Patricia Churchland, *Neurophilosophy: Towards a Unified Science of the Mind-Brain*, MIT Press, Cambridge MA, 1986.

63. Paul Ricœur, Interview with J-P Changeux, *Le Monde*, 31 October 1982. Also see J-P Changeux and P. Ricœur, *Ce qui nous fait penser. La nature et la règle*, Paris, Odile Jacob, 2000.

64. Karl Popper and John Eccles, *The Self and its Brain*, Springer, Berlin, 1977.

65. See David Chalmers, *The Conscious Mind: in Search of a Fundamental Theory*, Oxford University Press, 1996. Another major work by Chalmers on this subject, *The Character of Consciousness*, appeared in September 2010.

66. See, for example, J. R. Searle, *The Rediscovery of the Mind*, MIT Press, 1992, and *The Mystery of Consciousness*, New York Review Press, 1997.

67. Though recent work in the University of California, Berkeley, by neurologists Jack Gallant and Shinji Nishimoto claims to demonstrate that functional MRI measurements of brain activity contain far more information than was believed previously, and suggest that MRI might permit reconstruction of perceptual experiences via a new Baysian decoder. (See for example K. N. Kay et al. 'Identifying natural images from human brain activity', *Nature*, 452, 352–5, 20 March 2008.).

68 See Yves Rosetti's Preface to Jean Pillon, *Neurosciences cognitives et conscience: Comprendre les propositions de neuroscientifiques et des philosophes*, Chronique Sociale, Lyon, 2008.

69. W. V. Quine, *Quiddities. An Intermittently Philosophical Dictionary*, Belknap Press of Harvard University Press, 1987. Quine's logical empiricism can perhaps be seen as an enlightened new way of looking at the eternal questions of philosophy, and many of his images seem to bear this out, as when he borrows an image from Otto Neurath and compares philosophers to 'sea-farers who must rebuild their ship in open sea'.

70. See Francis Crick, *The Astonishing Hypothesis: The Scientific Search for the Soul*, Charles Scribner's Sons, New York, 1994, and Christof Koch, *The Quest for Consciousness: A Neurobiological Approach*, Roberts and Company Publishers, Colorado, 2003.

71. J-P Changeux, *Raison et Plaisir*, Odile Jacob, Paris, 2002.

72. See note 63 on Ricœur and Changeux.

73. See *L'Homme de la verité*, Odile Jacob, 2002. Changeux has also engaged in a published dialogue with mathematician Alain Connes (in *Matière à penser*, Odile Jacob, 1989) over the fundamental question of whether mathematical realities are invented or discovered. Quantum physicist Bernard d'Espagnat (in *La Matière aujourd'hui*, Seuil, 1979) also denies that Changeux's materialist reductivism can describe physical reality adequately.

74. See *Esprit où es-tu? Psychanalyse et neurosciences*, Odile Jacob, 1996.

75. Odile Jacob, 2002.

76. Ibid.

77. *Qu'est-ce que l'homme – sur les fondamentaux de la biologie et de la philosophie*, Odile Jacob, 2002.

78. Ibid.

79. Ibid.

80. See *Descartes' Error: Emotion, Reason, and the Human Brain*, 1994, and *The Feeling of what Happens: Body and Emotion in the Making of a Consciousness*, 1999. Damasio's work has been explored in this context by Slavoj Zizek, in *The Parallax View*, MIT Press, 2006, where he gives an exciting and far more detailed exploration of it than I can here. See in particular, 'Emotions lie, or, where Damasio is wrong', pp. 222–231.

81 *The Feeling of what Happens*, p. 191.

82. Ibid. p. 283.

83. Daniel C. Dennett, 'Review of Antonio R. Damasio, *Descartes' Error*, 1994, TLS, August 25, 1995, pp. 3–4.

84. Ibid.

85. See Nicholas Humphrey, *A History of the Mind*, Chatto and Windus 1992, Simon and Schuster 1992, and *The Mind Made Flesh: Essays from the Frontiers of Evolution and Psychology*, Oxford University Press, 2002. Humphey's work was discovered by Damasio somewhat belatedly, and he recognized him immediately as a precursor.

86. F. Nietzsche, *Thus Spoke Zarathustra*, trans. W. Kaufman, Random House, USA, 1954, p. 146. See also, David Hume, *A Treatise on Human Nature*, 'Reason is, and ought only to be, the slave of the passions'.

87. Jacques Derrida, *L'Ecriture et la différence* (Paris: Editions du Seuil, 1967), 427/369.

88. Jacques Derrida, *Spectres de Marx: L'Etat de la dette, le travail du deuil et la nouvelle Internationale* (Paris: Galilée, 1993), 119/68 and back cover.

89. Jacques Derrida, '"Il faut bien manger" ou le calcul du sujet', entretien avec Jean-Luc Nancy, in *Confrontations. Après le sujet qui vient?*, 20 (1989); translated as '"Eating Well", or the Calculation of the Subject', in *Points . . . Interviews, 1974–1994*, ed. Elisabeth Weber, trans. Peggy Kamuf et al. (Stanford: Stanford University Press, 1995), 92/255.

90. Michel Foucault, *Les Mots et les choses* (Paris: Gallimard, 1966), 397/421.

91. As Auden himself later recognized. The quotation is from 'September 1, 1939'.

2 Phenomenology of Emotion and Forgetfulness of Death

Jean-Paul Sartre, Maurice Merleau-Ponty, Simone de Beauvoir

1. Simone de Beauvoir, 'Merleau-Ponty et le pseudo-sartrisme', in *Privilèges*, Gallimard, 1955, p. 207.
2. 'Une idée fondamentale de la phénoménologie de Husserl: l'intentionnalité', collected in *Situations I*, Gallimard, Paris, 1947.
3. For extended discussions of Sartre's conception of emotions, see Joseph Fell, *Emotion in the Thought of Sartre*, New York, Columbia University Press, 1965, and also Strasser (1956/1977) and Solomon (1976), both in the bibliography. Three interesting articles on the subject by Glen Mazis, Hazel Barnes and Bruce Baugh are collected in volume 4 of the series *Sartre and Existentialism*, edited by W. L. McBride, Garland Publishing, New York and London, 1997.
4. See *L'Etre et le Néant*, pp. 428–84/361–412. I have discussed this in another context in 'Sartre: desiring the impossible', in *Philosophy and Desire*, ed. Hugh Silverman, Routledge, New York and London, 2000.
5. The English translation misreads 'morte' as 'mort'; in fact 'la fausse morte' refers to the woman in post-orgasmic slumber, as in the Valéry poem of that title, taken from *Charmes*.
6. This subtitle is taken from Elaine Scarry's book of that name to which we will return in the final chapter. See note 10 below.
7. See, for example, Joseph Fell's substantial *Heidegger and Sartre*, Columbia University Press, 1979.
8. *L'Etre et le Néant*, 629/544–5.
9. Ibid., 631/546–7.
10. 'Death is the possibility of the absolute impossibility of Dasein', Heidegger, *Being and Time*, §50, p. 294 [250].
11. For an essential discussion of this matter, and one to which we will return in our discussion of Jean-Luc Nancy, see Elaine Scarry, *The Body in Pain: The Making and Unmaking of the World*, London, Oxford University Press, 1985.
12. *Situations IX*, Gallimard, Paris, 1972, pp. 100–1.
13. For two interesting recent critiques see John Ireland, 'Sartre and Scarry: Bodies and Phantom Pain', in Revue internationale de Philosophie: le théâtre de Jean-Paul Sartre, 1–2005, vol. 59, no. 231, January 2005, pp. 85–106; and Guillaume Seydoux, 'De la douleur 'physique' comme 'contre-exemple flagrant' au postulat sartrien de la liberté', in *Le Portique: Sartre, conscience et liberté*, no 16, 2005, pp. 33–52.
14. I am indebted here to Margaret Whitford's analysis in *Merleau-Ponty's Critique of Sartre's Philosophy*, French Forum, Lexington, Kentucky, 1982, pp. 65–70.

15. This is not to say that many critics have not simply swallowed Merleau-Ponty's critique of Sartre without much apparent reflection. See the list provided by Margaret Whitford, p. 150.
16. Again, see Whitford, p. 150.
17. Ibid.
18. 'La Phénoménologie de la perception' in Les Temps modernes, no. 2, (Nov. 1945), pp. 366–7.
19. In *Privilèges*, Gallimard, 1955, pp. 201–72.
20. E.g., Judith Butler, 'Sex and gender in Simone de Beauvoir's Second Sex, in *Simone de Beauvoir: A Critical Reader*, ed. Elizabeth Fallaize, Routledge, London and New York, 1998, p. 32.
21. Toril Moi, *Simone de Beauvoir: The Making of an Intellectual Woman*, Blackwell, Oxford UK and Cambridge USA, 1994, p. 164.
22. Ibid. p. 173.
23. 'Pyrrhus et Cinéas' in *Pour une morale de l'ambiguïté*.
24. Ibid., p. 11/7.
25. Oliver Davis, *Age Rage and Going Gently: Stories of the Senescent Subject in Twentieth-Century French Writing*, Rodopi, Amsterdam, New York, 2006, p. 33. He is quoting Penelope Deutscher, 'Beauvoir's *Old Age*' in *The Cambridge Companion to Simone de Beauvoir*, ed. Claudia Card, Cambridge University Press, 2003, pp. 286–304, p. 302.
26. S. de Beauvoir, *La Vieillesse*, Gallimard, Paris, 1970, p. 41.
27. See Terry Keefe, *Simone de Beauvoir: A Study of her Writings*, Harrap, London, 1983, p. 60.

3 Religious Philosophy: Keeping Body and Soul Together

Gabriel Marcel, Paul Ricœur, Vladimir Jankélévitch, Emmanuel Levinas

1. See the Jewish Encyclopedia which claims that at the Rabbinical conference in Philadelphia the doctrine of the resurrection of the body was replaced by that of the immortality of the soul. (http://www.jewishencyclopedia.com/view.jsp?artid=233&letter=R&search=Resurrection).
2. It is interesting that Marcel recognizes the possibility for misunderstanding his own philosophical position on precisely this issue, and writes in *Du refus à l'invocation* (republished as *Essai de philosophie concrète*): 'Although I have explicitly repudiated everything that might in some way resemble or be connected with materialism, I would not be surprised if my radical rejection of dualism seems to some as necessarily establishing such strong ties between man and his earthly environment that the doors opening onto transcendence are thereby closed to him.' (p. 252/169).

3. _Le mort de demain_, 1919, collected in _Trois pièces_, Plon, 1931, p. 161.
4. _Essai de philosophie concrète_, p. 215/143. (Idées re-publication of _Du refus à l'invocation_, 1940.).
5. _Fragments philosophiques, 1909–1914_, ed. Nauwelaerts, Louvain and Paris, 1961, p. 78.
6. _Gabriel Marcel et Karl Jaspers: philosophie du mystère et philosophie du paradoxe_, Temps présent, 1948.
7. See Corinthians I, 15, v.35 et seq.
8. We will see Derrida address the question of Husserl and the problem of translating the Leib/ Korper terminology in Chapter 5.
9. Ricœur is quoting Heidegger's _Sein und Zeit_, 275, and gives references to French translations by Martineau, p. 199, and Vezin, p, 332. In the Macquarrie and Robinson (Blackwell, Oxford) translation, the relevant passage is p. 320.
10. It was dedicated to his wife Simone who died in 1996.
11. Ricœur also discusses Spinoza's claim in _La Mémoire, l'histoire, l'oubli_, pp. 465–6/357.
12. _Soi-même_, pp. 49–50/36, citing Strawson's _Individuals_, Methuen, London, 1957, p. 89.
13. See also Jankélévitch's _Philosophie première_: 'Regret regrets not being able to prolong an irreversible moment; but remorse suffers from not being able to annul that which has been irrevocably done (_fecisse_)', p. 164.
14. V. Jankélévitch, 'Pardonner?'[1971], reprinted in _L'Impréscriptible_, Seuil, Paris, 1986; 'Should We Pardon Them?', trans. Ann Hobart, in _Critical Inquiry_, vol. 22.3, 1996, p. 50/567.
15. Avertissement to 'Pardonner?' Ibid. pp. 14–15/553, and quoted in Ricœur's _La Mémoire_, p. 613/598.
16. It is true that Ricœur already uses the distinction in volume III of _Temps et Récit_ (1985), but the Jankelevitch usage is still decades earlier.
17. See for example _Autrement qu'être ou au-délà de l'essence_, pp. 91–102/64–74.
18. When we explore the work of Didier Anzieu in the next chapter, we will see an extraordinary development of such a theorization of skin.
19. At this point we may perhaps understand the qualms of Michael de Saint-Cheron when, in his interviews in the 1990s, he suggests to Levinas that his ethics may seem more Christian than Jewish (_Entretiens avec E. Levinas_, 1992–4, Librairie générale française, Livre de Poche, 2006, e.g. p. 32). I must leave it to theologians to decide on this difficult issue.
20. See, for example, _Soi-même comme un autre_, pp. 408–9/337.

21. Republished, together with some essays on God and onto-theology, as *Dieu, la mort et le temps*, Grasset, 1993. All references are taken from this republished edition.

4 Psychoanalytic Thought: Eros and Thanatos, Psyche and Soma

Jacques Lacan, Didier Anzieu, Julia Kristeva

1. Julia Kristeva, *Histoires d'amour*, p. 83/67.
2. Jacques Lacan, *Ecrits*, p. 99/80.
3. See *Civilisation and its Discontents*, vol. 12, p. 304, and *Group Psychology*, vol. 12, p. 130: 'Perhaps with the solitary exception of the relation of a mother to her son, which is based on narcissism, is not disturbed by subsequent rivalry, and is reinforced by a rudimentary attempt at sexual object-choice.'
4. See too 'Beyond the pleasure principle', p. 327 for a discussion of the element of sadism present in the sexual instincts. Freud's argument is that this does not derive from Eros but is rather a death instinct which has been 'forced away from the ego and has consequently only emerged in relation to the object'.
5. Borrowing a term from Barbara Low.
6. Freud describes his own discoveries as 'bewildering and obscure' (333), and suggests that they might seem more acceptable if he was 'already in a position to replace the psychological terms by physiological or chemical ones' (334). Laplanche and Pontalis give an illuminating overview of Freud's thinking on this topic in their *Vocabulaire de la psychanalyse*, PUF, 1967, especially in 'Pulsions de mort', pp. 371–8.
7. 'Courtly love [. . .] is a highly refined way of supplementing the absence of sexual relationship, by feigning that we are the ones who erect an obstacle thereto' (XX, 65/69). See also *Séminaire VII*.
8. This will, of course, not deter us: 'The point is that love is impossible and the sexual relationship drops into the abyss of nonsense, which doesn't in any way diminish the interest we must have in the Other' (XX, 81/87).
9. Lacan speaks appreciatively of Sartre's phenomenology of love in *Séminaire I*, pp. 241–2/216, and calls it 'irrefutable'.
10. There is much humour to be found in Lacan, though it is often overlooked. Here for example, as in note 6 above, we see his amused recognition that sexual relations, or love-making, in the usual sense of the term, continue as normal whatever psychoanalysis may say about their inadequacy: 'that bear an astonishing resemblance to love'. Earlier in the Seminar we see his mockery of a particularly naive feminist reaction to his claim that 'Woman does not exist'.

Quoting an Italian journalist, 'According to Dr Lacan, Ladies – *le donne* – Do Not Exist!', he continues wryly: 'It's true – what did you expect? – If the sexual relationship doesn't exist, there aren't any ladies' (SXX, 54/57).

11. Lacan accuses Freud of ignoring feminine *jouissance* in his insistence that the libido is solely masculine (SXX, 75/81).

12. Lacan's claim that the phallus is a 'privileged signifier' (E, 693/581), described in 'La signification du phallus' as 'the signifier that is destined to designate meaning effects as a whole' (E, 690/579), in 'Sur la théorie du symbolisme d'Ernest Jones' as 'the signifier of the very loss that the subject suffers due to the fragmentation brought on by the signifier' (E, 715/599), and in *Séminaire XX*, (p. 75/81) as without a signified, is what led Derrida to accuse him of phallogocentrism.

13. Despite attractive arguments which link him to Marcuse. See for example Daniel Cho, 'Thanatos and Civilization: Lacan, Marcuse, and the death drive', in *Policy Futures in Education*, vol. 4, no. 1, 2006, pp. 18 – 30.

14. Malcolm Bowie, *Lacan*, London, Fontana Press, 1991, p. 199.

15. Bowie, *Lacan*, pp. 202–3.

16. On this occasion, when he is answering questions for the radio in 1970, Lacan's formula is clearer and possibly less controversial: 'There is no sexual relation, by which it is understood: formulable within the structure' (AE, 413). A little later, in 1972, in 'L'Etourdit', he writes: '*There is no sexual relation*. This presupposes that there is only the utterance of relation (of relation 'in general')' (AE, 455).

17. Freud's description of the sexual experience of the child, who does not (yet) seek genital satisfaction.

18. 'Homage to Marguerite Duras, on *Le ravissement de Lol V. Stein'*, Paris: Seuil, 2001, transl. by Peter Connor in *Duras by Duras*, City Lights Books, San Francisco, CA, 1987.

19. We should note that Lacan has made the gender of love feminine here, in a way that is archaic, at least in the singular, and continues only in a few songs.

20. Though he does claim to believe that the super-ego is structured like a language. See *Une peau pour les pensées*, p. 72.

21. See *Le Moi-Peau*, chapter 6, especially p. 107/85.

22. Marc Lafrance, in his Oxford University doctoral thesis of 2006 entitled *(Re)covering the Body: A Critical Introduction to Didier Anzieu and the Psychoanalysis of Skin*, shows how, in *Gender Trouble*, Butler distorts Freud's remarks in order to argue that the body is a product of the ego, rather than vice versa (pp. 82–4). I would like to take this opportunity to record my thanks to Marc Lafrance for

all I learnt from him about Anzieu in the course of supervising his doctoral work.

23. Abraham and Torok, *L'Ecorce et le noyau*, referred to by Anzieu in *MP*, 31/9.
24. Deleuze also questions the hierarchy of depth and surface, profundity and superficiality in *Logique du sens* of 1969.
25. It is true that in *Le Penser*, Anzieu gives an apparently less surface-centred account when he writes: 'the kernel of the mind is the thinking ego; the shell is the skin-ego' (p. 14) but this does not affect his conception of the *moi-peau* which has been, from the outset, a stage on the path to subjectivity.
26. *Une peau pour les pensées*, p. 65.
27. Ego psychology is, of course, a particular school of psychology and not a general term for all psychological approaches that concentrate on the ego. It is to be distinguished from self psychology, for example. These issues are technical and, although interesting, would be a distraction from our present purposes which attempt to remain philosophical rather than properly psychoanalytic or therapeutic.
28. *L'Epiderme nomade*, pp. 92–3.
29. *Ecrits*, p. 94/76.
30. It is worth noting that Sartre too, despite describing the ego as an imaginary construct, does not thereby deny either its existence or even its value. See Hazel Barnes in *The Cambridge Companion to Sartre*, (ed. C. Howells), Cambridge University Press, 1992.
31. See *Une Peau pour les pensées*, where religion is described as a necessary illusion (p. 61), as is group identity (p. 107); and *Créer/Détruire*, where the couple is similarly described (p. 254). We might note that in *L'Idiot de la famille*, Sartre says much the same of mother-love: by masking our contingency it gives us a (necessary) illusion of necessity.
32. See for example *Psychanalyse des limites*, p. 50–2: 'Logical paradoxes are figures of the death drive.'
33. *Le Penser*, p. 6.
34. See above, pp. [3–4].
35. See pp. 31–5/21–4. Here Kristeva seems closer to Anzieu than to Lacan in so far as she seems to view the strengthening of the ego in a positive light.
36. Kristeva is careful to distinguish her usage from that of Lacan or Heidegger, where the Thing is extensively theorized, but this is not the place to discuss the detail of these different definitions.
37. A. Green, *Narcissisme de vie, narcissisme de mort*, ed. de Minuit, 1983, p. 255.

38. As Anzieu points out in relation to Freud's notion of the 'psychic apparatus': 'Freud uses the terms "psychischer" and "seelischer Apparat" interchangeably', *Le Moi-Peau*, p. 96, footnote 3/74, footnote 2.

39. This example is drawn from an article by Z. Pylyszyn entitled 'Computation and cognition. Issues in the foundation of cognitive science', published in the *Journal of Behavioural Brain Sciences*, 1980, pp. 111–69.

40. Michael Dummett, *Origins of Analytical Philosophy*, Cambridge MA, Harvard University Press, 1993, p. 193. Dummett was speaking of the divide between Continental and analytic philosophy.

5   The Deconstruction of Dualism: Death and the Subject

Jacques Derrida and Jean-Luc Nancy

1. *Les Muses*, 1994, 2001, p. 64/35.
2. *Une pensée finie*, Galilée, 1990, p. 239/255.
3. *A Taste for the Secret*, p. 88.
4. Based on his Master's thesis of 1954 on the problem of genesis in Husserl, this paper was first published in 1964 by Gandillac, Goldmann and Piaget in the ensuing conference proceedings (edited by Mouton), and was republished in 1967 in *L'Ecriture et la différence*.
5. This is a constant preoccupation for Derrida. See also, for example, 'Edmond Jabes et la question du livre' (*L'Ecriture et la différence*): 'Si le livre n'était que l'oubli le plus sûr de la mort?', p. 115.
6. Derrida explores this through an analysis of Freud's account of Jensen's *Gradiva* in an account which might, despite its exemplarity, distract us from our purpose here.
7. Collected in *L'Ethique du don*, ed. J-M Rabaté and M. Wetzel, Metailié-Transition, 1992.
8. See again ED, p. 169. Indeed, there could be no gift possible except between mortals ('Donner la mort', p. 49/49).
9. We discussed this in the chapter on Religious Philosophy.
10. Jacques Derrida, 'Donner la mort', in *L'Ethique du don. Jacques Derrida et la pensée du don*, Colloque de Royaumont, December 1990, edited by J-M Rabaté and M. Wetzel (Paris: Metailié-Transition, 1992, pp. 43/41, 45/43.
11. Jacques Derrida, *De la grammatologie* (Paris: Editions de Minuit, 1967), 159. I have discussed this in more detail in my *Derrida: Deconstruction from Phenomenology to Ethics* (Cambridge: Polity Press, 1998), 128–30.
12. Jacques Derrida, 'Donner la mort', p. 61/60.

13. 'Donner la mort', p. 108/78, n.6.
14. 'Donner la mort', p. 62/61.
15. See also *Etats d'âme*, p. 83.
16. This is discussed by Derrida on many occasions, including of course 'L'animal que donc je suis', in *L'Animal autobiographique*, 1999; *L'Animal que donc je suis*, Galilée, 2006; and *Séminaire: La bête et le souverain, vol. 1 (2001–2002)*, 2008.
17. It would be interesting to consider this question in conjunction with similar issues raised in *De l'Esprit*.
18. 'In Memoriam', *Yale French Studies*, vol. 69, 1985, not included in the English translation of *Mémoires*.
19. Jacques Derrida, *Adieu: à Emmanuel Levinas*, Galilée, Paris, 1997; *Adieu: to Emmanuel Levinas*, trans. Pascale-Anne Brault and Michael Naas. Stanford University Press, Stanford, 1999. p. 16/6.
20. *Adieu*, 18/7.
21. Ibid. 33/132.
22. Ibid. 17/9.
23. 'The laws of love', to use the wonderful phrase coined by Arundhati Roy in *The God of Small Things*.
24. Cf: Sartre's criticism of Heidegger, discussed in Chapter 2.
25. Derrida's relationship with religion, Jewish and Christian in particular, is extremely complex. Like Jean-Luc Nancy, with his recent 'deconstruction of Christianity', Derrida can certainly not be identified with any simple rejection of religion; indeed, both philosophers arguably attempt to combine atheism with faith, understood as something other than belief. Both write incessantly about questions of religion, prayer, sacrifice, sacrament etc., and subscribe to positions that seem remarkably close to those of contemporary 'death of God' theologians. Although there are significant differences between their (different) views and those of Vattimo, many similarities are evident, for example in their understanding of the way in which Christianity in its historicity becomes increasingly self-deconstructive, an aspect which Vattimo is happy to call nihilism and interpret in a positive sense. Vattimo and Nancy were, of course, both very committed Catholics in their youth. Their current attitudes to religion are sophisticated, complex, and would certainly warrant an extended discussion in another context. Janicaud's study of *The Theological Turn* in recent French philosophy does not consider either Nancy or Derrida, but rather a set of thinkers whom he believes smuggle religion and theology into phenomenology while denying it. The relationship between these approaches would merit a study in its own right. Perhaps I will one day undertake it.

26. See below, and 'Responsabilités – du sens à venir', a discussion between Derrida and Nancy in *Sens en tous sens*, Galilée, 2004, p. 167.
27. See below.
28. Nancy's text is studded with unreferenced quotations from Derrida's work. These come from *Mémoires d'aveugle. L'autoportrait et autres ruines*, ed. Réunion des Musées Nationaux, Paris, 1990, p. 72/68–9.
29. Michel Henry would vigorously disagree. See for example *Incarnation: une philosophie de la chair*, Seuil, 2000. His conception of the flesh is resolutely positive, and seems to ignore St Paul.
30. In French, of course, 'esprit' has to do duty for both mind and spirit, which makes it much harder for it to throw off its spiritualist overtones, and gives 'la philosophie de l'esprit' a range of connotations quite out of keeping with the Philosophy of Mind for which it serves as a translation. See the Introduction for a further discussion of this question.
31. Jean-Luc Nancy, 'Thought as a Gap that Touches', interview with Chantal Pontbriand in *Poiesis*, vol. 3, 2001.
32. Elaine Scarry, *The Body in Pain: the Making and Unmaking of the World* (Oxford University Press, 1985).
33. *Dédale*, nos. 9 and 10, automne 1999, *La venue de l'étranger*, 'L'Intrus', pp. 440–50.
34. Until very recently it seemed that in both philosophy and science the brain had entirely taken over from the heart as the seat of selfhood, memory, emotion and thought, and that the heart had been definitively relegated to the realm of metaphor, as in expressions such as 'heart-broken' or 'I know in my heart.' But heart-transplant surgery seems to have put the nature of this shift in question, for the experience of a number of heart-transplant patients has been one of a significant personality change, and an influx of new memories, feelings, emotions, desires and even traumas which, upon investigation, have been found to be uncannily close to those of the donor – too close and too frequent to be explained by mere coincidence. The area is of course still highly controversial, but some contemporary neurologists maintain that the heart, like the brain, contains memory neurons and hormones, has areas of long and short-term memory, and is arguably more constitutive of our sense of selfhood and identity than we have recognized for centuries.
35. See, for example, J. Derrida, *Cosmopolites de tous les pays, encore un effort!*, Galilée, 1997.
36. Jean-Luc Nancy, 'Thought as a Gap that Touches', interview with Chantal Pontbriand in *Poiesis*, vol. 3, 2001.

37. Jacques Derrida, '"Il faut bien mange", ou le calcul du sujet', in *Points de suspension, Entretiens*, Paris, Galilée, 1992; translated as '"Eating Well", or the Calculation of the Subject', in *Points . . . Interviews, 1974–1994*, ed. Elisabeth Weber, trans. Peggy Kamuf et al. (Stanford: Stanford University Press, 1995).

Epilogue

1. In its original form, 'Life is a sexually transmitted disease and the mortality rate is one hundred per cent', the quip is attributed to R. D. Laing.
2. See, in particular, my essay on 'Sartre and the Deconstruction of the Subject', in *The Cambridge Companion to Sartre*, Cambridge University Press, 1992, pp. 318–52.
3. See Derrida's contribution to the special issue of *Confrontations*, entitled *Après le sujet, qui vient?*, no. 20, Winter 1989, p. 92.
4. J. Lacan, *Ecrits*, p. 99. And see above, Chapter 4 on Psychoanalysis.
5. J. Derrida, 'In Memoriam: de l'âme', *Mémoires pour Paul de Man*, pp. 18–19.
6. M. Foucault, *Surveiller et punir: Naissance de la prison*, Gallimard, 1975.
7. 'Sartre and the Deconstruction of the Subject', p. 321.
8. J. Lacan, 'Tuché et automaton', in *Le Séminaire, Livre XI, Les Quatre concepts fondamentaux de la psychanalyse*, Paris, Seuil, 1973, p. 53–4/53–4.
9. Sarah Kofman, *Mélancolie de l'art*, Galilée, 1985. Back cover.
10. Jacques Rancière, 'Aesthetic Separation, Aesthetic Community: Scenes from the Aesthetic Regime of Art', text of a plenary lecture delivered on 20 June 2006 to the Symposium *Aesthetics and Politics: with and around Jacques Rancière* at the University of Amsterdam. http://www.artandresearch.org.uk/v2n1/pdfs/ranciere.pdf, accessed 9 November 2010.
11. See J-P Sartre, 'Prière pour le bon usage de Genet', *Saint Genet, comédien et martyr*, Gallimard, 1952.
12. Saint Teresa of Avila, *Interior Castle*, Wilder Publications, 2008, p. 81.

Bibliography

Abraham, Nicholas and Maria Torok. *L'Ecorce et le noyau*, Aubier Flammarion, 1978; *The Shell and the Kernel, vol. 1: Renewals of Psychoanalysis*, ed. and trans. Nicholas T. Rand. Chicago: University of Chicago Press, 1994.

Agacinski, Sylviane, *Corps en miettes*, Paris: Flammarion, 2009.

Agamben, Giorgio and Valeria Piazza. *L'Ombre de l'amour: le concept de l'amour chez Heidegger*, trans. Joël Gayraud. Paris: Rivages, 2003.

Ameisen, J-C, *La Sculpture du vivant: le suicide cellulaire ou la mort créatrice*, ed. du Seuil, Paris, 1993.

Anzieu, Didier. *Le Groupe et l'inconscient*. Paris: Dunod, 1975.

—— *Le Corps de l'oeuvre*. Paris: Gallimard, 1981.

—— *Le Moi-peau*, [1985] nouvelle édition revue et augmentée. Paris: Dunod, 1995; *The Skin Ego*, trans. Chris Turner. New Haven: Yale University Press, 1989.

—— *Une Peau pour les pensées: entretiens avec Gilbert Tarrab*. Paris: Apsygée, 1986.

—— *L'Epiderme nomade et la peau psychique*. Paris: Apsygée, 1990.

—— *Le Penser: du Moi-peau au Moi-pensant*. Paris: Dunod, 1994.

—— *Créer-Détruire*. Paris: Dunod, 1996.

—— *Psychanalyser*. Paris: Dunod, 2000.

—— *Psychanalyse des limites* (textes réunis et présentés par C. Chabert). Paris: Dunod, 2007.

—— and M. Monjauze, *Francis Bacon ou le portrait de l'homme désésperé*. Paris: Seuil/Archimbaud, [1993] 2004.

Aristotle, 'De Anima', in *The Complete Works of Aristotle*, ed. J. Barnes. Princeton: Princeton University Press, 1984.

Avila, Saint Teresa, *Interior Castle*, Wilder Publications, 2008.

Baldwin, T. (ed.), *Maurice Merleau-Ponty: Basic Writings*, London: Routledge, 2004.

Barnes, J., M. Schofield and Richard Sorabji, eds. *Articles on Aristotle*, vol. 4, 'Psychology and Aesthetics', Duckworth, London, 1979.

Barthes, R. *La Chambre claire: note sur la photographie*, Gallimard, Paris, 1980; *Camera Lucida: Reflections on Photography*, trans. Richard Howard (New York: Hill and Wang, 1982)

—— *Journal de Deuil, 26 octobre 1977–15 septembre 1979*, Paris: Seuil, 2009.

Beauvoir, Simone de, *Tous les hommes sont mortels*, Paris: Gallimard, 1946.

—— *Pour une morale de l'ambiguïté*, suivi de *Pyrrhus et Cinéas*. Paris, Folio/Gallimard, 1947; *The Ethics of Ambiguity*, trans. Bernard Frechtman. New York: Citadel, 2000.

—— *Le Deuxième sexe, vols I and II*, [1949] Paris, Folio/Gallimard, reprinted 1976; *The Second Sex*, trans. Constance Borde and Sheila Malovaney Chevalier. New York: Alfred Knopf, 2010.

—— *Privilèges*, Paris, Gallimard, 1955, (includes 'Merleau-Ponty et le pseudo-sartrisme')

—— *Mémoires d'une jeune fille rangée*, Paris, Gallimard, 1958; *Memoirs of a Dutiful Daughter*, trans. James Kirkup. Harmondsworth: Penguin, 2001.

—— *La Force de l'âge*. Paris, Gallimard, 1960; *The Prime of Life*, trans. Peter Green. Harmondsworth: Penguin, [1962] 2001.

—— *La Force des choses*. Paris: Gallimard, 1963.

—— *Une Mort très douce*. Paris: Gallimard, 1964.

—— *La Vieillesse*. Paris: Gallimard, 1970.

—— *Tout compte fait*. Paris: Gallimard, 1972.

—— *La Cérémonie des adieux*. Paris: Gallimard, 1981.

Bennett, Maxwell, Daniel Dennett, Peter Hacker and John Searle. *Neuroscience and Philosophy: Brain, Mind, and Language*. New York: Columbia University Press, 2003.

Bernasconi, R. and David Wood, eds. *The Provocation of Levinas*, London: Routledge, 1988.

Bianchi, H. et al. *La Question du vieillissement: perspectives psychanalytiques*, Paris: Dunod, 1989.

Borch-Jacobsen, Mikkel. *Le Sujet freudien*. Paris: Flammarion, 1982.

Bossi, L. *Histoire naturelle de l'âme*. Paris: PUF, 2003.

Bowie, Malcolm. *Lacan*. London: Fontana Press, 1991.

—— *Psychoanalysis and the Future of Theory*. Oxford: Blackwell, 1993.

Cabanis, P-J-G, *Rapports du physique et du moral de l'homme*, vol 1. Paris: L'Harmattan, [1802] 2005.

Cain, S. *Gabriel Marcel*. London: Bowes and Bowes, 1963.

Caputo, John, *The Prayers and Tears of Jacques Derrida: Religion without Religion.* Bloomington: Indiana University Press, 1997.
—— *On Religion.* London: Routledge, 2001.
——, Mark Dooley and Michael Scanlon, eds. *Questioning God.* Bloomington: Indiana University Press, 2001.
——, ed. *The Religious.* Oxford: Blackwell, 2002.
—— and Gianni Vattimo. *After the Death of God.* New York: Columbia University Press, 2007.
Carman, T and Mark Hansen. *The Cambridge Companion to Merleau-Ponty.* Cambridge: Cambridge University Press, 2005.
Cassam, Qassim, ed. *Self-Knowledge.* Oxford: Oxford University Press, 1994.
Chalmers, David J. *The Conscious Mind: in Search of a Fundamental Theory.* Oxford: Oxford University Press, 1996.
—— *The Character of Consciousness.* Oxford: Oxford University Press, 2010.
Changeux, J-P. *L'Homme neuronal.* Paris: Fayard, 1983.
—— *Raison et Plaisir.* Paris: Odile Jacob, 2002.
—— *L'Homme de la vérité.* Paris: Odile Jacob, 2002.
Changeux, Jean-Pierre and Alain Connes. *Matière à penser.* Paris: Odile Jacob, 1989.
Changeux, Jean-Pierre and Paul Ricœur. Interview in *Le Monde,* 31 October, 1982.
—— *Ce qui nous fait penser. La nature et la règle,* Paris: Odile Jacob, 2000; *What Makes Us Think,* trans. M. B. DeBevoise. Princeton: Princeton University Press, 2000.
Chanter, Tina. *Time, Death, and the Feminine: Levinas with Heidegger.* Stanford: Stanford University Press, 2001.
Cho, D. 'Thanatos and Civilization: Lacan, Marcuse, and the death drive', in *Policy Futures in Education,* vol. 4, no. 1, 2006, pp. 18–30.
Choron, Jacques. *Death and Western Thought.* Paris: Collier-Macmillan, 1963.
Churchland, Patricia. *Neurophilosophy: Towards a Unified Science of the Mind-Brain.* Cambridge, MA: MIT Press, 1986.
Churchland, Paul. *Matter and Consciousness: a Contemporary Introduction to the Philosophy of Mind.* Cambridge MA: MIT Press, 1984.
Clarke, Desmond M. *Descartes's Theory of Mind.* Oxford: Clarendon, 2003.
Clark, Steve. H. *Paul Ricœur.* London: Routledge, 1990.
Crick, Francis. *The Astonishing Hypothesis: the Scientific Search for the Soul.* New York: Simon and Schuster, 1994.
Cyrulnik, Boris. *De Chair et d'âme.* Paris: Odile Jacob, 2006.
Dastur, Françoise. *Chair et langage: Essais sur Merleau-Ponty.* Fougères: Encre marine, 2001.

Damasio, A. *Descartes' Error: Emotion, Reason, and the Human Brain.* New York: Putnam 1994.

—— *The Feeling of What Happens: Body and Emotion in the Making of Consciousness.* London: Heinemann, 1999.

Davis, C. *Levinas: An Introduction.* Cambridge: Polity Press, 1996.

Davis, O. *Age Rage and Going Gently: Stories of the Senescent Subject in Twentieth-Century French Writing.* Amsterdam and New York: Rodopi, 2006.

Deleuze, G. *Logique du sens,* Paris: Minuit, 1968.

Dennett, D. C. 'Review of Antonio R. Damasio, *Descartes' Error*', 1994, TLS, August 25, 1995, pp. 3–4.

Derrida, J. *Introduction à L'*Origine de la géométrie *de Husserl.* Paris: PUF, 1962; *Edmund Husserl's Origin of Geometry: An Introduction,* trans. John P. Leavey, Jr. Lincoln: University of Nebraska Press, 1989.

—— *L'Ecriture et la différence.* Paris: Seuil, 1967; *Writing and Difference,* trans. Alan Bass. London: Routledge, 1978.

—— *De la grammatologie.* Paris: Minuit, 1967.

—— *La Voix et le phénomène,* Paris: PUFs, 1967; *Speech and Phenomena,* trans. David B. Allison. Evanston: Northwestern University Press, 1973.

—— *Glas.* Paris: Galilée, 1974.

—— *La Carte postale: de Socrate à Freud et au-delà.* Paris: Aubier-Flammarion, 1980; *The Post Card: From Socrates to Freud and Beyond,* trans. Alan Bass. Chicago: University of Chicago Press, 1987.

—— *Psyche: inventions de l'autre.* Paris: Galilée, 1987.

—— *De l'esprit: Heidegger et la question.* Paris: Galilée, 1987.

—— *Mémoires: pour Paul de Man.* Paris: Galilée, 1988; *Mémoires for Paul de Man,* trans. Cecile Lindsay, Jonathan Culler and Eduardo Cadava. New York: Columbia University Press, 1986.

—— '"Il faut bien manger" ou le calcul du sujet', entretien avec Jean-Luc Nancy, in *Confrontations. Après le sujet qui vient?,* 20. Paris: Aubier, 1989, pp. 91–114, reprinted in *Points de suspension, Entretiens.* Paris: Galilée, 1992; translated as '"Eating Well", or the Calculation of the Subject', in *Points…Interviews, 1974–1994,* ed. Elisabeth Weber, trans. Peggy Kamuf et al. Stanford: Stanford University Press, 1995.

—— *Mémoires d'aveugle: l'autoportrait et autres ruines.* Paris: Louvre/ Réunion des Musées Nationaux, 1990; *Memoirs of the Blind: the Self-Portrait and Other Ruins,* trans. Pascale-Anne Brault and Michael Naas. Chicago: Chicago University Press, 1993.

—— 'Donner la mort', in *L'Ethique du don. Jacques Derrida et la pensée du don,* Colloque de Royaumont, December 1990, ed. J.-M. Rabaté and M. Wetzel. Paris: Metailie-Transition, 1992; *The Gift of Death,* trans. David Wills. Chicago: Chicago University Press, 1995.

—— *Spectres de Marx: 'L'Etat de la dette, le travail du deuil et la nouvelle Internationale*, Paris: Galilée, 1993; *Specters of Marx*, trans. Peggy Kamuf. New York: Routledge, 1994.

—— *Khôra*. Paris: Galilée, 1993.

—— *Sauf le nom*. Paris: Galilée, 1993.

—— *Passions*. Paris: Galilée, 1993.

—— *Politiques de l'amitié; suivi de l'oreille de Heidegger*. Paris: Galilée, 1994; *The Politics of Friendship*, trans. George Collins. London: Verso, 1997.

—— *Mal d'Archive: une impression freudienne*. Paris: Galilée, 1995; *Archive Fever*, trans. Eric Prenowitz. Chicago: Chicago University Press, 1996.

—— *Apories*. Paris: Galilée, 1996; *Aporias*, trans. Thomas Dutoit. Stanford: Stanford University Press, 1993.

—— *Résistances: de la psychanalyse*. Paris, Galilée, 2000; *Resistances of Psychoanalysis*, trans. Peggy Kamuf. Stanford: Stanford University Press, 1998.

—— *La Religion: Séminaire de Capri*, ed. Jacques Derrida and Giannni Vattimo. Paris: Seuil, 1996.

—— *Adieu: à Emmanuel Levinas*. Paris: Galilée, 1997; *Adieu: to Emmanuel Levinas*, trans. Pascale-Anne Brault and Michael Naas. Stanford: Stanford University Press, 1999.

—— *Cosmopolites de tous les pays, encore un effort!* Paris: Galilée, 1997.

—— 'L'animal que donc je suis (à suivre)', *L'Animal autobiographique*. Paris: Galilée, 1999, pp. 251–301.

—— *Etats d'âme de la psychanalyse*. Paris: Galilée, 2000; 'Psychoanalysis Searches the States of its Soul', in *Without Alibi*, ed. and trans. Peggy Kamuf. Stanford: Stanford University Press, 2002.

—— *Le Toucher: Jean-Luc Nancy*, Paris: Galilée, 2000; *On Touching – Jean-Luc Nancy*, trans. Christine Irizaray. Stanford: Stanford University Press, 2005.

—— *Chaque fois unique, la fin du monde*. Paris: Galilée, 2003; *The Work of Mourning*, trans. Pacale-Anne Brault and Michael Naas. Chicago: University of Chicago Press, 2001.

—— *Genèse, généalogies, genres et le genie*. Paris: Galilée, 2003.

—— *Apprendre à vivre enfin*. Paris, Galilée, 2005.

—— *L'Animal que donc je suis*. Paris, Galilée, 2006.

—— *Séminaire; La Bête et le souverain, vol. 1 (2001–2002)*. Paris: Galilée, 2008.

—— *Demeure, Athènes. Photographies de Jean-Francois Bonhomme*. Paris: Galilée, 2009 [1996]; *Athens, Still Remains: The Photographs of Jean-François Bonhomme*, trans. Michael Naas and Pascale-Anne Brault. New York: Fordham University Press, 2010.

—— and Maurizio Ferraris. *A Taste for the Secret*. Cambridge: Polity, 2001.

Descartes, René. *Les Passions de l'âme* [1649] in *Œuvres et lettres*, ed. A Bridoux. Paris: Pléiade Gallimard, 1953.

—— *Meditations on First Philosophy* [1640], trans. John Cottingham, Cambridge University Press, Cambridge, 1997.

—— *Descartes: Philosophical Letters*, trans. Anthony Kenny, Clarendon Press, Oxford, 1970.

d'Espagnat, B. *La Matière aujourd'hui*. Paris: Seuil, 1979.

Dummett, Michael. *Origins of Analytical Philosophy*. Harvard: Harvard University Press, 1993.

Dumoulié, C. *Le Désir*. Paris: Armand Colin, 1999.

Evans, Dylan. *An Introductory Dictionary of Lacanian Psychoanalysis*. London: Routledge, 1996.

Fallaize, Elizabeth. *Simone de Beauvoir: A Critical Reader*. London: Routledge, 1998.

Felman, Shoshana, ed. *Literature and Psychoanalysis: The Question of Reading: Otherwise*. Baltimore: Johns Hopkins University Press, 1982.

Foucault, M. *Les Mots et les choses*, Paris: Gallimard, 1966; *The Order of Things*, trans. Alan Sheridan. London: Routledge 1989.

—— *Surveiller et punir*. Paris: Gallimard, 1975.

Frere, J. 'L'Ame et le corps selon Platon', in *Le Corps et l'esprit*, ed. R. Quilliot. Paris: Ellipses, 2003.

Freud, Sigmund. *The Standard Edition of the Complete Psychological Works of Sigmund Freud*, trans. James Strachey. London: Allen and Unwin, 1963. Edition cited: Pelican Freud Library.

—— vol. 1, *Introductory Lectures on Psychoanalysis*. Harmondsworth: Penguin, 1973.

—— vol. 11, *On Metapsychology: The Theory of Psychoanalysis*. Harmondsworth: Penguin, 1984.

—— vol. 12, *Civilization, Society and Religion*. Harmondsworth: Penguin, 1991.

—— vol. 14, *Art and Literature*. Harmondsworth: Penguin, 1985.

Gray, Jeffrey. *Consciousness: Creeping up on the Hard Problem*. Oxford: Oxford University Press, 2004.

Green, A. *Narcissisme de vie. Narcissisme de mort*. Paris: Minuit, 1983.

—— *Pourquoi les pulsions de destruction ou de mort?*. Paris: Panama, 2007.

—— et al. *L'Avenir d'une désillusion*. Paris: PUF, 2000.

Frey, Jean-Marie. *Le Corps peut-il nous rendre heureux?* Paris: Pleins Feux, 2001.

Guillaumin, J. et al. *L'Invention de la pulsion de mort*. Paris: Dunod, 2000.

Harsym, Sarah, ed. *Levinas and Lacan: the Missed Encounter*. Albany: SUNY Press, 1998.

Hassoun, J. *La Cruauté melancolique*. Paris: Aubier, 1995.

Heidegger, Martin. *Being and Time*, trans. J. Macquarrie and E. Robinson. Oxford: Blackwell, 1978.

Heller-Roazen, Daniel. *The Inner Touch: Archeology of a Sensation*. New York: Zone, 2007.

Henry, Michel. *Incarnation: une philosophie de la chair*. Paris: Seuil, 2000.

Howells, Christina. *The Cambridge Companion to Sartre*. Cambridge: Cambridge University Press, 1992.

— *Derrida: Deconstruction from Phenomenology to Ethics*. Cambridge: Polity, 1998.

Hume, David. *Inquiry Concerning the Human Understanding*. Oxford: Clarendon, [1748, 1777] 1997.

Humphrey, Nicholas. *A History of the Mind*. New York: Simon and Schuster, 1992.

—— *The Mind Made Flesh: Essays from the Frontiers of Evolution and Psychology*. Oxford: Oxford University Press, 2002.

Irigaray, Luce. *Speculum. De l'autre femme*. Paris: Minuit, 1974.

—— *Ce sexe qui n'est pas un*. Paris: Minuit, 1977; *This Sex Which Is Not One*, trans. Catherine Porter. Ithaca: Cornell University Press, 1985.

Jacquet, Chantal. *Le Corps*. Paris: PUF, 2001.

James, Ian and Patrick ffrench, eds. *The Oxford Literary Review, vol 27, Exposures: Critical Essays on Jean-Luc Nancy*, 2005.

James, Susan. *Passion and Action: The Emotions in Seventeenth-Century Philosophy*. Oxford: Clarendon, 1997.

Janicaud, Dominique et al. *Phenomenology and the 'Theological Turn': The French Debate*. New York: Fordham University Press, 2000.

Jankélévitch, Vladimir. *Philosophie Première: Introduction à une philosophie du 'presque'*. Paris: PUF, 1953.

—— *La Mort*. Paris: Flammarion, 1966.

—— *Le Pardon*. Paris: Aubier, 1967.

—— 'Pardonner?', in *L'Imprescriptible*, Paris: Seuil, [1971] 1986; "Should We Pardon Them?', trans. Ann Hobart, in *Critical Inquiry*, vol. 22.3, 1996.

—— *L'Irréversible et la nostalgie*. Paris: Flammarion, 1974.

—— *La Méconnaissance, le malentendu*. Paris: Seuil, 1980.

—— *Le Sérieux de l'intention*. Paris: Flammarion, 1983.

—— *Penser la mort*. Paris: Seuil, 1994.

Jeannerod, M. and J. Hochman. *Esprit ou es-tu? Psychanalyse et neurosciences*. Paris: Odile Jacob, 1996.

Jeannerod, M. *Le Cerveau intime*, Paris: Odile Jacob, 2002.

—— *La Nature de l'esprit*, Paris: Odile Jacob, 2002.

Kant, Immanuel. *Critique of Pure Reason*, trans. Norman Kemp Smith. London: Macmillan, [1781] 1980.

Kay, K. N. *et. al.* 'Identifying Natural Images from Human Brain Activity', *Nature*, 452, 20 March 2008, pp. 352–5.

Koch, Christof. *The Quest for Consciousness: A Neurobiological Approach.* Denver: Roberts and Company, 2003.

Kofman, Sarah. *Mélancolie de l'Art.* Paris: Galilée, 1985.

Kristeva, Julia. *Histoires d'amour.* Paris: Denoël/Folio, 1983; *Tales of Love*, trans. Leon S. Roudiez. New York: Columbia University Press, 1987.

—— ed. *The Kristeva Reader.* Oxford: Blackwell, 1986.

—— *Soleil noir: dépression et mélancolie.* Paris: Gallimard/NRF, 1987; *Black Sun: Depression and Melancholia*, trans. Leon S. Roudiez. New York: Columbia University Press, 1992.

—— *Etrangers à nous-mêmes.* Paris, Gallimard, 1988.

—— *Les Nouvelles maladies de l'âme.* Paris: Fayard, 1993; *New Maladies of the Soul*, trans. Ross Guberman. New York: Columbia University Press, 1997.

—— *Sens et non-sens de la revolte: pouvoirs et limites de la psychanalyse I.* Paris: Fayard, 1996.

—— *La Révolte intime: pouvoirs et limites de la psychanalyse II.* Paris: Fayard, 1997.

Kwant, R. *The Phenomenological Philosophy of Merleau-Ponty.* Pittsburgh: Duquesne University Press, 1963.

Lacan, Jacques. *Ecrits.* Paris: Seuil, Paris, 1966; *Ecrits: The First Complete Edition in English*, trans. Bruce Fink. New York: W. W Norton, 2007.

—— *Autres Ecrits*: Paris, Seuil, 2001.

—— *De la psychose paranoïaque dans ses rapports avec la personnalité, suivi de Premiers écrits sur la paranoia.* Paris: Seuil, 1975.

—— *Télévision.* Paris: Seuil, 1973; *Television: A Challenge to the Psycho-analytic Establishment*, trans. Joan Copjec. New York: W. W. Norton, 1990.

—— *Le Séminaire, I, Les écrits techniques de Freud.* Paris: Seuil, 1975; *The Seminar of Jacques Lacan, book I: Freud's Papers on Technique*, trans. John Forrester. New York: W. W. Norton, 1991.

—— *Le Séminaire, II, Le Moi dans la théorie de Freud et dans la technique de la psychanalyse.* Paris: Seuil, 1978; *The Seminar of Jacques Lacan, book II: The Ego in Freud's Theory and in the Technique of Psychoanalysis, 1954–55*, trans. Sylvana Tomaselli. New York: W. W. Norton, 1991.

—— *Le Séminaire, VII, L'Ethique de la psychanalyse.* Paris: Seuil, 1986; *The Seminar of Jacques Lacan, book VII: The Ethics of Psychoanalysis*, trans. Dennis Potter. New York: W. W. Norton, 1997.

—— *Le Séminaire, XI, Les Quatre concepts fondamentaux de la psychanalyse.* Paris: Seuil, 1973; *The Seminar of Jacques Lacan, book XI: The Four*

Fundamental Concepts of Psychoanalysis, trans. Alan Sheridan. New York: W. W. Norton, 1998.

—— *Le Séminaire XVIII, D'un discours qui ne serait pas du semblant.* Paris: Seuil, 2006.

—— *Le Séminaire, XX, Encore.* Paris: Seuil, 1975; *The Seminar of Jacques Lacan, book XX: On Feminine Sexuality, the Limits of Love and Knowledge*, trans. Bruce Fink. New York: W. W. Norton, 1999.

Lafrance, M. *(Re)covering the Body: A Critical Introduction to Didier Anzieu and the Pychoanalysis of Skin*, unpublished doctoral thesis of University of Oxford, 2006.

La Mettrie, J. O. de, 'La Volupté' [1746], and 'L'Art de jouir' [1753], in *Œuvres philosophiques*, tome II. Paris: Fayard, 1987.

Laplanche, Jean. *Vie et mort en psychanalyse.* Paris: Flammarion, 1970.

—— *La Sexualité humaine: biologisme et biologie.* Paris: Institut Synthélabo, 1999.

—— and Jean-Baptiste Pontalis. *Vocabulaire de la psychanalyse.* Paris: PUF, 1967.

Lavie, J-C. *L'Amour est un crime parfait.* Paris: Gallimard, 1997.

Lazar, P. *Court traité de l'âme.* Paris: Fayard, 2008.

Lear, Jonathan. *Open Minded: Working Out the Logic of the Soul.* Harvard: Harvard University Press, 1988.

Leclaire, Serge and M. Chapsal. *Apprendre à aimer.* Paris: Fayard, 2007.

Leibniz, G.W. 'Discourse on Metaphysics' [1686] and 'A New System of the nature and communication of substances, as well as of the union existing between the Soul and Body' [1695], in *Philosophical Writings*, ed. G. H. R Parkinson. London: Everyman/Dent, 1995.

Levinas, Emmanuel. *Le Temps et l'autre.* Paris: PUF, 1948/1979; *Time and the Other*, trans. Richard A. Cohen. Pittsburgh: Duquesne University Press, 1987.

—— *Totalité et Infini.* The Hague: Martinus Nijhoff, 1961; *Totality and Infinity*, trans. Alphonso Lingis. Dordrecht: Kluwer Academic, 1991.

—— *Humanisme de l'autre homme.* Paris: Fata Morgana, 1972.

—— *Autrement qu'être ou au-délà de l'essence*, (1974), The Hague, Martinus Nijhoff, 1978 (2nd edition); *Otherwise than Being, or Beyond Essence*, trans. Alphonso Lingis. The Hague: Kluwer Academic, 1991.

—— *Noms propres.* Paris: Fata Morgana, 1976.

—— *Ethique et infini.* Paris: Fayard, 1982.

—— *De Dieu qui vient à l'idée.* Paris: Vrin, 1982.

—— *Hors sujet.* Paris: Fata Morgana, 1987; *Outside the Subject*, trans. Michael B. Smith. Stanford: Stanford University Press, 1993.

—— *Dieu, la mort et le temps*, Paris, Grasset, 1993; *God, Death and Time*, trans. Bettina Bergo. Stanford: Stanford University Press, 2000.

—— *Cahiers d'Etudes Levinassiennes*, 2006 - no. 5, Levinas–Sartre.

—— and Michael de Saint Cheron. *Entretiens avec E. Levinas 1992–4.* Paris: Librairie générale de France, 2006.

Lloyd, Genevieve. 'What a Union!', in *The Philosophers' Magazine.* 29, 1st quarter, 2005.

MacCannell, J. F. *Figuring Lacan: Criticism and the cultural unconscious,* London and Sydney: Croom Helm, 1986.

Macquarrie, John. *Heidegger and Christianity.* London: SCM Press, 1994.

Malebranche, Nicolas. 'Méditations sur l'humilité et la pénitence' [1677], in *Conversations chrétiennes.* Paris: Gallimard, 1994.

—— *Dialogues on Metaphysics and Religion* [1688] trans. N. Tolley and D. Scott. Cambridge: Cambridge University Press, 1997.

Marcel, Gabriel. *Fragments philosophiques, 1909–14.* Louvain: Nauwelaerts, 1961.

—— *Journal Metaphysique.* Paris: Gallimard, [1927] 1935.

—— *Trois pièces* (includes 'Le Mort de demain'). Paris: Plon, 1931.

—— *Etre et Avoir*, Paris: Aubier Montaigne, 1935; *Being and Having*, trans. Katharine Farrar. London: Dacre, 1949.

—— *Du Refus à l'invocation* (1940), reprinted as *Essai de Philosophie concrète*, Paris: Gallimard, 1967; published in English as *Creative Fidelity*, trans. Robert Rosthal. New York: Fordham University Press, 2002.

—— *Homo Viator: prolégomènes à une métaphysique de l'espérance.* Paris: Aubier Montaigne, 1944.

Margel, S. *Corps et âme. Descartes. Du pouvoir des représentations aux fictions du Dieu trompeur.* Paris: Galilée, 2004.

McBride, W., ed. *Sartre and Existentialism*, vol. 4, Existentialist Ontology and Human Consciousness, etc. New York: Garland, 1997.

—— *Sartre and Existentialism*, vol. 8, Sartre's French contemporaries and enduring influences. New York: Garland, 1997.

Merleau-Ponty, Maurice. *La Structure du comportement*, Paris, PUF, 1942/1972; *The Structure of Behaviour*, trans. Alden L. Fisher. London: Methuen, 1965.

—— *Phénoménologie de la perception*, Paris, Gallimard, 1945; *The Phenomenology of Perception*, trans. Colin Smith. New York: Routledge, 2002.

—— *Les Aventures de la dialectique.* Paris: Gallimard, 1955.

—— *Signes.* Paris: Gallimard, 1960.

—— *L'Œil et l'esprit.* Paris: Gallimard, 1964; 'Eye and Mind' trans. Carleton Dallery in *The Primacy of Perception*, ed. James Edie. Evanston: Northwestern University Press, 1964, pp. 159–190.

—— *Le Visible et l'invisible*, Paris, Gallimard, 1964; *The Visible and the Invisible*, trans. Alphonso Lingis. Evanston: Northwestern University Press, 1968.

—— *Sens et non*-sens. Paris: Nagel, [1948] 1966; *Sense and Non-Sense*, trans. Hubert Dreyfus and P. A. Dreyfus. Evanston: Northwestern University Press, 1964.

—— *Résumés de cours, Collège de France, 1952–60*. Paris: Gallimard, 1968.

—— *La Prose du monde*. Paris: Gallimard, 1969; *The Prose of the World*, trans. Alphonso Lingis. Evanston: Northwestern University Press, 1973.

—— *L'Union de l'âme et du corps chez Malebranche, Biran et Bergson*, Paris: Vrin, [1978] 2002.

Miller, Gérard, ed. *Lacan*. Paris: Bordas, 1987.

Moi, Toril. *Sexual/Textual Politics: Feminist Literary Theory*. London: Methuen, 1985.

—— ed. *The Kristeva Reader*. Oxford: Blackwell, 1986.

—— *Simone de Beauvoir: The Making of an Intellectual Woman*. Oxford: Blackwell, 1994.

Muller, John. P. and William J. Richardson, eds. *Lacan and Language: A Reader's Guide to the Ecrits*. New York: International Universities Press, 1982.

Montmollin, I de. *La Philosophie de Vladimir Jankélévitch*. Paris: PUF, 2000.

Nancy, Jean-Luc. *Les Lieux divins, suivi de Calcul du Poète*. Mauvezin: TER, [1987] 1997.

—— *Une pensée finie*. Paris: Galilée, 1990; *A Finite Thinking*, ed. and trans. Simon Sparks. Stanford: Stanford University Press, 2003.

—— *Corpus*. Paris: Metailie, 1992, reprinted 2000; *Corpus*, including 'Extension of the Soul' and '58 Indices on the Body', trans. Richard A. Rand. New York: Fordham University Press, 2008.

—— *Le Sens du monde*. Paris: Galilée, 1993; *The Sense of the World*, trans. Jeffrey S. Librett. Minneapolis: Minnesota University Press, 1997.

—— *Les Muses*. Paris: Galilée, [1994] 2001.

—— 'L'Intrus', in *Dédale, La venue de l'étranger*, nos. 9 and 10, Autumn 1999, pp.440–450.

—— 'Thought as a gap that touches', interview with Chantal Pontbriand, *Poiesis*, vol. 3, 2001.

—— *L' 'il y a' du rapport sexuel*. Paris: Galilée, 2001.

—— *La Création du monde*. Paris: Galilée, 2002.

—— 'Le Judéo-chrétien', *Judéités*. Paris: Galilée, 2003, pp. 303–321.

—— *Noli me tangere, essai sur la levée du corps*. Paris: Bayard, 2003; *Noli Me Tangere*, trans. Sarah Clift, Pascale-Anne Brault and Michael Naas. Fordham University Press, New York, 2008.

—— *58 indices sur le corps et Extension de l'âme*, Nota bene, 2004; in *Corpus*, trans. Richard A. Rand. New York: Fordham University Press, 2008.

—— *La Déclosion: (Déconstruction du Christianisme, 1)*. Paris: Galilée, 2005.

—— *La Naissance des seins*. Paris: Galilée, 2006.

—— *A plus d'un titre, Jacques Derrida*. Paris: Galilée, 2007.

—— *Tombe de sommeil*. Paris: Galilée, 2007; *The Fall of Sleep*, trans. Charlotte Mandell. New York: Fordham University Press, 2009.

—— *Je t'aime un peu, beaucoup, passionnément*. Paris: Bayard, 2008.

—— *L'Adoration: (Déconstruction du Christianisme, 2)*. Paris: Galilée, 2010.

—— and Jacques Derrida. 'Responsabilités – du sens à venir', in Jean-Clét Martin and Francis Guibal, eds. *Sens en tous sens, autour des travaux de J-L Nancy*. Paris: Galilée, 2004, pp. 165–200.

Nancy, Jean-Luc and Philippe Lacoue-Labarthe. *Le Titre de la letter*. Paris: Galilée, 1973.

Nault, Francois, *Derrida et la théologie: Dire Dieu après la deconstruction*. Montreal: Mediaspaul/Du Cerf, 2000.

Nietzsche, Friedrich. *Thus Spoke Zarathustra*, trans. W. Kaufman. New York: Random House, 1954.

Ogilvie, B. *Lacan: Le Sujet*. Paris: PUF, 1987.

Parfit, Derek. *Reasons and Persons*. Oxford: Clarendon, 1984.

Phillips, Adam. *Darwin's Worms*. London: Faber and Faber, 2000.

Pillon, J. *Neurosciences cognitives et conscience: Comprendre les propositions des neuroscientifiques et des philosophes*, Lyon: Chronique Sociale, 2008.

Popper, K. and John C Eccles. *The Self and its Brain: An Argument for Interactionism*, Berlin: Springer, 1977.

Quilliot, Roger. *Le Corps et l'esprit*. Paris: Ellipses, 2003.

Quine, W.V. Interview with Brian Magee in *Men of Ideas: Some Creators of Contemporary Philosophy*. Oxford: Oxford University Press, 1982.

—— *Quiddities. An Intermittently Philosophical Dictionary*. Harvard: Belknap, 1987.

Rabaté, Jean-Michel. *Jacques Lacan: Psychoanalysis and the Subject of Literature*. Basingstoke: Palgrave, 2001.

Revault d'Allonnes, M. *Merleau-Ponty: La Chair du politique*, Paris: Michalon, 2001.

Revel, F. *La Passion*. Paris: Belin, 2004.

Ricœur, Paul. *Gabriel Marcel et Karl Jaspers: philosophie du mystère et philosophie du paradoxe*. Paris: Temps présent, 1948.

—— *Philosophie de la Volonté, I, Le Volontaire et l'Involontaire*. Paris: Aubier Montaigne, 1950.

—— *Philosophie de la Volonté, II, Finitude et Culpabilite* (contains 'L'Homme faillible'). Paris: Aubier Montaigne, 1960.

—— *Entretiens: Paul Ricœur, Gabriel Marcel*, Paris, Aubier Montaigne, 1968; 'Conversations between Paul Ricœur and Gabriel Marcel', in *Tragic Wisdom and Beyond*, trans. Peter McCormick and Stephen Jolin. Evanston: Northwestern University Press, 1973.

—— *Soi-même comme un autre*. Paris: Seuil, 1990; *Oneself as Another*, trans. Kathleen Blamey. Chicago: Chicago University Press, 1992.

—— (with J-P Changeux) *Ce qui nous fait penser. La nature et la règle*, Paris: Odile Jacob, 2000; *What Makes Us Think*, trans. M. B. DeBevoise. Princeton: Princeton University Press, 2000.

—— *La Mémoire, l'histoire, l'oubli*. Paris: Seuil, 2000; *Memory, History, Forgetting*, trans. Katherine Blamey and David Pellauer. Chicago: Chicago University Press, 2004.

—— *Vivant jusqu'à la mort, suivi de Fragments*, Paris: Seuil, 2007; *Living Up To Death*, trans. David Pellauer. Chicago: Chicago University Press, 2009.

Rilke, R. M. *Duino Elegies* [1922], trans. Edward Snow. New York: North Point, 2000.

Rogozinski, Jacob. *Le Moi et la chair: introduction à l'ego-analyse*. Montreal: Du Cerf, 2006.

Rose, Gillian. *Mourning Becomes the Law: Philosophy and Representation*. Cambridge: Cambridge University Press, 1996.

—— *Love's Work*. London: Vintage, 1997.

Ryle, Gilbert. *The Concept of Mind*. Harmondsworth: Penguin Books, [1949] 1990.

Sartre, Jean-Paul. *La Transcendance de l'Ego*. Paris: Vrin, [1936] 1965; *The Transcendance of the Ego*, trans. Andrew Brown. London: Routledge, 2004.

—— *Esquisse d'une théorie des émotions*. Paris: Hermann, 1939; *Sketch for a Theory of the Emotions*, trans. Philip Mairet. London: Routledge, 1994.

—— *L'Etre et le Néant*, Gallimard, Paris, 1943; *Being and Nothingness*, trans. Hazel E. Barnes. Routledge, London, 1958.

—— *Situations II: Qu'est-ce que la littérature?*, Paris: Gallimard, 1948; *'What Is Literature?' and Other Essays*, ed. and trans. Steven Ungar. Harvard: Harvard University Press, 1988.

—-*Saint Genet, comédien et martyr*. Paris: Gallimard, 1952.

Scarry, Elaine. *The Body in Pain: the Making and Unmaking of the World*. Oxford: Oxford University Press, 1985.

Schmidt J., *Maurice Merleau-Ponty: Between Phenomenology and Structuralism*. Basingstoke: Macmillan, 1985.

Schneider, M. *La Cause amoureuse: Freud, Spinoza, Racine.* Paris: Seuil, 2008.

Searle, John. R. *The Rediscovery of the Mind.* Harvard: MIT Press, 1992.

—— *The Mystery of Consciousness.* New York: New York Review Press, 1997.

—— *Freedom and Neurobiology: Reflections on Free Will, Language, and Political Power.* New York: Columbia University Press, 2007.

Sherwood, Yvonne, and Kevin Hart, *Derrida and Religion.* New York: Routledge, 2005.

Simms, Karl. *Paul Ricœur.* London: Routledge, 2003.

Solomon, Robert C. *Continental Philosophy Since 1750: The Rise and Fall of the Self.* Oxford: Oxford University Press, 1988.

—— *True to Our Feelings: What Our Emotions Are Really Telling Us.* Oxford: Oxford University Press, 2007.

Sorabji, Richard. *Self: Ancient and Modern Insights about Individuality, Life, and Death.* Oxford: Clarendon, 2006.

Spinoza, Baruch. 'Short Treatise on God, Man and his Well-being', [1662], in *The Essential Spinoza. Ethics and Related Writings,* ed. Michael Morgan. Indianapolis: Hackett, 2006.

—— *The Ethics* [1677], trans. S. Shirley and ed. Seymour Feldman. Indianapolis: Hackett, 1992.

Stanton, M. *Outside the Dream: Lacan and French Styles of Psychoanalysis.* London: Routledge and Kegan Paul, 1983.

Storr, Anthony. *Freud.* Oxford: Oxford University Press, 1989.

Strawson, P. F. *Individuals.* New York: Doubleday, [1959] 1963.

Taylor, Charles. *Sources of the Self: The Making of the Modern Identity.* Cambridge: Cambridge University Press, 1989.

Turkle, Sherry. *Psychoanalytic Politics: Jacques Lacan and Freud's French Revolution.* London: The Guilford Press, 1992.

Vasey, G. N. A. *Body and Mind.* London: Allen and Unwin, 1964.

Vincent, J-D. and Luc Ferry. *Qu'est-ce que l'homme? Sur les fondamentaux de la biologie et de la philosophie.* Paris: Odile Jacob, 2002.

Vincent, J-D. *Biologie des passions.* Paris: Odile Jacob, 2002.

—— *Le Cœur des autres: une biologie de la compassion.* Paris: Odile Jacob, 2003.

Watkin, William. *On Mourning: Theories of Loss in Modern Literature.* Edinburgh: Edinburgh University Press, 2004.

Weatherill, Rob, ed. *The Death Drive: New Life for a Dead Subject?* London: Rebus, 1999.

Weiskrantz, Lawrence and Martin Davies, eds. *Frontiers of Consciousness.* Oxford: Oxford University Press, 2008.

Whitford, Margaret. *Merleau-Ponty's Critique of Sartre's Philosophy.* Lexington: French Forum, 1982.

Wittgenstein, Ludwig. *Philosophical Investigations*, trans. G. E. M. Anscombe. Oxford: Blackwell, 1953.

Wright, Elizabeth. *Psychoanalytic Criticism: Theory in Practice*. London: Methuen, 1984.

Zielinski, A. *Lecture de Merleau-Ponty et Levinas: le corps, le monde, l'autre*, Paris: PUF, 2002.

Zizek, Slavoj. *The Parallax View*. Harvard: MIT Press, 2006.

—— and John Milbank. *The Monstrosity of Christ: Paradox or Dialectic?* Harvard: The MIT Press, 2009.

Index